Urban Education in Social Perspective

Urban Education in Social Perspective

Alfred Lightfoot
Loyola Marymount University

Rand McNally College Publishing Company
Chicago

Rand McNally Education Series
B. Othanel Smith, Advisory Editor

78 79 80 10 9 8 7 6 5 4 3 2 1
Copyright © 1978 by Rand McNally College Publishing Company
All Rights Reserved
Printed in U.S.A.
Library of Congress Catalog Card Number 77-77744

This book is a two-fold dedication:

- to my mother, in appreciation for sacrificing all
  so that I might have an education, and in whose
  retirement years I wish her greater happiness
  yet to come;

- to MacGregor, whose presence and memory will be
  with me forever.

Table of Contents

Preface

I am convinced that the ultimate test of public education is the degree to which urban schools meet or fail to meet the needs of their urban inhabitants. Do they meet the challenges of urban life? Do they effectively demonstrate that all youngsters, regardless of background, can have an equal education? Can educators be confident that going to a public urban school will educate youngsters for the real world and give them the essential skills for survival in that real world? Can we say with accuracy that poverty-ridden youngsters, blacks, Chicanos, Asian-Americans, Puerto Ricans, and American Indians are receiving a relevant, meaningful education in urban schools? In other words, are our urban schools meeting the needs of the majority of youngsters attending them?

I feel no desire or professional need to expound on the virtues, strength, and tremendous potential of the public school system as it has evolved and transformed American life. I am committed to the system, yet critical of it. I take an advocacy position, but in taking this position, I have not deliberately turned my back on certain data and realities, nor have I ordered my statistics to set up a straw man. Data and facts speak for themselves, and I make no apologies for some of their tragic results. I am more concerned about the social dysconnectionism or dys-functionalism of the urban school system, the social distance that it has exhibited from the realities of American life. The purpose of this book is to help teachers and educators understand more about and come to accept certain realities of urban life and urban schools and the subcultures from which an increasing number of urban students come.

There are still many uncertainties about the field of urban education, and it is neither my intent nor purpose to suggest that I have all the answers. So much has been written about urban education that it is difficult to sort out the valid from the invalid. Many well-based generaliza-tions have emerged about urban schools. It is my objective in this book to look at as many as possible. To admit that I have covered all would be far from the truth; to suggest that I've covered only those that I wished to cover to prove a viewpoint would also be untrue and unfair.

Social foundation courses in teacher education should be among the most interesting, challenging, and thought-provoking offerings in a teacher's training program. Unfortunately, they are not. All too often students get bogged down in the philosophy of education or the history of education or the purely theoretical sociology of education and are dulled by the irrelevancy and uselessness of such studies in relation to the situations that they are going to face on the battlefield that urban schools have become. Unless foundation courses alert students to the realities of the urban teaching world, the schools and the thousands of "captured" youngsters in urban city classrooms will continue to be victimized.

The purpose of this book is to alert teachers to the tasks and challenges awaiting them in an urban setting. I will be challenged by many educational critics about my tone, my approach, and my observations, but I leave it to the reader, the prospective teacher, to decide the truth and wisdom in what I have had to say. You will be the fatality or survival figures in our urban schools, make no mistake about that. On your shoulders rests the future of urban education.

I wish personally to thank Charles Heinle, editor at Rand McNally, for his encouragement of this project over the years. I also wish to thank B. Othanel Smith for his counsel in making this a better work. I reserve a special word of thanks and gratitude to Lillian Roberts, who typed the manuscript, not only for being an able typist, exceptional secretary, but also for being a warm, compassionate, caring human being. This project would never have become a reality without her. And a word of special thanks to Patricia Ingalls for her wisdom and skills in putting this all together. Last, I wish to thank Loyola Marymount University and the Department of Education for never pressuring me by threats of "publish or perish," and for continuing to place emphasis in teacher education where the emphasis should be placed: on teaching.

Alfred Lightfoot
Loyola Marymount University
Los Angeles, California

Introduction to Urban Schooling

Chapter 1

Each chapter will list several behavioral learning goals. After reading each chapter, you should be able to understand the key elements or ideas by referring to these objectives. For Chapter 1, you should be able to do the following tasks when you have completed its reading:

1. Describe several social and cultural changes that have modified urban life and urban schooling.

2. List and describe the major differences between the urban schools of a generation ago with those of today.

3. Define those features of urban life that should be of prime concern to the urban school curriculum.

4. Logically describe how the population of urban schools has changed to one of a multicultural setting.

5. State and describe how future teachers in urban schools can become urban specialists.

The student entering the teaching profession today will in all likelihood be entering an urban school. The jobs, as well as the challenges, exist in the urban centers of America rather than the suburban or rural areas. Today's students will be entering a profession that is totally different from the one entered into by students ten to twenty years ago. This textbook is an attempt to give these students an overview of the educational world that he or she will be entering. By doing this, the teacher in today's urban school setting will be armed with more professional skills and will be prepared for stresses and strains that are unlike those faced by other teachers in two hundred years of educational growth.

A generation ago, a school was typically a neighborhood unit that drew people from a homogeneous cultural, social, economic, and, in some cases, linguistic background. The school could be found in the city, in the countryside, in the suburbs, in a village, or even in an embryonic city. One-room schools were already being consolidated, and middle schools and junior high schools and comprehensive high schools were becoming realities. Schools had a "one-ness," an equilibrium, a focus about them; they were future-oriented; and they offered a graduate the world for the asking. Segregation was a matter of fact in almost everything the schools did, whether it was ability grouping and tracking, orientation of the curriculum, or the use (or abuse) of standardized tests. People lived their entire lives without the inconvenience or pain that comes today from urban congestion, shortages of food, energy problems, water shortages, air pollution, and lack of funds to operate their metropolises.

The 1970 census indicated how complete the shift from rural to urban living was. Education and educators felt the trauma of change produced by the shift from the homogeneous equilibrium of former days to the multigeneous chaos of the present urban scene. Seventy percent of all Americans now live in cities and the population density in urban areas varies from 5,408 to 3,376 persons per square mile.[1]

Social Change and the Schools

Social change characterized America in the late 1960s and early 1970s. It also changed the character of the schools. The thesis that the urban environment modifies sociocultural behavior is the most prominent influence on educators' thinking today. The urban milieu has produced tremendously diverse social factors which have had their impact upon the school, changing it from a public school to a public urban school.

The following set of factors has contributed to the quality of life in urban communities and has qualitatively and quantitatively changed education and teaching in the schools:

1. Poverty and related health and welfare costs
2. Crime and vandalism
3. Unemployment and underemployment

---

1. *Los Angeles Times,* March 31, 1977.

4. High-density housing and the housing-development complex

5. Noise, air pollution, and congestion

6. Need for increased social, civil, sanitation, police, and welfare services

7. Migration and emigration, including a serious illegal alien problem

8. Exodus of economically upward families to the suburbs

9. Family instability due to unemployment, greater sexual freedom, and greater liberation awareness (e.g., women's rights movement)

10. Absence of adult role models in the home as a result of the newer concepts of family life

11. Heavier reliance on the mass media for the communication of ideas and news

12. Isolation of diverse cultural and racial groups into ghettos

13. Languages other than English being spoken in the home, with peers, and in school

14. Judicial court decisions affecting all aspects of life from protection of legal rights (*Miranda* decision) to school desegregation (*Brown* v. *Board of Education* decision)

15. Transportation systems that are overburdened

16. Difficulty of financing city services and other fiscal problems of major cities

The movement toward urbanization has brought with it the aforementioned social realities and has taken its toll on the behavior and attitudes of students, parents, and teachers. The growth of urbanization also has brought depersonalization, alienation, and a sense of anonymity. Sociologists call these conditions dysfunctionalism or anomie. The modern city, facilitated by industrialization, has resulted in a more highly concentrated population, and these diverse groups have crowded the urban classrooms. The neighborhood school has lost its identity and is becoming more broadly based and more openly strained, and paradoxically, more stratified and segregated. Minority groups have crowded into the cities, and the identity of the public urban school has changed dramatically in its makeup to that of a school composed largely of minority group and lower socioeconomic-class members.

Realities of Urban Education
There is no question that the school of a generation ago was far different from the school that today's young teacher experiences. The urban school is different in many ways, and future urban teachers must adjust to these simple realities if they are to find a job in today's market and survive in it. Although this text explores these urban teaching realities, a few basic realities can be pointed out that make urban schools of today different from those of yesteryear:

Reality 1. Urban schools serve a multicultural population that is different from schools in the past. White flight to the suburbs, the influx of rural populations to the cities, the concentrations of minority groups in large urban centers, and the continuous flow of illegal aliens into some parts of the country have turned urban classrooms into international centers for such diverse groups as Caucasians, Black Americans, American Indians, Asian-Americans, Mexican-Americans, Puerto Ricans, Cubans, and Vietnamese. The schools are no longer institutions of a monocultural or monolingual nature. Cultural identities, which have traditionally centered around history, language, traditions, values, and attitudes, have made urban centers pluralistic institutions whose success depends upon the flexibilities of enculturation and socialization. The two large school systems in Chart 1–1 are good examples of this population shift and this multicultural flavor.[2]

Chart 1–1. School Populations

Chicago	Los Angeles
28.2% Caucasian	37% Caucasian
57.9% Black	32% Hispanic
.2% American Indian	24% Black
1.0% Asian-American	5% Asian-American
6.7% Mexican	1% Vietnamese
6.2% Puerto Rican	1% American Indian
.5% Cuban	

Source: *Chicago Tribune,* November 26, 1974.

2. *Los Angeles Times,* March 31, 1977; *Chicago Tribune,* November 26, 1974. See also, Johanna Lemlech, *Handbook for Successful Urban Teaching* (New York: Harper and Row, 1977), p. 4.

The Director of Research and Evaluation for the Los Angeles Public School System noted that since 1966 the Anglo population has declined from 56 percent to 37 percent, and at the same time, the Latin population enrolled in the schools has increased from 18.6 percent to 32 percent. He believed that by 1981 the Latin enrollment will have increased to 43.2 percent, while the Anglo enrollment will have dropped to 24.4 percent. In terms of this shifting ethnic mix, he suggested "It would all but be impossible to integrate the district by any method if only 24.4 percent of its students are white."[3]

Reality 2. The urban school serves numerous student needs because of its multicultural population, and these needs are unique to urban students. Language, obviously, becomes the main concern in schools, because if teachers are not bilingual or multilingual, as well as bicultural or multicultural, learning will come to a standstill. Language protects the person, personalizes the culture, and provides a framework for one's day-to-day peer relationships. Any school that imposes a monolingual or monocultural system of instruction on its pupils is far from the world of reality and may actually retard students, forcing them into alinguality or aculturality. Several years ago, Riessman (1972), summarized some of the unique characteristics of urban students, characteristics that future urban teachers should be alert to and prepared to handle.[4]

Reality 3. Urban schools are larger, more complex institutions with structures, student bodies, and staffs that hardly resemble the schools of a generation ago. Elementary schools frequently range from 1,000 pupils up to 1,200 pupils, while junior high schools can be as large as 1,700 to 2,500 students. Secondary schools often have more than 2,500 students and some can be found in the 3,500 pupil range, depending on the neighborhood schools that feed into it.[5] Some schools that are six-year institutions, junior-senior high school combinations, have populations of more than 4,500. One such school is the John Marshall Junior Senior High School in Milwaukee, Wisconsin.

---

3. John W. Wright, Director of Research, LA Public School System, interview in *Los Angeles Times,* March 31, 1977.

4. Frank Riessman, "The Overlooked Positives of Disadvantaged Groups," in Ronald Shinn, ed., *Culture and School* (Scranton: Intext, 1972), Chapter 16; chart taken from Johanna Lemlech, *Handbook for Successful Urban Teaching* (New York: Harper and Row, 1977), pp. 174–75.

5. Lemlech, *Successful Urban Teaching,* p. 2.

Chart 1–2. Characteristics of Urban Students

Verbal ability	Extremely verbal in out-of-school situations. Articulate in conversation with peers. Descriptive, expressive, colorful use of slang.
Attitude toward education	Positive attitude about education; value education as a means for personal achievement. However, a negative attitude often exists about the institution of the school.
Cooperativeness and mutual aid	This characteristic is a result of the extended family.
Avoidance of competitiveness	Informality and humor prevail in out-of-school relationships and carry into the classroom.
Freedom from self-blame	The student wastes little time crying over "spilled milk."
Lessened sibling rivalry	Children enjoy each other's company and derive security from the extended family.
Enjoyment of music, sports, games, cards	Greater enjoyment seems to be derived from creative and expressive activities.
Emotional expressions	Children express anger and other emotions readily. They lack emotional deviousness.
External orientation	Rather than introspective outlook.
Spatial perspective	Rather than temporal perspective.
Expressive orientation	Rather than instrumental orientation.
Consent-centered	Rather than form-centered mental style.
Problem-centered	Rather than abstract-centered approach.
Physical and visual style	The student may be a slow learner, but this is not to be confused with "dullness." It is descriptive of his learning approach.

Source: Johanna Lemlech, *Handbook for Successful Urban Teaching* (New York: Harper and Row, 1977), pp. 174–75.

These are large schools, and large schools require a variety of structures ranging from lunch programs, welfare and psychological services, sanitary and recreational facilities, instructional facilities, drama and fine arts facilities, to the external devices such as bell systems, public address systems, security systems, and parking facilities. Many large urban schools are in fact small urban centers. Plant facilities are overpowering as are the plant maintenance and the financing of them. Vandalism has taken its toll on most large urban school budgets, to the point where a system such as Los Angeles pays out over $2 million yearly for vandalism.

These complex urban schools require many people filling a variety of jobs. In addition to the principal and several vice-principals, some schools have a guidance director, a staff of counselors, social workers, psychologists, and medical personnel. Besides clerical staff and janitorial staff, these schools have welfare and attendance directors, curricula coordinators, career counselors, cafeteria workers, paraprofessional teaching aides, security officers, and student teachers. Besides classroom teachers, there are reading specialists, bilingual specialists, title-aide program specialists, teachers for the emotionally and physically handicapped, and substitute teachers (long and short term), to name only a few.

Running a large urban school is not unlike running a large corporation. Such schools of necessity require large budgets. The operating budget for the Los Angeles City School System in 1977 was 1.3 billion dollars, which is larger than the operating budget for the entire city of Los Angeles and larger than the operating budget of several states. The Superintendent of the Los Angeles School System gets a higher salary than the governor of California.

Reality 4. Urban schools have had to change their instructional thrust to cope with the realities of urban life. This has meant leaving behind many of the cherished fundamentals of a by-gone era. For example, the multicultural child no longer accepts social studies taught without some enthnocentric emphasis on his or her own cultural heritage, nor does the child want the exclusion of his language from the instructional tools of learning. Black English is as relevant as White English to many urban youngsters, and unless the urban teacher recognizes this, failure will take place in the classroom. Curricular emphasis has shifted from preparation for the future to coping with the present. Emphasis on the immediate utility of learning, and skills that can be used now have replaced deferred gratification in urban schools.

Ochoa and Allen (1972)[6] have suggested concepts representative of urban life, which could be incorporated into urban curricula and used by urban teachers to teach attitudes, values, and content about city life. They are as follows:

---

6. Anna Ochoa and Rodney Allen, "Creative Teacher-Student Learning Experiences About the City," in Richard Wisniewski, ed., *Teaching About Life in the City* (Washington, D.C.: National Council for the Social Studies, 42nd Yearbook, 1972), p. 91. See also Lemlech, *Successful Urban Teaching,* p. 59.

alienation	de facto segregation
anonymity	ghetto
city	integration
civil rights	megalopolis
class mobility	metropolitan area
community control	standards of living
rural	subculture
segregation	unemployment
slum housing	anomie
slum landlord	urban
social activist	urban renewal
social class	race
pollution	racial strife
power	welfare
prejudice	ecology
protest	energy crisis
congestion	

Because of this new thrust in subjects and content, many critics of education have led the battle against the "new relevancy" and are calling for a return to the basic fundamental skills of reading, writing, and math. Using as their arguments the continuing declining achievement scores of students in urban schools, they cry out for greater accountability. Tomorrow's urban teacher will be caught between the advocates of more relevancy in the urban curriculum and the advocates of a return to the fundamentals. Regardless of the eventual outcome of this struggle, education in urban centers will never be the same again. Educators will be forced to look over their constituencies a little more carefully than they have in the past, and they may have to alter their contradictory results regarding the effectiveness of special placement and ability grouping. They will have to reevaluate the entire testing program, as well as the entire student labeling process, and they will have to give more importance to the effect of the environment upon learning. From this process, a new spirit of humanistic education may evolve.

Reality 5. Urban schools still largely remain segregated by race and ethnic group, although many school districts have implemented desegregation plans. Yet, segregated schools by their very nature go against the validity of equal educational opportunity.

Data from the Department of Health, Education, and Welfare reveal that, in districts sampled from 1970 to 1974, four out of every ten black students and three out of every ten Hispanic students attended schools in which at least 90 percent of the students belonged to minority groups. There were, of course, wide regional variations: blacks were 23 percent of the student population in the South, 58 percent in border and northeastern states, 62 percent in the Midwest, and 45 percent in the West.[7] The report concluded: "Segregation remains a problem, particularly in large districts . . . [which] tend to be more segregated than small ones." In school districts with more than 100,000 pupils, three out of every five black students in northern schools and two out of every five black students in southern schools attended schools with a minority enrollment that was greater than 50 percent. Over 30 percent of the black students in these northern districts and 15 percent in the southern districts attended schools with minority enrollments of more than 90 percent.[8] The following charts provide additional information of the status of segregation in the schools.[9]

Chart 1–3. Black Enrollment in Schools 50 Percent or More Black in Districts 20 to 40 Percent Black

Enrollment		Percent Black Enrollment of School Attended	
		Over 50%	Over 90%
Less than 2,000	South	0.0	0.0
	North	0.0	0.0
Greater than 100,000	South	40.3	15.0
	North	60.6	30.2

Source: *Desegregation,* p. 153, and *Congressional Record,* p. 9938.

Adjusting to the realities of urban schools will not be easy for the new teacher. The future professional will have to be a multicultural expert, a language specialist, and a person of diverse talents and abilities. He

---

7. *Desegregation of the Nation's Public Schools, A Report of the U.S. Commission on Civil Rights, 1976* (Washington, D.C.: U.S. Government Printing Office, August, 1976), p. 153. See also, *Congressional Record,* 94th Congress, 2nd Session, Vol. 122, #95, June 18, 1976, p. 9938.

8. *Desegregation,* p. 153, and *Congressional Record,* p. 9938.

9. *Desegregation,* p. 153, and *Congressional Record,* p. 9938.

Chart 1–4. Districts that Desegregated, by Source of Intervention and Year of Greatest Desegregation

Time Period	Courts No.	%	HEW No.	%	State-Local No.	%	Total No.	%
1901–53	*	*	*	*	7	3	7	1
1954–65	13	6	18	12	53	21	84	13
1966–67	8	4	19	12	46	18	73	12
1968–69	53	26	42	28	34	13	129	21
1970–71	107	51	61	40	46	18	214	35
1972–73	12	6	5	3	38	15	55	9
1974–75	15	7	7	5	31	12	53	9
Total	208	100	152	100	255	100	615	100

* None in Sample.
Source: *Desegregation,* p. 153, and *Congressional Record,* p. 9938.

or she will have to be skilled at human relations. Teachers will have to deal with students in a confrontation atmosphere, parents in the community setting, and also with the forces of urban life that will constantly be eroding the very foundation that the school will be building. As such, future teachers will have to develop what Lemlech (1977) calls "urban teaching specializations."[10] These specializations involve training in language, reading, mathematics, early childhood education, remedial strategies, discipline procedures, multicultural understanding, and sensitivity training as an urban specialty. The task will be no small undertaking; future urban teachers had better be aware of their responsibilities and the specialized training involved.

If you are a future teacher preparing for a career in education, you are preparing for a world that may be very different from the world you may have come from. It also may be different from the world that you, unfortunately, may be hearing about in teacher training courses. Many teacher training programs have not come to grips with this world. Unfortunately, the victims are the student teachers who think that they will be teaching in middle-class suburban schools where things have remained unchanged for years.

---

10. Lemlech, *Successful Urban Teaching,* pp. 72f.

Social Foundations and Urban Schools

Chapter 2

By the time you have finished studying this chapter, you should be able to perform the following tasks. Read these goals now and then check yourself after you finish the chapter.

> 1. Describe the features of the public school system that are unique to it and the functions that characterize these features.
>
> 2. Define the changes in urban education since the 1970s.
>
> 3. Describe the realities that urban teachers must be prepared to deal with in the schools of tomorrow.
>
> 4. List the crises in the urban schools that are apparent today and the diversified populations affected by and effecting these crises.
>
> 5. State and briefly define how the public school is a social institution and how it reflects and affects society as a whole.

The American public school system is unique. The schools are locally controlled by the lay public with no central federal system that can tell educators what to do, what to teach, whom to hire, how long to keep the schools open, or what materials to use. Whereas most foreign school systems are national systems, the United States is made up of thousands of regional and local systems. The public exercises its direct control over the schools through the election of school board members or through the election of politicians who appoint school board members. The public, through local bond issues, also controls the finances of public education. Without question, the most "public" of public institutions in America today is the public school system. As such, it is the epitome of the American democratic process.

The public school system in the United States is unique in other ways as well. The school system is inclusive and comprehensive; it is free for all young people from kindergarten through twelfth grade, and it is a non-selective system. Students pursuing academic and vocational goals are all housed under one roof. Although public education in America is not under a central or national system, and what we know as the public education system is in reality a combination of systems, there is nonetheless a marked uniformity in the pattern education takes within these systems. The following diagram illustrates this basic uniformity.

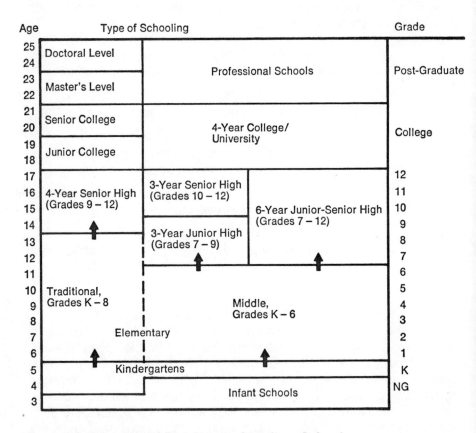

Figure 2-1. Educational Divisions in American Schools

Our school systems are also unusual in the following ways:

1. Public schools are co-educational through the university and graduate levels.

2. Public schools are nonsectarian and do not support any religious organization.

3. Public schools receive financial support from a combination of sources that include the federal government, state government, and local community government.

4. Public schools have competing school systems, such as private schools, alternative schools, parochial schools, free schools, and military schools interacting with them.

5. Public schools are open to all children from kindergarten through college.

6. Public schools are professionally staffed by teachers and administrators who have been trained by national standards (via accrediting agencies and affiliations) and state and by local standards (via state credentialing requirements and local schools of education standards for preparing qualified teachers).

Aside from the peculiarities of a school system that is actually a combination of school systems, there is, nonetheless, a remarkable uniformity within the public schools. Public schools have seemingly integrated their functions, and what has emerged has been some rather specific roles or functions that society expects the schools to fill. Among the most specific roles[1] are the following:

1. To keep students aware of social change and the nature of emerging society in light of the present economic and technological revolution.

2. To help students develop an understanding and awareness of democracy and the role that they can play in implementing democratic principles.

---

1. See Robert Stalcup, *Sociology and Education* (Columbus, Ohio: Merrill Publishing Co., 1968); Alfred Lightfoot, *Schools and Society* (New York: Simon and Schuster, SAR, 1969); Cole Brembeck, *Social Foundations of Education* (New York: Wiley and Sons, 1971).

3. To help students develop to their maximum potentiality through the various guidance and instructional facilities offered in the schools.

4. To provide a varied and differentiated curricula so that all students will have an opportunity to learn.

5. To help students and society adjust to the social, political, economic, and religious realities of life and to make unique contributions to each.

Functions of the Public Schools

Among the most notable functions performed by the public schools, the following[2] are most often mentioned by educators and social scientists:

1. *Socialization.* The school is like a sociostat, with varying inputs and outputs that eventually reach a comfortable "temperature level." The primary role of the school is to induct a youngster into society and to teach that youngster the ways of society. This process, in which the schools preserve and change the culture by passing it on to the new agents, is called socialization.

2. *Allocation.* The school has as one of its main objectives the defining of role formation in order to maximize or minimize social mobility. It is in essence the economic and social positioning of persons in society, the status allocations, so to speak, that determine the functioning order of institutions. Persons with minimal education and training are allocated a less important role within society than are persons with a greater education.

3. *Functionalizing.* The school has as its prime responsibility the induction of youth into its culture and the providing of youth with the tools of competency to function within that society. It has the responsibility for balancing the realities of self-realization with those of societal realization. It provides youngsters with the tools of knowledge and literacy that enable

---

2. See Wilbur Brookover and Edsel Erickson, *Society, Schools and Learning* (Boston: Allyn and Bacon, 1969); Alan Bates, *The Sociological Enterprise* (New York: Houghton Mifflin, 1967); Alfred Lightfoot, *The Socio-Psychological Dimensions of Learning* (New York: MSS Educational Publishing Co., 1971).

them to engage in realistic problem solving for themselves and for society.

4. *Democratization.* The school has the responsibility for enhancing the participation of youngsters in the democratic process, specifically, in their roles as citizens in a democratic society. The blending of views regarding the conformist vs. the individual or the welfare of others (group/collectivity) vs. the welfare of self (individual responsibility) are key concerns of the school system if democracy is to work.

5. *Experimentation.* The school should provide opportunities for youth to prepare, experiment, and perform adult roles for later life. Education should develop key capabilities and the schools should be centers for experimentation and change. Only through experimentation can people learn adaptation, acceptance, and innovation.

Uniformities of Public Education

Although American public education is in many ways unique, it does nonetheless have many built-in faults because of its slow pace in reacting to social change. These faults detract from the unique character of the schools and tend to produce the drabness that so many critics of education have noted.

From first glance, one would think that public education in America is highly individualized, even fractured, because of its many varied systems. Yet, given the local community nature of public schools, a remarkable uniformity pervades public education in the United States. Although in principle, Americans have no national system of education, in practice, they have moved slowly towards a system of control in which the Educational Establishment rivals that of the Military-Industrial Complex. Since the 1950s, state legislatures have promulgated new school laws and have established departments of education to control and supervise local schools. They have maintained control over teacher certification, curricula, graduation requirements, testing procedures, finances, and general guidelines for methodological procedures of instruction (one example being the New Social Studies State Framework, California).

Credential controls exercised by the states have been reinforced by professional evaluation and accreditation agencies such as National

Council for Accrediting Teacher Education or through professional agencies and semiprofessional organizations such as the National Education Association, the Parent-Teachers Association or the American Federation of Teachers. Educational publishers have added to this uniformity by publishing materials that are adopted on statewide or school system-wide bases. Little opportunity is left for multiple-text adoption procedures. Departments of education and schools of education at colleges and universities have a remarkable oneness about their teacher education programs and offer few, if any, distinctly different or innovative credentials programs. Educational journals and research have defined the semantics of education and have given to educators the terminology that is requisite for being a professional in this field. Like medicine or law with their distinct professional vocabulary, education has carefully distinguished itself as a discipline worthy of attention and worthy of study. Separate professional degrees such as the Master of Education degree and the Doctor of Education degree have been added to graduate study at many colleges, and schools everywhere have identified themselves as being in the academic field of "Education." Contrary to what many would have you believe, the academic field of "Education" has become a potent discipline to contend with and many a university that formerly held this discipline in disrespect or thought of it as an illegitimate academic partner have come to learn the hard realities of economic survival regarding student enrollments, government grants, and/or consultantship requests. Federal government involvement alone over the last several years, whether it be a result of the legislative branch (in financial aid programs), the executive branch (the overseeing of problems under Health, Education, and Welfare), or the judicial branch (literally hundreds of court decisions dealing with everything from finances, student rights, to corporal punishment), has led to a gradual erosion in the "differentness" of our school systems. The only result of all of this has been a greater trend towards uniformity within our school systems.

One other factor is also a force towards a greater uniformity. School systems are basically conservative, representing the status quo more than social change. Such a conclusion is reasonable when you consider that the school is the most public of all our institutions, that the greatest tax bite in local areas generally goes to education, that the societal and community pressures on administrators, school board members, and teachers are large, and that the red tape of a large urban school bureaucracy fosters a desire to maintain the status quo.

Traditionally, education has been a social agency of reaction, one that responds to the complex of pressures brought to bear on it. Since a social institution both influences and is influenced by all other social institutions, it is safe to assume that the community as a whole provides the climate for education. That climate or setting is determined by the educational level of the community, the occupational pattern of the community, the population composition of the community, the social structure of the community, and the economic and political foundations of the community. School and community interact and have many publics: parents, taxpayers, voters, business people, interest groups, professionals, all of whom can potentially bring intense pressures upon the schools.

The Educational Revolution

Alienation is the word that best describes American education today. It can be witnessed and evidenced everywhere. It took hold in the 1960s on the college and university campuses and manifested itself in student unrest, and then filtered down in an unprecedented scale during the 1970s to the public schools. City schools will be the target of youth for social reform, whether that reform be over student civil rights or over the revelancy and control of the school program. Relevancy will be the shibboleth of the 1980s school-age generation while accountability will be the shibboleth of the general public.

Just who are these alienated, unnerved, restless, dissatisfied populations? They are seemingly everywhere and everyone.[3]

- *The taxpayer,* who is in open revolt against taxes in general and the nonproductive results from the tax increases for schools in particular.
- *The student,* who is seeking greater relevancy in the curriculum, greater decision-making powers in the school, and a

3. See Alfred Lightfoot, *American Urban Education: Inquiries into Changing Patterns* (New York: MSS Educational Publishing Co., 1970); Ornstein, Levine, and Wilkerson, *Reforming Metropolitan Schools* (Pacific Palisades, California: Goodyear Publishing Co., 1975).

greater voice in the judgments being made about his/her civil rights as opposed to his/her student rights.

- *The parent,* who is increasingly bitter and resentful over declining achievement scores balanced by rising costs for education and is concerned about the consequences of social decisions such as busing and the neighborhood school concept.
- *The school administrator,* who is desperately trying in vain to hold on to the last remnants of the status quo and who has to fight teachers, students, parents, public, and the school board for survival.
- *The general public,* who is collectively antagonized over the supposed failure of the schools to educate youth and to successfully place them into the labor market.
- *The politicians,* who rush to fill the power vacuum in the schools by proposing legislation that has as its intention reform and instead brings confusion and added chaos to an already chaotic public school system.
- *The teacher,* who is upset over everything from teacher surpluses and job insecurity to desegregation, decentralization, and deschooling trends.
- *The urban poor,* who receive less than their share of the nation's resources, are blamed for many of our school's woes, and generally receive an inferior education that will ultimately retard their degree of social mobility.
- *The minority student,* who receives a segregated education and is discriminated against because of race, culture, and language and who is often victimized by the "self-fulfilling prophecy."
- *The societal and/or school dropout,* who views the Establishment as his natural enemy and who seeks to overturn the foundations of society and the schools.
- *The conservative,* who views everything in terms of red, white, and blue and attacks as unpatriotic and communist everything from sex education to water fluoridation and who wants greater control over everything from teacher hiring to textbook selection.

- *The liberal,* who views education simply as change for the sake of change, who does not consider the consequences of radical change upon traditional standards.
- *The school board and superintendent,* who often are nonrepresentative of the community or the schools and who seek to preserve the status quo and educational traditions that are deemed by many as outdated or representative of special interest groups.

The urban school system of the 1980s will have to contend with these and many more forces. One prevailing concern is obviously whether or not consensus is possible.

How can urban schools fail to become the battlefields for the many, oncoming feudal wars? As cities grow and the middle class continues its flight to the suburbs and to the comfortable middle-class schools, urban school crises will mount in intensity and scope. Some of these crises appear to be:[4]

1. The quality of inner-city education as opposed to middle-class education and suburban education.

2. The overwhelming predominance of lower-class children and minority youngsters inhabitating urban schools and thus regenerating a "resegregation" pattern before schools have even tackled the problems of desegregation.

3. The financial plight of large city systems as they seek to pass on the minimum needs of youth and witness the widening financial plight of the city itself as it moves closer towards bankruptcy (see Figure 2–2).[5]

4. The dropout rate among youth.

5. The outmoded and inflexible nature of the school structure and curriculum and the glaring irrelevancy of subject matter to real life and social realities.

---

4. An excellent text dealing with the multiple problems of urban schools is Allan Ornstein's *Urban Education* (Columbus, Ohio: Charles Merrill Co., 1972).

5. A case in point: the Los Angeles Public School system's budget for 1976 was over one billion dollars, a budget for a school system that is larger than the budget for the City of Los Angeles and larger than the budget of several of our states in the Union.

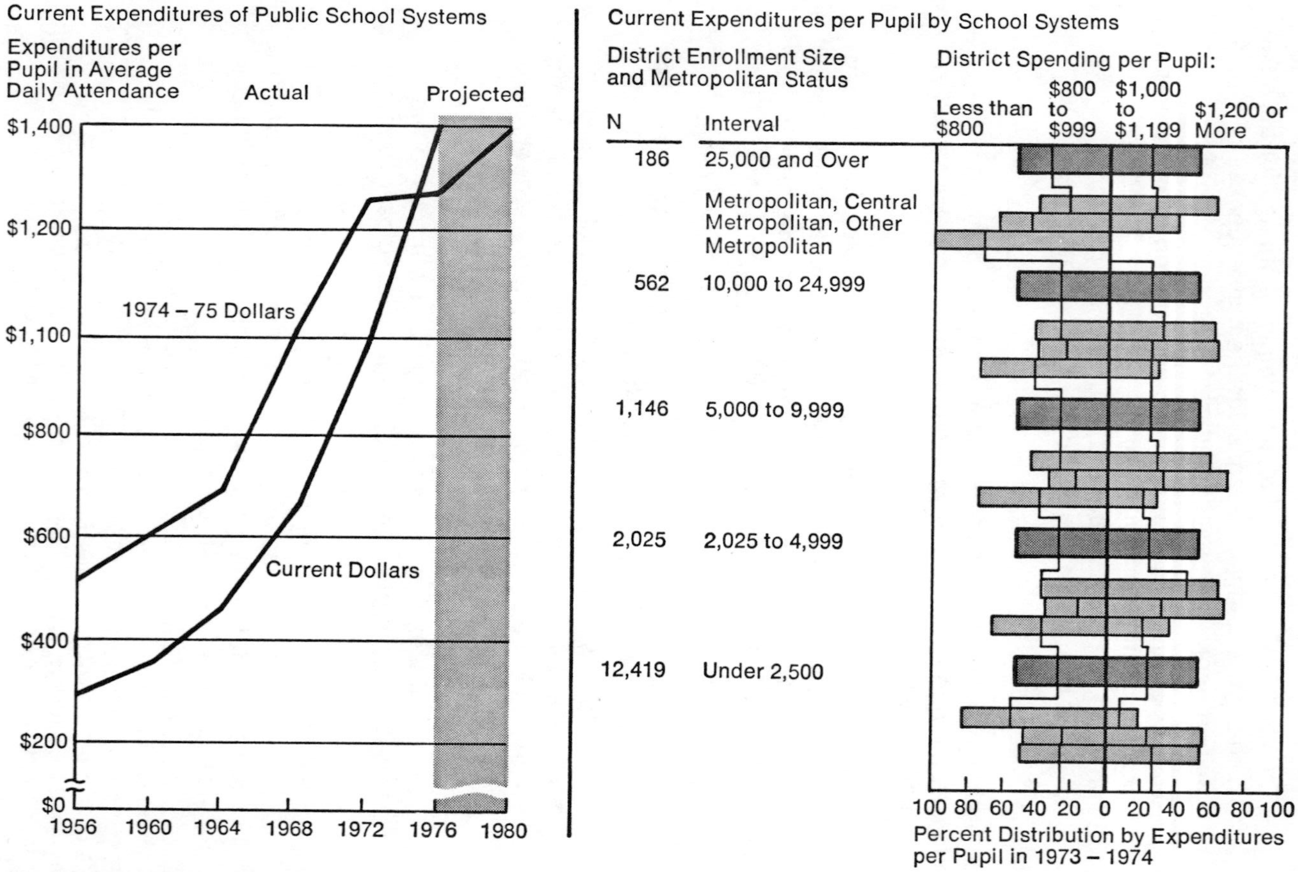

Figure 2-2. Expenditures of Public Schools

Source: The National Center for Education Statistics, *The Conditions of Education*

6. The inability of teachers to deal effectively with urban school problems or to even unite in a common front to attack school problems.

7. The growing violence and unrest in city schools.

8. The declining achievement rates of students, and, in particular, the decline in minority youngsters' reading scores.

9. The failure to come to terms with the influence of varying cultures and languages upon learning.

10. The misuse of standardized testing procedures and their obvious bias against minority youth.

11. The questions of decentralization and local community control that plague large, monstrous urban city systems such as New York, Chicago, Los Angeles, and Detroit.

12. The financial cutbacks urban school systems are forced to make (see Chart 2–1).

Many educators and public-minded critics have said that, unless the urban schools change dramatically during the 1970s and early 1980s, America may witness the emergence of a two-track system of education, with one track for the haves and another for the have-nots. Experts caution that urban schools are synonymous with inferior education and that the problems of urban areas and their schools are so intermixed that they have conditioned educators into a state of immobilization. If this is true, then quality education has indeed been reserved for the few, namely, the white, middle-class suburban school or the private school. Seemingly then, the very concept of an American open-class structure, where social mobility is an ideal as well as a practice, is threatened by the one institution that has historically created that mobility and opportunity—the American public school.

Changes in Urban Education Since the 1970s

Contemporary society is constantly changing, and so are the schools. The schools basically are in a state of cultural lag. They do change as society changes, only at a much slower rate than does society.

Several significant trends or changes can be summarized as evident of American public education since the early 1970s.

Chart 2–1. Budget Committee's Cutback Recommendations to the Los Angeles Board of Education, 1975

1. Elimination of approximately 1,200 teaching positions including 345 secondary inner-city teachers, 250 elementary off-norm teachers, 88 secondary off-norm positions, and a 50 percent cut in supplemental counseling in senior high schools.
2. A 20 percent cut in area counselors for elementary schools.
3. The elimination of permissive home-to-school transportation.
4. Supplemental pay, both academic and athletic, cut 50 percent.
5. The complete closing down of the district for two weeks in August.
6. A modification of the district's health and medical benefit package, either to establish a limit of board contribution per employe, or to provide coverage for the employe only or other options not yet determined.
7. The elimination of 126 secondary school deans.
8. The elimination of approximately 300 non-school located classified and certified administrative positions located in area and central office locations, including elimination of two assistant superintendent positions, several deputy area administrator positions and administrative coordinator positions.
9. The district's contribution to the Gifted Program of $500,000 will be eliminated.
10. All principals who are currently on an "A" basis will be reduced to a "B" basis.
11. School Determined Needs will be cut 25 percent.
12. Coordinator differentials for elementary schools to be eliminated.
13. The coordinator differential for counseling and libraries at the secondary schools eliminated.
14. An 18 percent cut in sabbatical leaves.
15. Forty-six Pupil Service and Attendance counselors to be eliminated.
16. The entire Traffic and Safety Program eliminated.
17. One hundred fourteen school nurses, 14 school physicians and 12 audiometrists eliminated.
18. The district's Preventive Maintenance Program eliminated.

Source: *Spotlight,* Office of Communications, Los Angeles City Schools, Feb. 28, 1975.

First and perhaps the most important change is the movement toward a fuller conceptual view of the culturally different child, one that is more positive in terms of the successes and creativity of the children and away from a view that has been totally negative and self-fulfilling.

Second, there is a movement away from the methodology of memorization or learning by doing, toward an emphasis on learning how to think and using the inquiry process and inductive reasoning. Although the cognitive concerns will probably always dominate curricula, the affective concerns are beginning to demand equal attention and values education is frequently considered part of the thinking process.

Third, there is a movement away from the concept of the school as part of a total system that is somehow isolated from the community and toward more direct integration with the community, local community control, and decentralization. There is increased support for the belief that the school is part of the community and not in isolation to it. This has, of course, created numerous new problems with regard to such issues as desegregation. How can one desegregate the schools and bus youngsters to different neighborhood schools and still maintain local community control?

Fourth, the use of modern technology, especially computers, as educational tools that can help to cut down on error, improve competency-based programs, eliminate overlapping procedures and methods, and reduce manpower hours has been introduced. At the same time, technology has retarded the movement of education from a mass to an individual approach.

Fifth, there is a preoccupation with performance and the need for an accountability method that specifies the competencies to be demonstrated by the student. This, in turn, would lead to a specification of the criteria to be used in assessing these competencies; students and their teachers would be held responsible for meeting these standards. Competency-Based Teacher Education (CBTE) has become the dogma of teacher training institutions throughout the U.S.

Sixth, flexible curricula models, such as the open classroom, the alternative or free school, and modular or flexible scheduling, as well as the use of resource centers, inquiry centers, or media areas, have become important. The educational materials available to educators have multiplied, requiring more than a cursory knowledge on the part of teachers of new curricular developments and models.

Even given some of these basic, vital changes, urban education is still in trouble. Educational critics such as Jencks, Holt, Kozel, Kohl, Glasser, and Coleman point out that the urban schools have complicated problems that seem to defy solution. They may be right. Urban educators have carefully delineated the problems festering in urban America, and the schools and these problems are the primary domain of the urban teacher. Briefly, the major problems are as follows:

Some students, primarily low-income and ghetto youth, are not receiving an adequate education. The forces of race, culture, language, biased standardized testing, ability grouping, and social class still largely dominate educational decision making and serve to differentiate the haves from the have-nots.

Teachers are not teaching, or so achievement tests show. Teachers, in fact, tend to be least credible in the eyes of their students when it comes to tackling the relevant problems of sex and drugs, the inequities in society and school, ecology and the environment, the political process and structure, and social and legal justice.

Schools seem to be driving students away by increasing their dissatis-faction and alienation. Free schools crop up continuously; dropout rates by the tenth grade remain abnormally high among minority youth; achievement and reading scores remain consistently low; and the basic validity of compulsory education comes into question. School systems have had to contend with legal suits against them for willfully damaging their students and negligently and carelessly failing to notice the pupils' reading disabilities while graduating students from high school who are unable to read above the eighth-grade level, as required by Educational Codes in more than several states.[6]

Intense conflicts riddle the urban schools. They are battles of (a) students vs. teachers, with an ever increasing student assault rate upon teachers; (b) teachers vs. teachers, with one teacher organization fighting another teacher organization even to the point of invalidating the successes of one organization over the other;[7] (c) students vs. students, with gang warfare in some systems reaching epidemic proportions;[8] (d) parents vs. teachers and administrators, with the battle lines being drawn over de-centralization, local community control, teacher hiring and firing, and accountability; and (e) politicians vs. educators, with legislation that

---

6. See the findings of the New York State Commission on Educational Reform, Department of Education (Albany, New York, October, 1972), reported in the *Los Angeles Times,* October 20, 1972.

7. California is a case in point. The California Legislature has passed a collective bargaining authorization for teachers, and yet, several teacher organizations are taking the matter to court for fear that one teacher organization or another will become too powerful.

8. It is estimated that in the Los Angeles area alone there are 150 well-organized gangs that are fighting small-scale wars for control of territory. See the *Los Angeles Times,* November 12, 1975.

mandates teacher accreditation, teacher accountability, collective bargaining, tenure, student rights, and budgeting procedures.

Teacher training is largely outdated and self-serving, and there is little concern for the realities of the "real world" outside urban schools or the "real world" of the employment market. Teachers trained in schools of education today are still largely middle-class persons who are taught middle-class procedures and methodologies. They are ill-prepared in reading specialization and discipline procedures and controls. They have little exposure to culturally different youngsters and their cultural heritage. Prepared in their own current discipline only, many urban teachers lack awareness of the actual realities of the psychological and counseling tasks that will be required of them.

The final sources of educational funds are still largely undetermined. Do these funds come from local property taxes or some other source, what is the degree and dimension of state support, what is the degree, dimension, and role of federal support? Every major urban school system faces financial cutbacks throughout the 1980s, and some school systems in California, Oregon, and Wisconsin may have to close down before the end of 1978 because of a shortage of funds.

The structures of urban school systems are frequently called bureaucratic, rigid, and conservative. The system itself seems to be preventing change and reform. School boards tend to be less representative of the school community as a whole; they have little in common with teachers, students, and minority youngsters. Although the ranks of administrators are constantly changing, especially in central city schools, in many states the vast number of administrators were educated during the 1940s and are little in touch with the realities of today. The huge systems, such as New York, Chicago, and Los Angeles, defy the imagination in size, amount of red tape, bureaucratic structure, and the order of decision making.

Exercises

I. The questionnaire that follows will help you evaluate your attitudes and views with regard to many of the issues you will be confronted with if you teach in an urban school system. Many of these issues will also be discussed in later chapters of this book. Complete the questionnaire now and then review it again later to see if and how your attitudes and views may have changed.

Questionnaire

Yes	No	Don't Know	
☐	☐	☐	1. Blacks and Latins receive the same quality of education as do whites in the public schools.
☐	☐	☐	2. The present low reading achievement scores of school pupils are due to poor teaching and poor teaching methods.
☐	☐	☐	3. The drug problem in the schools is chiefly in inner-city schools rather than in suburban or rural schools.
☐	☐	☐	4. Violence and vandalism in schools is merely a small-scale imitation of violence and vandalism in our society as a whole.
☐	☐	☐	5. Student success in school is directly related to the teacher's perception of the child's capabilities.
☐	☐	☐	6. The property tax is an equitable means of financing public education in our urban schools.
☐	☐	☐	7. Public funds should be used to help finance private and parochial education.
☐	☐	☐	8. Schools should address themselves to teaching the basic fundamental skills only and leave the electives and frills to other social agencies.
☐	☐	☐	9. Compensatory aid to education has the effect of reinforcing the separate but equal doctrine.
☐	☐	☐	10. Segregated education is detrimental to the education and the psychological self-image of all pupils concerned.
☐	☐	☐	11. Heredity plays the most dominant role in determining intellectual differences among youngsters.
☐	☐	☐	12. Blacks are genetically inferior to whites in certain areas of intellectual capacity.

Yes	No	Don't Know	
☐	☐	☐	13. The culturally different are educationally disadvantaged because of home and family backgrounds.
☐	☐	☐	14. Busing children to achieve integration is an important and healthy means of achieving educational equality.
☐	☐	☐	15. Forced integration of races and cultures is desirable.
☐	☐	☐	16. Black children bused to white schools tend to show greater achievement gains than they did in their all-black schools.
☐	☐	☐	17. Children generally acquire approximately one-third of their intellectual capacity before they reach age five.
☐	☐	☐	18. Since English is the formal, acceptable language for social mobility in the mainstream of American society, its acquisition and comprehension must be required of all students before they can successfully acquire a high school diploma.
☐	☐	☐	19. Our schools should be stressing vocational skills rather than academic skills for the reality of today's society.
☐	☐	☐	20. Children with different language backgrounds should be taught only by bilingual or multilingual teachers.
☐	☐	☐	21. Because of the current teacher surplus market, teacher training institutions should limit the numbers they train to meet the realities of the market.
☐	☐	☐	22. Good teaching is an instinctive ability and cannot be taught.
☐	☐	☐	23. Ability grouping is a far more effective means of instruction than heterogeneous grouping.
☐	☐	☐	24. Only blacks can effectively teach blacks, only Chicanos can teach Chicanos, and only whites can teach whites.
☐	☐	☐	25. Teachers should have the right to strike to gain their educational and personal objectives.

	Don't	
Yes	No	Know	
☐	☐	☐	26. Students do not give up a portion of their civil and human rights when they enter school.
☐	☐	☐	27. Local schools should be controlled by the local community.
☐	☐	☐	28. Minority students in inner-city schools tend to be behind their white counterparts by three full years in reading.
☐	☐	☐	29. Blacks tend to score 15 points below whites of the same age in I.Q. tests.
☐	☐	☐	30. Teachers should be held accountable for their teaching effectiveness through competency-based testing.
☐	☐	☐	31. Compulsory education should be abolished and students should be given the option of alternative education.
☐	☐	☐	32. Standardized testing is one of many effective means of grouping youngsters for appropriate tasks.
☐	☐	☐	33. School boards are not truly reflective of the population of our urban schools.
☐	☐	☐	34. Ethnic-study programs and classes in college departments are largely unacademic and of little value.
☐	☐	☐	35. Textbooks used in urban schools today do not accurately depict the views and attributes of minorities.

II. Following is a partial list of urban school problems. As an educator, what five would have your priority rating for attention? In what order? Why?

_____ 1. Segregated teaching faculties.

_____ 2. Segregated student bodies in most school systems.

_____ 3. Segregation based on wealth and income; inequity between rich and poor school districts.

_____ 4. Lack of effective programs for bilingual education.

_____ 5. Lack of curricular attention toward multicultural experiences.

_____ 6. Sexism in the schools; perpetuation of male-dominance patterns.

_____ 7. Overuse of standardized testing for determining outcomes and potentials.

_____ 8. Role of public financing of education inadequately defined and/or supported.

_____ 9. Lack of public aid to private and parochial education.

_____ 10. Need to decentralize large urban school systems.

_____ 11. Need for more local community control over schools.

_____ 12. Overstaffing of administrators and understaffing of teachers.

_____ 13. The use of some system of busing to achieve racial balance in schools.

_____ 14. Lack of teacher cohesiveness, power, and control over school matters and personal professional matters.

_____ 15. Need for more Competency-Based Education and accountability for teachers.

_____ 16. The detachment of local schools from state or federal politics.

_____ 17. Increase in the amount of school violence and crime.

_____ 18. Increase in rates of school dropouts.

_____ 19. Widespread use of drugs and selling drugs at schools.

_____ 20. Widespread teacher surplus.

_____ 21. Developing struggle over students' rights at school.

_____ 22. Better election procedures and broader representation on school boards.

_____ 23. Increased need for federal finances in compensatory aid programs.

_____ 24. Rapid increase in alternative schools and free schools.

_____ 25. Declining achievement scores of students, especially in reading.

The Urban Setting for Educational Decision Making

Chapter 3

When you have finished this chapter, you should be able to perform the following tasks.

1. Describe why public education can be characterized as "urban education."

2. Describe demographic changes taking place in major urban centers.

3. Identify the critical social systems within an urban area.

4. Explain the contradictions in urban society that hinder education.

5. List the persistent characteristics of public education that have dominated the schools since the beginning of the twentieth century; indicate what trends seem likely to emerge in urban schools.

6. List and characterize the six types of schools found in urban society and relate them to housing and economic patterns.

7. Summarize the changing portrait of the urban citizenry.

Urban education refers to the school systems in the large urban centers throughout the U.S. Each of these urban centers has a population in excess of a quarter of a million citizens and a public school enrollment that exceeds 50,000 pupils. Each urban school system has had to cope with the social problems and consequences of inflation and economic decline, population shifts due to less or more mobility and a declining birthrate, racial tensions due to desegregation programs, physical decay in the facilities, an increasing need for greater social services, and a political and bureaucratic complexity that stifles reform and change.[1]

Demographic Changes

Two hundred years ago, less than 10 percent of the population lived in urban centers. Today, 75 percent of all people live in urban areas, and 30 percent of these live in or immediately around a central city. Eighty percent of all students in public schools are in urban schools, and approximately 45 percent of all students in public schools are in one of the 30 large urban centers shown in Chart 3–1.

Figure 3–1 shows the racial composition of schools in various regions of the U.S.; Chart 3–2 shows population changes in large cities; and Chart 3–3 shows the cities where most of the student population is black.

It should be noted that the Census Bureau recently reported (*Los Angeles Times,* April 14, 1977) that the only major urban centers that are gaining population are in the South and the West, while 20 of the largest cities in the nation are losing population. Houston, San Diego, San Antonio, Honolulu, Phoenix, and Memphis are growing, while the others are losing population. St. Louis had a drop of 15.6 percent, Cleveland 14.9 percent, Pittsburgh 11.8 percent, Detroit 11.8 percent, and Newark 11 percent. New York fell 5.2 percent, while Chicago fell 8 percent, and Los Angeles 3 percent. Demographic figures are in such a state of flux that it is difficult to predict with accuracy what urban growth patterns will be in the next ten years. One thing, however, is certain: wherever the population shifts take place, all such shifts will eventually follow the same social patterns and realities of inner decay. Serious urban disease will permeate the older, larger urban centers as well as the "boom towns" of the future. Generally, population estimates showed older cities in the East and Midwest dropping in population, while the largest growth patterns are in the Southeast and West. The population estimates of

1. See Raymond Hummel and John Nagle, *Urban Education in America* (New York: Oxford University Press, 1973), Preface.

Chart 3–1. United States Standard Metropolitan Statistical Areas

Area	Rank	1975 Population
New York, N.Y.-N.J.	1	9,973,577
Los Angeles-Long Beach, Cal.	2	7,032,075
Chicago, Ill.	3	6,978,947
Philadelphia, Pa.-N.J.	4	4,817,974
Detroit, Mich.	5	4,431,390
San Francisco-Oakland, Cal.	6	3,109,519
Washington, D.C.-Md.-Va.	7	2,908,801
Boston, Mass.	8	2,899,101
Nassau-Suffolk, N.Y.	9	2,533,030
St. Louis, Mo.-Ill.	10	2,410,163
Pittsburgh, Pa.	11	2,401,245
Dallas-Ft. Worth, Tex.	12	2,377,979
Baltimore, Md.	13	2,070,670
Cleveland, Ohio	14	2,064,194
Newark, N.J.	15	2,054,928
Houston, Tex.	16	1,999,316
Minneapolis-St. Paul, Minn.-Wis.	17	1,965,159
Atlanta, Ga.	18	1,597,816
Seattle-Everett, Wash.	19	1,412,869
Anaheim-Santa Ana-Garden Grove, Cal.	20	1,420,386
Milwaukee, Wis.	21	1,403,688
Cincinnati, Ohio-Ky.-Ind.	22	1,384,851
San Diego, Cal.	23	1,357,854
Buffalo, N.Y.	24	1,349,211
Kansas City, Mo.-Kan.	25	1,271,515
Miami, Fla.	26	1,267,792
Denver-Boulder, Col.	27	1,237,208
Riverside-San Bernardino-Ontario, Cal.	28	1,143,146
Indianapolis, Ind.	29	1,109,882
Tampa-St. Petersburg, Fla.	30	1,088,549

Source: *Chronicle of Higher Education,* April 25, 1977.

25 cities listed here are for single cities, as now required by the federal revenue-sharing law, the figures do not include the metropolitan areas surrounding the city limits. In the ranking of metropolitan areas, which include a city's suburbs and sometimes combine parts of two states, the New York City-New Jersey metropolitan area would be the nation's largest with a 1970 population of 9,973,577.

Some cities that were not considered among the ten major metropolitan areas in terms of population would be if their metropolitan area popula-

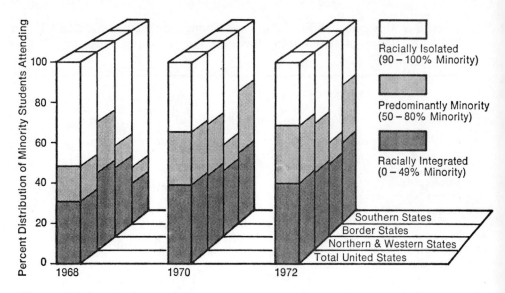

Figure 3-1. Racial Composition of Schools

Source: The National Center for Education Statistics, *The Conditions of Education,*
1976 (Washington, D.C.: U.S. Government Printing Office, 1976): 67.

tions were considered. The San Francisco-Oakland area, with a population of 3,109,519, would rank sixth in size among metropolitan areas,
for example.

The growth of towns into cities and cities into sprawling metropolitan
complexes has had a tremendous impact on society and schools. Urban
areas have developed systems within systems. There are varying levels
of government systems serving an area, such as county, state, and
local governments; there are various welfare agency systems, transportation systems, and economic systems.

Trends in Society and Schools
Among the educational systems, there are often public school districts,
church-related private schools, independent school districts, free school
districts, and teacher's organizations, all of which require financing for
their survival and contribute to the crucial social and cultural interactions
that either promote or hinder education. While these systems define
the quality of urban life and the degree to which a person is mobile
within a society, they also produce severe social and educational contradictions. These contradictions are assigned to our public schools for

Chart 3–2. Comparative Percentage of Change Between 1960 and 1970 in Total Population of Twenty-nine Selected Large Central Cities and Their Respective Suburbs

Central City	Percent of Change in Population of Central City Between 1960 and 1970	Percent of Change in Population of Surrounding Suburbs Between 1960 and 1970
St. Louis	−17.0	+28.5
Cleveland	−14.3	+27.1
Pittsburgh	−13.9	+ 4.4
Minneapolis	−10.0	+55.9
Detroit	− 9.5	+28.5
Boston	− 8.1	+14.7
New Orleans	− 5.4	+61.8
Chicago	− 5.2	+35.3
Seattle	− 4.7	+64.3
Baltimore	− 3.5	+34.7
San Francisco	− 3.3	+31.9
Philadelphia	− 2.7	+20.7
Washington, D.C.	− 1.0	+61.9
New York	+ 1.1	+25.7
Denver	+ 4.2	+63.7
Los Angeles	+13.6	+20.0
Columbus	+14.5	+32.8
San Diego	+21.6	+43.8
Dallas	+24.2	+61.8
Houston	+31.4	+56.7
In all central cities of U.S. SMSA's	+ 5.3	+28.2

Source: U.S. Department of Commerce, Bureau of the Census, *Census of Population,* 1970.

resolution. Because of the nature of urban survival, the following contradictions in urban society have been identified by social scientists:

1. Interdependence of urban life vs. isolation and segregation of subcultural groups.

2. Cultural pluralism vs. separate community control.

3. Urban middle class wealth vs. minority and ethnic poverty.

4. Belief that a good education leads to a good, secure job vs. the economics of present-day unemployment.

5. Belief in a well-rounded education (liberal arts) vs. vocational and career training.

Chart 3–3. Big Cities Where Most Students are Black

School District	Black Enrollment Number	As Percentage of All Students
Washington	133,638	95.5%
Atlanta	73,985	80.0%
New Orleans	77,504	74.6%
Newark	56,736	72.3%
Richmond	30,746	70.2%
Gary	31,200	69.6%
Baltimore	129,250	69.3%
St. Louis	72,629	68.8%
Philadelphia	173,874	61.4%
Oakland	39,121	60.0%
Birmingham	34,290	59.4%
Memphis	80,158	57.8%
Cleveland	83,596	57.6%
Chicago	315,940	57.1%
Kansas City, Mo.	35,578	54.4%
Louisville	25,078	51.0%

Source: U.S. Dept. of Health, Education and Welfare, 1976.

6. Rising demands for law and order vs. rising demands for police and court justice.

7. Slum and ghetto housing and high rents vs. high property costs, urban renewal, and suburban living.

8. Extensive highway and auto usage vs. pollution, overcrowding and lack of public transportation.

9. Greater expenditures for education vs. lower achievement scores.

10. Racial and ethnic justice vs. segregated institutions.

11. Belief in a national spirit and cohesiveness vs. regionalism and narrow geographic enculturation (ethnocentrism).

12. Democratic participation in decision making vs. concentration of political and economic power.

13. Belief in a free capitalistic economic system vs. monopoly and great wealth at the expense of the consumer.

14. Belief in open, free elections vs. lobbying, money interests, and seniority systems within political parties.

15. Energy crisis vs. the environmentalist crusade.

These contradictions have led some within our society to forecast social and economic disruption ahead for urban America. The Trend Analysis Program Report of the Institute of Life Insurance noted that "people increasingly want to be insured against such risks as loss of jobs, breakup of families, inadequate or incorrect medical attention, and unsafe or faulty products." The report noted that a transition will take place during the next two decades in our urban centers. It will be a move toward new but undefined culture that will ultimately "lead to more public frustration and worker alienation and with increased potential for slowdowns, sabotage, and riots." The report added that there would be more regulation by government in our daily lives, but that this could be offset by "increased disenchantment with the regulatory process, coming not only from business, but from the liberal political and academic communities."[2]

The report cites such things as the liberalization of criminal penalties without adequate programs to rehabilitate offenders, the substitution of methadone for heroin without tackling the underlying problems related to drugs, employment practices that lead to reverse discrimination, and, perhaps most important, the creation of large agencies, originally designed to carry out programs related to people's needs in urban areas, that have become so unwieldy that they are unable to cope with their internal problems, let alone meet the public's needs.[3]

The contradictions in urban society will probably foster several educational trends that may in coming years transform our public schools into new entities. In urban schools today, there is a remarkable consistency, uniformity, dullness, and drabness. Any trend that can break up the sameness of the public schools would be a change for the better. That sameness in public urban schools can be identified by the following characteristics that have been a persistent part of public urban education since the 1930s:

---

2. Institute of Life Insurance Report (Washington: Trend Analysis Program, 1975); *Los Angeles Times*, Dec. 22, 1975.
3. Institute of Life Insurance Report, *Los Angeles Times*, Dec. 22, 1975.

Organizational Characteristics

1. All students tend to take the same subjects in a required sequence; there are fairly uniform requirements for graduation.

2. Students are assigned into grades, time periods, and subjects with little variation or room for individualized instruction.

3. Ability grouping seems to dominate most schools, making clear distinctions between the academically talented and the remedial students.

4. Rules and regulations for school systems tend to be fairly uniform and do not vary much from school to school within a system.

5. Schools tend to operate on a two-semester schema and are open approximately nine months of the year; schools are generally organized for daylight hours only.

6. Most school systems are organized around the neighborhood school concept, which creates problems regarding desegregation.

7. The tax base for schools comes largely from local property taxes and state aid; inequities arise as a result of wealthy districts that are able to provide more school aid than are poor districts.

8. Schools are largely segregated in faculty and student bodies.

9. School systems are still largely centralized, with school boards either elected or appointed; there is little decentralization or local community control.

Curricular Characteristics

1. Systems still largely depend upon standardized testing and their results.

2. School systems still use the grading system as established during the 1940s with very little variation; few systems use a credit/no credit or pass/fail.

3. Curriculum content still tends to be largely monolingual and monocultural, although some recent changes have come about as a result of the bilingual movement.

4. Secondary and junior high schools tend to overemphasize

subject specialization and content coverage rather than skills and inquiry learning.

5. School systems still tend to use system-wide textbook adoptions with few opportunities for multiple texts. This tends to complicate the effective teaching of reading skills.

6. Schools tend to be academically oriented, past-oriented, and future-oriented; very little concern is given to present realities and adjustments.

7. Curriculum guides rarely effectively tap community resources or the mass media.

Instructional Characteristics

1. Guidance counselors do more paperwork than guidance, and guidance facilities are severely limited.

2. Teachers tend to teach to the group and group standards prevail; teachers tend to stay away from individualized instruction or the open classroom.

3. There is very little value clarification; more often, value instruction is centered around middle-class values such as deferred gratification, school/society structure and organization, time factors, competition, the work motive, and the importance of grades.

4. Methods and teaching approaches are largely unchanged, and contemporary social issues are excluded in part from the curriculum or watered down so that they are no longer controversial.

5. Students are largely powerless in making instructional revisions, and to a large extent, so are teachers; administrators and school boards determine decision making processes.

6. Dropout statistics for public schools are very high, and the dropouts tend to blame the teachers and the schools for their lack of interest in education.

7. Males still dominate the junior high and secondary levels while females dominate the primary and pre-primary levels.

Most educators believe that the 1980s will bring substantial changes to urban public education. The time is right, the need is great, and the cry for reform and change is loud.

Several present trends will predictably continue to gain strength in the future.[4]

Financial problems will become more acute as there are additional assaults on the property tax as a means of financing schools. Federal support will probably increase, but it will continue to be categorical rather than general. State control over school finances will probably increase.

Population mobility will also increase, as the flight to the suburbs continues to cause declining urban school enrollments. This will create problems in achieving integration in urban systems and lead to declining financial revenues, which, in turn, leads to deterioration of school property.

Minorities will gain greater representation on school boards and in administration, thus widening the split over the controversy of local community control of schools vs. integration.

Teachers will be held to a greater accountability level than ever before, with Competency-Based Programs reaching their peak. On the other hand, teacher militancy will be less effective due to continued teacher surplus, which will continue through the 1980s, and financial problems of city systems. Teachers will probably have a lesser role in decision and policy making.

The trend toward increasing school bureaucracies will continue as the government demands more special programs and credentials, e.g., bilingual programs and teachers. This will require more and more reports and additional educational staffs.

Instruction and curricula will focus more on individualization and emphasize identification of academic capability, learning inquiry techniques and skills, and clearly defined, workable behavioral objectives.

---

4. Irving Melbo, "Educational Trends in the 1970's," *Los Angeles Times,* Jan. 18, 1970; Harold Shane & June Shane, "Forecast for the Seventies" and John H. Fischer, "Realities of Education in Our Time," in Alfred Lightfoot's *Inquiries Into Social Foundations of Education* (Chicago: Rand McNally, 1972): pp. 74–88; Reform of Public Education in California, Recommendations (Sacramento: Dept. of Education, 1974).

Classrooms will be more open, nontraditional, and there will be greater emphasis on value-laden concerns.

Emphasis will be placed upon early childhood education and the crucial elementary years, while emphasis at the secondary level will be placed upon developing marketable occupational skills. Career education will occupy as strong a position as college preparatory. Students will be leaving school and entering college or the employment market earlier.

There will be an increased concern for insuring student rights, as well as a call to end compulsory education, corporal punishment, and rigid school operations.

Types of Urban Schools: Their Characteristics

The study of urban education is based on the belief that there is a part of education that is purely urban and that the teacher must be familiar with the culture and language of those being taught. As a recent addition to the educational vocabulary, the term *urban education* is used to describe contemporary problems and practicalities of urban schooling. It encompasses the vital social and psychological factors in the urban community that reflect upon schooling and associated institutional practices. Family backgrounds and traditions, self-concept, role playing and role expectations, value systems and peer group pressures, goals and levels of aspirations all are knowledge areas for understanding by urban teaching specialists.[5]

Urban life has as many varieties of life-styles as it has differing institutions. The same is also true of its schools. There are many types of urban schools, and it would be difficult to oversimplify urban education by forcing all schools into some sort of convenient mold. It can be said, however, with some degree of accuracy, that some schools more appropriately fall into a sociological and educational grouping than do others. Most educators and social scientists tend to group schools according to a certain criteria, which include socioeconomic class, parental and community involvement, emphasis of curriculum, and equal educational opportunity.

5. See Eugene Kruszynski, "The Nature of Urban Education," *School and Society,* March 1970. See also William Brickman and Stanley Lehrer, *Education and the Many Faces of the Disadvantaged* (New York: Wiley & Sons, 1972), Part I, pp. 19–64.

Socioeconomic class places students in schools according to their family's socioeconomic status. Since most public schools have some sort of neighborhood school system, the economic status of the parent is important. Since a child goes to school where he or she lives, family residence is a crucial factor. Basic to any housing pattern is family income and occupation. Schools, then, can be classified according to the socioeconomic status of its students. Faculty, on the other hand, is a less reliable indicator, since teachers do not often live in the school neighborhood in which they teach.

Parental and community involvement also seems related to socioeconomic class since a higher degree of involvement seems more evident on the higher social levels than on the lower levels. This can be due to a number of variables, but it tends to accent the social distance between classes all the more. School and community seem to be farther apart in lower socioeconomic classes than in higher socioeconomic classes.

The emphasis of the curriculum reflects the actual instructional process in the schools and tends to characterize the objectives and philosophy of the individual urban school. Is the curriculum concerned exclusively in preparing students for college entrance, or is it vocationally and career-education oriented? What academic courses are offered, and what electives are provided? What is the quality of the staff, their turnover rates, fatality rates, or tenure service? What are the attitudes, objectives, and aspirations of the faculty and how do these relate to the stereotypes they have regarding the youngster they are teaching (especially in the case of minority youngsters, culturally different youngsters, and the poor)? Relevancy and effectiveness of instructional offerings often reflect teacher turnover and transient rates of students.

Equal educational opportunity relates to socioeducational problems such as segregation, decentralization, school financing, compensatory educational programs, and experimental and/or innovative programs within a school system. In short, one school may have distinct advantages over another school simply because it receives more funds, more attention, and more publicity. This, in turn, influences the type of curriculum it offers, the materials it uses, the competency of the staff, and the types of accountability required to complete the program. Contrary to Coleman, few in urban education today would deny the influence of such external variables.

Most urban schools can fall into certain characteristic types. Urbanologists tend to divide these urban schools into six general types: high-status schools, main-line schools, common-man schools, transitory schools, inner-city schools and private schools.[6]

High-status schools constitute about 3 percent of the public school population, and in living patterns and life style, typify the upper-middle and middle classes, according to the Lloyd Warner Social Class Scale.[7] On the whole, these schools are located in the outer edges of urban areas or suburban areas. The curriculum is highly academic and college oriented. Such schools are largely segregated in terms of student body and staff. Class sizes are small, averaging from 10–25 students. School facilities are new and well-equipped. The average teacher tenure, approximately 15 years, shows a high degree of stability. In reading score tests, youngsters generally are above the 50 percentile. Dropout statistics are fairly low—about 1–5 percent of the district—and there are few, if any, problems relating to absenteeism, truancy, and transient students. Well over 80 percent of classroom time is spent on instruction, and less than 20 percent of classroom time is spent on discipline. The middle-class philosophy dominates the high-status school.[8]

The second type, the main-line school, constitutes about 7–10 percent of the school population and is basically a middle-class school in makeup and objectives. These schools also are largely segregated on both student and staff levels. Achievement scores tend to be average on a

6. See Robert Havighurst and Daniel Levine, *Education in Metropolitan Areas* (Boston: Allyn and Bacon, 1971); David Alloway and Francesco Cardasco, *Minorities and the American City* (New York: David McKay, 1970); A Berstein, *The Education of Urban Populations* (New York: Random House, 1967); Philip Vairo and J. Perel, *Urban Education: Problems and Prospects* (New York: McKay, 1969).

7. See Alfred Lightfoot, "The Potency of Social Class in Determining Educational Opportunity and Achievement," in Lightfoot's *Inquiries Into the Social Foundations of Education: Schools in Their Urban Setting* (Chicago: Rand McNally, 1970).

8. See James B. Conant's *Slums and Suburbs: A Commentary on Schools in Metropolitan Areas* (New York: McGraw Hill, 1961); Elizabeth Eddy, *Walk the White Line: A Profile of Urban Education* (New York: Doubleday, 1967); R. Corwin, *A Sociology of Education: Emerging Patterns of Class, Status and Power in the Public Schools* (New York: Appleton-Century-Crofts, 1965); Herbert Rudman and Richard Featherstone, *Urban Schooling* (New York: Harcourt, Brace and World, 1968); Alfred Lightfoot, *American Urban Education: Inquiries Into Changing Patterns* (New York: N.S.S. Educational Co., 1970).

national scale (reading scores range around the 45–50 percentile), and dropouts are still low—around 5–10 percent of the total school population. Class sizes tend to average 25–30, and the average teacher's tenure is 13–14 years. Instruction occupies 80 percent of classroom time, and discipline accounts for less than 20 percent of classroom time. The main-line school is also a very desirable assignment for teachers, but judging from population shifts and current urban demographic figures, possible assignments in main-line and high-status schools in the future will be less and less likely.[9]

Common-man schools constitute about 30 percent of our public school population. Relatively close to the center of the city geographically, they are frequently in working class areas and are composed of the lower-middle class and upper-lower class on the Warner Scale. Curriculum has the greatest diversity in common-man schools since they differ from one another greatly in the degree of intensity with which they view education and community involvement. Class sizes vary from 30–35, and the dropout rate begins to climb substantially, constituting about 20 percent of the public school population. Teacher tenure averages about 5–10 years and is relatively stable. Teachers frequently transfer from inner-city assignments to the common-man schools. Achievement scores tend to be low, and the national reading scores tend to be at the 30–40 percentile, below the norm. Almost half the instructional time is devoted to discipline and organizational matters. Emphasis on either the academic and or the vocational spheres varies, depending on the neighborhood in which the school is located. Many common-man schools are integrated, yet there are tremendous racial and cultural pressures against integration. Most busing protagonists can be found in common-man school neighborhoods, and the areas become social battlegrounds over this and other issues.[10]

---

9. See the following: Martin Deutsch, *The Disadvantaged: Studies of the Social Environment and Learning* (New York: Basic Books, 1967; Robert Dentler, *Big City Dropouts and Illiterates* (New York: Praeger, 1963); A. Wise, *Rich Schools, Poor Schools* (Chicago: University of Chicago Press, 1968); Atron Gentry, et al., *Urban Education: The Hope Factor* (Philadelphia: W. Saunders Co., 1972).

10. See Robert Havighurst and Daniel Levine, *Education in Metropolitan Areas,* pp. 93–111; Robert Strom, *Teaching in the Slum School* (Columbus: Merrill, 1965); Richard Wisniewski, *New Teachers in Urban Schools* (Detroit: Wayne State University, 1968).

Transitory schools are the most explosive schools in any urban school system. They hover between the common-man school and the inner-city school, primarily because of changing housing patterns, enforced desegregation, community militancy, and increasing minority enrollments. Although only about 10 percent of the public school population, these students constitute the "social dynamite" which Conant referred to in his study, *Slums and Suburbs.* These schools have been common-man schools and are now moving toward a racial balance in student body and in staff. The transition from an all-white school to an integrated school presents problems for the school as well as for the community. Staff reorientation and inservice training on intergroup behavior becomes necessary. This transition period is often marked by disorder and violence in and around the school. Often school boards take emergency action to prevent "white flight." Transitory schools have acute problems, and they are no place for new, inexperienced, or nontenured teachers.

Inner-city schools now take in the majority of youngsters attending public school, about 40–50 percent of the population. As such, inner-city schools face the most complex problems of any type of school in the system. Class sizes vary from 30–50 students. In some cases, when substitute teachers simply cannot be obtained by an inner-city school, class sizes may go even higher. Achievement scores are generally lowest in the system, with reading percentiles at a crucially low level. Several inner-city high schools in Los Angeles found the twelfth graders had a reading percentile average of 7. Status-wise, the inner-city school tends to reflect a middle-lower and lower-lower class status on the Warner Scale. Dropout figures are the highest in public education; they reach the 50 percent figure in some school districts. Inner-city schools are not always in the inner or central city, but can be on fringe areas as well. The problems of an inner-city school are presented in more detail later.

Private schools are the sixth category. Since this discussion centers around urban education in a public setting, little need be said about private schools. In general, private schools are of three kinds: religious, socioeconomic, or alternative schools. Parochial schools constitute about 80 percent of all private schools. The largest single parochial system is the Roman Catholic school system. Parochial schools exhibit the same types of schools as public schools, having high-status, main-line, common-man, transitional, and inner-city school categories.

Problems in the parochial schools are not unlike those of the public schools, and there is a definite similarity between inner-city school problems in Catholic and public schools.[11] Approximately 15 percent of private schools cater primarily to the upper-class youngster whose life-styles demand segregation academically and socially. A vast variety of such schools exist; they range from private prep schools to the military schools. The smallest number of private schools, constituting only 5 percent of the group, are the alternative schools, which offer new approaches to education and curricular design that stand in sharp contrast to many public school systems.

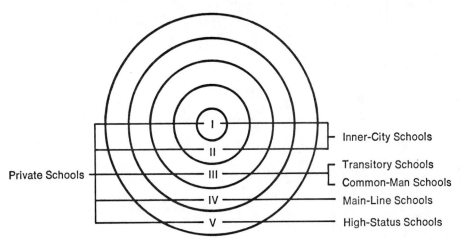

Figure 3-2. Concentric Zone Theory of School Organization

Schools follow housing patterns. The neighborhood school system is based, to a large extent, upon socioeconomic status, especially since the determining factors of class position are income, occupation, life-style, and housing. The five types of public schools just described are generally equated with the zones shown in Figure 3–2. As the central city begins to move outward, the next zone moves into a transitional zone and carries the characteristics of the former zone with it.

---

11. Alfred Lightfoot, "Inservice Training Program for Los Angeles Catholic Archdiocese Inner City Teachers," Los Angeles Archdiocese, October 1974, Loyola Marymount University.

Chart 3–4. Composite View of Types of Urban Schools

Type of School	Socio-Econ Class	Percent of Population in Public Schools	Curriculum Orientation	Dropout Rate (Percent)	Average Class Size	Teacher Tenure (By Years)	Percentile Average Reading Scores
High-Status	UM MM	3	academic	1–5	10–25	15	50+
Main-Line	MM	7–10	academic and career	5–10	25–30	13	45+
Common-Man	LM UL	30–40	academic and vocational	20	30–35	10	30+
Inner-City	ML LL	50	academic and vocational	50	30–50	3.1–5	5–20+
Private	All	17		Varies	Varies	10	45+

Not all cities follow a concentric zone pattern. Some follow a section zone approach or a multiple nuclei approach. Chicago represents a concentric zone pattern, while Los Angeles represents the multiple nuclei pattern.

By comparing the demographics on inner-city schools versus those of other kinds of schools, it is easy to sense the frustration of parents who send their children to these schools, as well as that of the faculties who deal with these students. In the 1970s, with social problems more magnified than ever before and solutions more elusive, many people feel that the American ideal of equal opportunity has somehow eluded them. Persons who plan to teach in these school systems will have to be prepared to cope with the numerous problems.

Exercises

I. Work on this problem individually or in small groups.

The Facts

1. School System A consists of 800,000 students.

2. The students are largely urban, minority groups are 55 percent of the school population.

3. The school system is spread out over an unusually large geographic area, covering 12 square miles.

4. There is a professional staff of 35,000 teachers, 7,000 administrators, and 6,000 paraprofessionals.

5. There are 250 elementary schools, 100 junior high schools, and 75 senior high schools in School System A.

6. Social problems the administration and teachers must cope with include declining student enrollment, minority students' unrest, growing teacher militancy as the staff senses that cutbacks may be in the offing if the school population continues to decline, and court-ordered desegregation.

7. There are also economic problems: three bond issues have failed to pass in as many years, and the administration is faced with the need to cutback operational costs before the end of the school year.

The Problem

You are a member of the Board of Education for School System A, and the superintendent has just presented you with the projected budget for next year. The budget is for only $768 million when school operating costs are really $900 million. The problem is how to balance the budget and make the necessary cuts. Use the following guidelines as you work on the problem.

1. Assuming that you will obtain no additional revenues, where should cuts be made? Be specific. Justify each cut economically, educationally, and sociologically.

2. If there were alternate revenue-raising plans, what would they be? Why would you use them?

3. How do you maintain quality service, solve some of the school system's internal problems, and survive the year?

4. What cuts should be made in the following areas:
   curriculum
   staff
   programs
   operating expenses

II. The following test was recently given at an inservice training program. How would you answer these statements?[11]

Fact Sheet on Inner City Schools

Place checks beside the statements that depict inner-city schools.

Inner-city schools:

____ (1) are largely composed of racial or cultural minorities.

____ (2) have the highest degree of teacher turnover.

____ (3) have the largest number of teacher substitute needs.

____ (4) have the highest incidence of gang violence.

____ (5) have the highest degree of administrative turnover.

---

11. Alfred Lightfoot, "Inservice Training Program for Los Angeles Catholic Archdiocese Inner City Teachers," Los Angeles Archdiocese, October 1974, Loyola Marymount University.

_____ (6) have the highest number of inexperienced, nontenured teachers.

_____ (7) have the greatest needs in terms of building maintenance and materials.

_____ (8) have the lowest achievement scores, especially in reading skills.

_____ (9) have the highest percentage of minority teachers.

_____ (10) have the largest overall class sizes.

_____ (11) have the greatest number of serious discipline disruptions.

_____ (12) have the greatest need in terms of health and social services.

_____ (13) have the highest dropout rates.

_____ (14) have the largest number of older buildings and outdated equipment.

_____ (15) have the greatest need for financial funds from compensatory aid.

_____ (16) have the greatest problem regarding social distance between parents and teachers.

_____ (17) can be parochial schools as well as public schools.

_____ (18) have the highest percentage of provisionally certified teachers.

_____ (19) have the highest percentage of overage children per grade.

_____ (20) have the greatest problems regarding attendance, truancy, and transient rates.

The Urban Teacher: Teaching and Surviving in the Urban Schools

Chapter 4

When you have finished this chapter, you should be able to perform the following tasks.

1. Explain the relationship between urban development and city growth and educational problems.

2. List the reasons for the teacher attrition rate in urban schools.

3. Describe the significant changes in youth since the 1940s and suggest their implications for the urban teacher of today.

4. State and describe the reasons for teacher surplus and list some possible implications for the profession and society.

5. Describe the component parts that make for a competent urban teacher and suggest reasons that some urban teachers are incompetent.

6. Tell why inner-city areas have problems different than other areas and why these problems are more comprehensive and acute than in other areas.

7. Identify components and strategies for improving instruction in urban areas.

Today's world is characterized by its complex social organization. Part of that organization is the public school system. Just as technology increases modern bureaucracy and the depersonalization of people, it also generates specialization and creates a greater desire for interdependence and cooperation. Developing an atmosphere where specialization, cooperation, and technology can be advanced is a key objective of contemporary education. The goal of education in any society is to empower persons to act in the interests of self and society, to give all citizens the skills, experiences, and understandings vital to maintenance and survival in contemporary society.

It has been recognized that today's emerging, complex urban society can actually restrict rather than expand personal living. Uselessness, monotony, depersonalization, prejudice, and anomie are, unfortunately, the by-products of economic affluence and urban development and evolution. In the context of social relevance, the many problems of the schools must have high priority among the overall complexities of urban society in the 1970s.

Cities are the communities of the future. Urbanization has become one of the most dominant aspects of modern society. The 1960 Census listed 212 metropolitan areas, encompassing 112 million people, or approximately 63 percent, of the total population. The 1970 Census has shown further growth concentrations. California, for example, increased its population by 25 percent, topping 19.5 million, with the greatest population increases in the metropolitan areas of Los Angeles, San Diego, San Jose, and Sacramento.

Approximately two-thirds of all U.S. schoolchildren and teachers are in city schools. This phenomenal urban development and city growth is the cause of numerous, difficult educational problems. For example:

> 1. As metropolitanism increases and people flood the cities, people become more stratified, segregated and ethnocentric. They are polarized in terms of social class, racial and ethnic composition, cultural background and interests, and housing patterns. The schools are then faced with the challenges of assimilation, desegregation, social mobility, decentralization, and the development of a meaningful, multicultural curriculum geared to all segments of society.
>
> 2. As urban areas increase in geographic and demographic size, their financial problems increase. Police and safety protection, recreation facilities, transportation, sanitation, and educational facilities are areas of mounting crisis.

3. As urban living becomes more complex, specialization and academic competence receive greater attention in our schools. The disadvantaged drop out, often only to join the unemployed.

4. As urban centers increase in size and social intensity, the schools must of necessity make students more aware of social realities. What seemingly still exists is a fantastic gap between Modern Urban Life and Modern Education. To meet these challenges, educational change and innovation must take place. In the 1970s more students will demand better education, in terms of less alienation and more reform.

Urban growth over the last several years has made it more difficult for youth to get a good education. School systems have become the victims of the growing metropolitanism; they have received little attention in comparison to other social institutions in urban society. Fundamental and substantial changes are needed if present-day educational policy, organization, and curriculum is to function well.

The motivations for entering the teaching profession are complex and exceedingly difficult to discern. Teachers enter the profession in large numbers for a variety of personal, social, economic, and humanitarian reasons—and they leave the profession in numbers just as large. Teaching in an urban classroom today is one of the more demanding professions. The attrition rate in the teaching profession is the highest of all professions and is even excessive compared to all other occupations.[1] Yet, there still exists a surplus of teachers. And even with the high professional mortality rate of teachers, a surplus will be a permanent characteristic of the 1970s.

Why Teachers Leave the Field
The causes of teacher attrition are, of course, only speculative. Nevertheless, several hypotheses can be advanced for the demographic

---

1. In the 1960s, Nelson and Thompson did a study on teacher attrition and concluded that only 75 percent of people prepared to teach actually enter the classroom (this is much higher today because of teacher surplus) and that less than 10 percent of those 75 percent will actually be found in the classroom ten years from now. See R.H. Nelson and M.L. Thompson, "Why Teachers Quit," *The Clearing House*, Issue 37, 1963, p. 467; see also, March, 1964, issue of *Educational Digest*. Teacher surplus, a reality of the 1970s, has changed this considerably.

turnover. First, many experts feel that the level of aspiration of teachers would be more realistic and the exodus from the profession far lower if teachers received financial remuneration equivalent to the status attached to teaching. Second, teachers have little choice over what tools they are to use or how and when to use them. Such control would undoubtedly benefit students, because teachers have the greatest degree of contact with them and are likely to be most sensitive to their needs. It would also improve the self-esteem of teachers. Third, teachers should receive realistic training that truly prepares them for what they will face in classrooms. If teachers were prepared as professionals *for the specific task of teaching,* fewer numbers—especially among beginners—would become dropouts. Fourth, if teachers were better able to understand children with backgrounds and cultures different from their own, they would be more capable of facing and coping with the pressures of contemporary urban and educational realities, and could manage and manipulate them into a more meaningful, relevant experience. This facet, too, could be part of a teacher's education.

Today's urban classroom teacher must be equipped with certain competencies. Among these are:

> 1. Knowledgeable and experiential exposure to disadvantaged pupils and the communities in which they live so as to prevent cultural shock and disorientation.

> 2. Analytical training balanced against a firm background of theoretical training to give the teacher the conceptual equipment necessary to be more than a reactor to trial and error, intuition, and common sense. Understanding classroom situations avoids classroom difficulties and mistakes.

> 3. Sensitization of the teachers to their prejudices and an effort to provide them with mechanisms to control them.

> 4. More systematic preparation in the skills needed to perform in the classroom, a better apprentice system, greater experiences with minority children, and a greater exposure to the social sciences and the answers they can provide to behavioral patterns.

Teacher education today has failed to prepare the teacher to work effectively with children of varying social and economic origins. This means failure for the teacher and failure for the youth. It ultimately means failure for the democratic system of public education—a system founded on the premise of equal educational opportunity.

As demographic patterns indicate a greater and greater concentration of youth from low socioeconomic groups in urban schools (these children are often minority children and culturally disadvantaged youth as well), one can only conclude that, to be effective, teachers in these schools must be effectively prepared.

Teaching in the urban school today can be at once the most frustrating and the most rewarding experience of one's professional career. Many teachers fall apart and fall out of the profession altogether—others stay, learn, and profit from their experiences and go on to greater professional competency.

Educators should be concerned about helping the teacher who is dropping out, as well as assisting the teacher who holds on too long. One thing schools of education should be doing is "telling it like it is."

Changes in Students Since the 1940s

Adolescents have changed since the 1940s, and today's youth present an altogether different set of problems. Unfortunately, teacher education too often deals with outdated attitudes, a fact that has contributed to the high teacher dropout rate. Teachers today are too often ill-prepared for the realities of urban teaching. C. Wayne Gordon, an educational sociologist long associated with the study of youth in the social context of the school, has described the features of the changing adolescent societies from the 1940s through the 1970s.[2]

Adolescent Societies of the 1940s, 1950s, and
Early 1960s

> 1. [Adolescent society] was a highly differentiated, highly stratified, and steeply ranked system, capable of providing

---

2. C. Wayne Gordon, "Prospects for the School Sociologist," paper presented at the National Invitational Conference on School Sociologists, May 1–3, 1975, Los Angeles, California, published by the University of Southern California, *Proceedings of the National Invitational Conference on School Sociologists*, pp. 29–33.

enormous satisfaction to its high-ranking members while delivering low satisfaction and deprivation to a very substantial proportion of its low-ranking members.

2. It was an internally oriented social system with its own elites, its own distinctive values, norms, activities, and its own sources of reward in social response of peers.

3. In relation to adults, parents, teachers, and administrators, it was in conflict. Collectively, it was in conflict with established authority.

4. In spite of substantial conflict, it was largely adult-sponsored in its values, leadership, and activities. While we have labeled it an adolescent-achieved status system, it may be accurately referred to as an adult-sponsored status system. Its activities, except for drinking and sexual experimentation, were legitimate.

5. From the view of adolescents, with the exception of lower-class youth, the goals and activities of the formal school system were also still legitimate. The core of basic values was shared by youth and adults. It was primarily in the realm of priorities of commitment where conflict occurred. The substantial variation in orientation to academic achievement and popular activities which Coleman found did not preclude the overlapping of values.

6. Adolescent societies were school-oriented. Social status was achieved in school-based activities. In current terms, school was where "it was at."

7. Although self-contained and varying considerably in the degree of autonomy and dependence of adult sponsorship and influence, adolescent societies were subject to a high degree of adult influence. Social and educational influence were monitored through the social elites.

8. The system served as a powerful control over behavior through its clearly defined norms and powerful sanctions. As such, it was an equally powerful socializer of expected behavior and new roles; the result bred uniformity. This feature of the system indicates its potential for learning if properly organized to serve educational purposes.

9. Status and identity resulted from the highly structured and patterned system of social interaction. Each member could derive a sense of who he was in the scheme of events. It should be noted that the system was productive of low self-esteem for many, but the sources of identity formation were inherent in the system.

10. The means for defining status were both visible and pervasive. The most detailed areas of behavior were patterned.

The color and style of shirt were subject to approval as well as the number of rolls of the sleeves at nine o'clock in the morning; further, there was an approved number of rolls of the sleeve at eleven o'clock. Predictability and stability of patterned behavior regulated the evaluation and allocation of status and undoubtedly had an important consequence for personality development of adolescents. The suggestion here is that the so called identity crisis which we hear about today is related to changes occurring in the social structure of youth societies.

11. Adolescent societies, with status systems based on either family-ascribed status or school-based, adolescent-achieved status, have been characterized in the past tense. These types of societies still represent present systems—particularly small and medium [sized] independent communities away from the large urbanized metropolitan centers.

12. The social system was characterized by the interplay of formal structures, especially the voluntary associations of the extra-curriculum; formal standards of academic achievements; and the student social structure and subculture in patterning the life of the student in school. In its normative basis and the ways in which it channeled student involvement and effort, this pattern was indeed alienated from the school's official expectations.

13. It is worthy of note that conformity to teachers' expectations influenced peer social status, and the power of teacher expectations arose largely from grade sanctions. But paradoxically, the student subculture redefined, through the extra-curriculum, the meaning of academic achievement.

14. The major implication of adolescent-achieved status is to intensify the dilemmas of the teacher role. The ways in which teachers attempt to resolve the dilemma will vary as an interaction effect of the student society, the school bureaucracy, and the strength and nature of collegial norms.

Adolescent Societies of the Mid to Late 1960s

1. Adolescent society tended to be oriented away from school. School was no longer the place "where it was happening." Whereas the earlier social structure of adolescent society was an elaborate status system, steeply ranked and created largely out of adult-sponsored, school-based activities, the new society had a more diffuse structure created out of off-campus activity influenced by leading figures of the mass media, popular music, cinema, television, art, and popular magazines.

2. The absence of highly structured relationships and patterned activity leading to a clearly defined status system may have accounted for the diffuse process of identity-seeking in

off-campus contexts. At the same time, a certain equally diffuse anomie pervaded the school.

3. Behavior appeared to be more manifestly psychological in content, whereas the earlier form appeared more social—at least in open expression; hence, youth were more concerned with self-identity than with status and conformity.

4. The search for personal identity was more prone to the use of drugs as a means of exploration. It also served as a manner of rejection of established values, rules, and authority.

5. Youth-adult conflict reflected not only a break with authority, but also a break with established values and belief systems.

6. The search for satisfaction was found in the mass gathering and the vast musical happening.

7. Adolescents sought immediate satisfaction; postponed gratification was no longer the motivating force.

Adolescent Societies of the 1970s

1. There appears to be some reorientation of youth to the school as a place of significance.

2. "Glitter is back" with heavy emphasis on conspicuous consumption and status validation through informal groups and formal extra-curricular participation.

3. Drug usage continues with an increase in the usage of alcohol.

4. Deviant ganging and gang violence is more prevalent.

5. Social goals are internal to the youth society and less directed toward the larger society.

Gordon's views about youth's transition from the 1940s to the 1970s is a significant contribution to the understanding of the educational milieu today. It is of profound importance to future urban teachers as they seek to comprehend the relationship between the sociological and psychological influences of society versus the school's influence. Gordon summarizes several important implications relative to the sociological content and the method of instruction in the secondary school.[3] They are as follows:

1. The classical bureaucratic model for classroom instruction with its assumptions of teacher authority, prescribed objects of

---

3. *Ibid.* See also S.L. Halleck, "Hypotheses of Student Unrest," in Alfred Lightfoot's *Inquiries Into the Social Foundations of Education* (Chicago: Rand McNally, 1972), pp. 89–103.

interest, and individualized systems of competitive achievement may no longer serve.

2. Educational activity which does not use the processes and sources of social reward inherent in youth society is unlikely to be successful.

3. The current malaise and apathy found in the typical high school social studies class provide evidence for the failures of current efforts.

4. If the school is ceasing to be the place of significant and meaningful activity for youth, we have a problem of legitimating our offering.

5. The context of adolescent society should dictate both the content and method of instruction.

6. An educational program consistent with the orientation of youth societies.

The Realities of Teacher Surplus

The nation's schools and the 2.1 million teachers are in the midst of hard times. The old adage that, if one got a teaching credential, one would never be in need of a job is no longer realistic. For the first time in a century, public school teachers are finding it difficult to secure teaching positions. It is no longer a buyer's market; teacher supply has not only caught up with but has suddenly and unexpectedly exceeded demand in almost every academic field on nearly all educational levels. This situation is likely to remain fairly constant throughout the 1970s and into the 1980s. This situation brings with it the always present danger that it may increase the already deteriorating state of public education.

Several years ago, educational systems, waiting for the supply of teachers to catch up with the demand, operated with starvation staffs. Large urban systems had the greatest difficulty in obtaining and keeping teachers. Teacher mobility was high. Districts such as Los Angeles, Chicago, New York, and Detroit often recruited teachers on a nationwide basis, using every device from campus visits to newspaper and radio appeals. In the more critical inner-city areas, the shortage of teachers was particularly acute.

Statistics in the middle to late 1970s revealed a reversed trend. Large urban systems no longer needed to extend themselves to obtain teachers.

Some experts estimate that by 1980, there may be as many as 240,000 teachers competing for 90,000 openings.[4] The National Educational Association estimated that in 1975 only 111,000 of the 234,000 persons who received teaching credentials were able to find jobs in teaching.[5] In 1975, in California alone, it was estimated that professional schools were turning out twice as many graduates as there were jobs—20,000 teachers for 10,000 positions.[6] A more current, conservative estimate is that the supply of teachers in 1977 will exceed demand by about 100,000 teachers.[7]

Figure 4-1 illustrates this imbalance. It is taken from the National Survey of the Preservice Preparation of Teachers (NSPPT) and the National Center for Educational Statistics (NCES).[8]

Chart 4-1[9] indicates the enrollments from 1975-76 in teacher training institutions. Although this was the worst period of surplus, these institutions were still turning out many teachers for nonexistent jobs:

Chart 4-1. Summary of Teacher Preparation Institutions, 1975-76

Institution Type	Number of Institutions	Pre-Service Enrollment	Number of Grads With Teaching Certificates
All Institutions Combined	1,151	411,000	227,000
Public	424	257,000	163,000
Private	727	154,000	64,000
Universities	150	83,000	69,000
Comprehensive Colleges	438	271,000	124,000
Liberal Arts	563	57,000	34,000

Source: *Condition of Teacher Education, 1977: Summary Report.* National Center for Educational Statistics (NCES).

4. *Los Angeles Times,* March 6, 1977.

5. *Los Angeles Times,* May 5, 1975.

6. *The Sacramento Bee,* December 3, 1975.

7. *Condition of Teacher Education, 1977: Summary Report,* report by the National Center for Educational Statistics (NCES), p. 7. See also Department of HEW, National Center for Education Statistics, *Projections of Education Statistics, 1984-85,* 1975 edition.

8. *Condition of Teacher Education,* 1977, p. 8.

9. *Condition of Teacher Education,* 1977, p. 6.

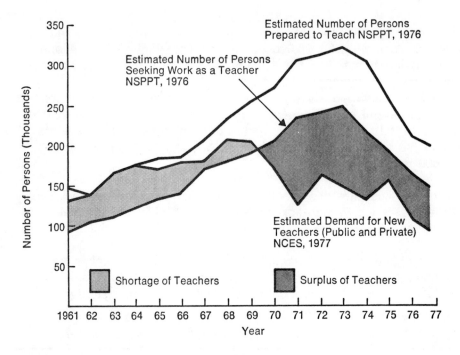

Figure 4-1. Supply and Demand for Teachers

Source: *Condition of Teacher Education, 1977: Summary Report,* Report by the National Center for Educational Statistics (Washington, D.C.: U.S. Government Printing Office, 1977): 7.

All academic fields are overcrowded, although some disciplines are more glutted than others. College placement offices indicate that the most difficult areas in which to place candidates are the social sciences, English, languages, and elementary and secondary education. Even math, science, and the vocational and fine arts are rapidly becoming overcrowded. The areas of special education, remedial reading, and some areas of vocational education are stabilizing, and the need for bilingual teachers is on the increase.[10] As a result, enrollments of teachers in elementary and secondary education in colleges has finally fallen off, as Figure 4–2[11] illustrates.

---

10. *Los Angeles Times,* March 2, 1977.

11. *Condition of Teacher Education, 1977,* p. 10.

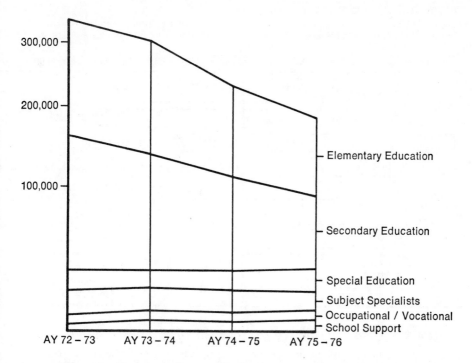

Figure 4-2. Supply of Trained Educational Personnel by Area of Specialization (Beginning Teachers)

Source: *Condition of Teacher Education, 1977: Summary Report*, Report by the National Center for Educational Statistics (Washington, D.C.: U.S. Government Printing Office, 1977): 10.

To better face the reality of supply and demand, the NSPPT asked teacher training institutions to forecast future trends in enrollment and got the results shown in Figure 4–3.[12]

What has caused this imbalance of supply and demand, and why has it occurred at this time? A number of sociological and economic reasons can be advanced to explain this change. The postwar baby boom is now being reflected in the job market. At the same time, enrollment figures in the public schools leveled off substantially as the baby boom subsided. National population statistics show a decrease

---

12. *Condition of Teacher Education*, 1977, p. 13.

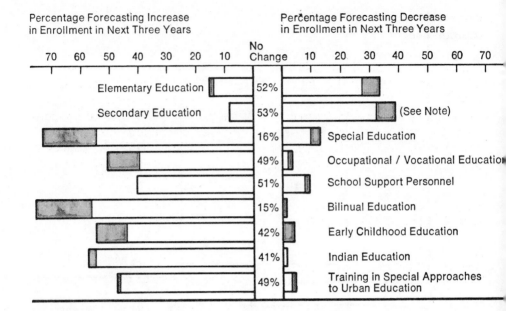

Figure 4-3. Anticipated Near-Term Trends in Supply

Note: 0.6% or 7 Institutions reported that secondary education would be eliminated.

Source: *Condition of Teacher Education, 1977: Summary Report*, Report by the National Center for Educational Statistics (Washington, D.C.: U.S. Government Printing Office, 1977): 13.

of over 1 million births since 1958. It will continue through the 1970s and well into the 1980s. The record birth levels of 1947–1967 peaked at 46.1 million in 1970–1971 and have been declining steadily since that period. Since the beginning of the 1970s, the number of children in the 5–13 age group has declined by about 3 million. This is a 10 percent drop in the population of elementary and junior high children, and it is being noticed in the surplus teacher market today. It is estimated that by 1983–1984 the school population will be down 5.8 million or 12.5 percent from the peak year. In California alone, the drop was very noticeable with a statewide loss of over 34,000 students, about 6,000 in the city of Los Angeles, and about 19,000 in the county of Los Angeles.[13] This change is particularly dramatic because the schools

13. *Los Angeles Times*, February 26, 1975; *Los Angeles Times*, March 6, 1976; Martin, *op. cit.*, p. 24.

were tightly geared from the 1960s on for continued increases in the population.

Another reason for the teacher surplus is that schools of education are still turning out record numbers of teachers and that teaching as a profession is still considered one of the more attractive careers. In 1974, the Gallup Poll listed teaching as the top career choice of college students; medicine was the second choice.[14] Although this has changed somewhat with the realities of the present market, teaching still remains a glamorous and humanitarian profession. Figure 4–4[15]

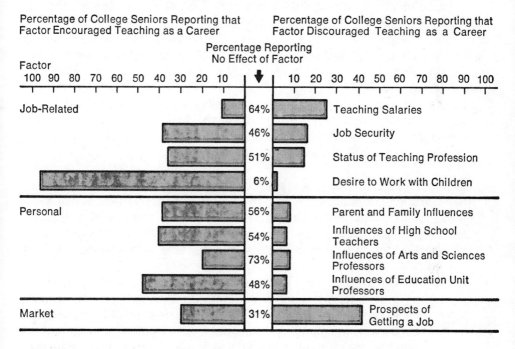

Percentage of College Seniors Reporting that Factor Encouraged Teaching as a Career

Percentage of College Seniors Reporting that Factor Discouraged Teaching as a Career

Percentage Reporting
No Effect of Factor

Factor		
Job-Related	64%	Teaching Salaries
	46%	Job Security
	51%	Status of Teaching Profession
	6%	Desire to Work with Children
Personal	56%	Parent and Family Influences
	54%	Influences of High School Teachers
	73%	Influences of Arts and Sciences Professors
	48%	Influences of Education Unit Professors
Market	31%	Prospects of Getting a Job

Figure 4-4. Factors Affecting College Student Choice in Careers

Source: *Condition of Teacher Education, 1977: Summary Report*, Report by the National Center for Educational Statistics (Washington, D.C.: U.S. Government Printing Office, 1977): 17.

14. *Los Angeles Times,* April 25, 1974.
15. *Condition of Teacher Education,* 1977, p. 17.

63   The Urban Teacher

illustrates this point when one considers that most people going into the profession are doing so because they want to work with children.

Finances are another contributing factor to the surplus. Because of the lack of money for urban school systems, boards of education have had to trim their budgets substantially. Teacher salaries have naturally become a prime target, as have many teacher benefits such as step increases and sick leave. Health benefits such as health insurance have increased tremendously with the rate of inflation and school systems simply cannot afford to find money for the many variables that the forces of inflation have created. Special educational programs have been cut, teaching staffs reduced, class sizes increased, and numerous cutbacks have been made in curricula. Taxpayers' rebellions against property taxes, alienation over declining achievement scores, angry feelings about desegregation and school busing, and increasing teacher militancy over declining teacher salaries and other benefits have led to a general, all-pervasive anti-education or anti-teacher attitude in many parts of the U.S. Increasingly conservative reaction from state legislatures and their reluctance to kick in more funds have led to an emergency situation in most urban school systems. The day of bankrupt school systems is close upon us.

Whether this national emergency can be turned around remains to be seen. Many educators think not. The future of education, as visualized now, seems particularly depressed for education in general and for teachers in particular. Both from an educator's and a sociologist's perspective, certain drastic implications become self-evident:

> 1. Teacher training institutions will have to adjust their programs to move more in line with the demand. Although fewer students are now going into teaching than did in the early 1970s and enrollments in schools of education are down, teacher training institutions seem capable of only gradual responses to this change. Built-in factors, such as survival and competition, add to the slow response. When one considers that 46 percent of the faculties in educational programs are tenured, one can see the problem.[16] In addition,

---

16. *Condition of Teacher Education*, 1977, p. 18.

up to two full years are often required to make a program change that involves different staffing, budgeting, and initiation. Also, commitments to students in existing programs must be met.

2. Through their recruitment practices, administrators, long felt to be the more conservative members of the educational establishment, can select those candidates who they consider most desirable. Obviously, with the surplus market and surplus of candidates for each job, an administrator will tend to select the ones who will follow procedures and play the game, rather than ones who may "rock the boat." The good teacher may be the safe teacher. One top administrator once confessed to this writer that he did not hire men who wore beards since he identified extremism with that image.

3. Financial cutbacks are going to restrict and hamper severely the educational progress of city schools. Los Angeles, for example, anticipates a deficit in 1978 in excess of 20 million dollars, which will result in a drastic cutback on services to the city. Even small school districts in California have faced these same realities and the consequent personnel cutbacks. Teacher's strikes are ineffectual if the money just is not there. Most systems are also facing further desegregation efforts, and that is also going to cost more money and, possibly, more loss of students to the system.

4. Professional pressures upon teachers will be more intense than ever. Noncredentialed and provisional teachers are in the greatest jeopardy. With the availability of credentialed and qualified teachers, school systems can select those who meet their standards. Graduate work will be required; teachers will have to go back to school for inservice training or for specialties that the schools now require. This does not mean, however, that the system will necessarily pay teachers for their graduate training with increases in the pay scale. It is more likely that additional education will be a minimal requirement just to hold a position. Many doctorates are already employed in urban school systems because of the surplus of persons with these degrees in higher education. Pressure to abolish tenure, which may very well be used as a ploy of the public and politician alike, could, if adopted, have

an ultimate effect on teacher militancy. Teachers will have to be constantly on guard to survive and to guard the advances made over the last century.

5. Teacher mobility, long a social characteristic of the teaching profession, may be severely restricted. The surplus of teachers and the financial difficulty of districts suggest that it will be far more difficult for a teacher to change jobs. The surplus will make it far more difficult to compete for positions in other school systems because they will not be able to afford to pay a higher salary to a transfer with more experience when they already have a surplus of qualified teachers willing to start at the bottom of the salary scale. For the new teachers, a willingness to go anywhere may be a must to secure that first job, but after that, their movements will be greatly restricted.

Obviously, there will be more pressure on teachers to retire early so that younger teachers can come into the system, presumably at lower salaries. As the market worsens, the new, unemployed teacher will become alienated by a system that protects the older teacher who has seniority and ignores the younger teacher. This friction can already be noticed in numerous teacher organizations and unions across the country.

The job picture is indeed bleak; a sort of Darwinian principle of survival of the fittest may prevail. Some optimists, although in the minority, view it differently. In 1970, Dr. Allan Ostar, then executive director of the American Association of State Colleges and Universities, noted: "There is no teacher surplus. There is an educational deficit which, for the first time since World War II, we now have an opportunity to correct ... this is an opportunity, not a calamity."[17] Many educators, however, fail to see the truth of this statement.

Teacher Training

Teachers exert a great deal of influence over the pupils they teach; other than the parents of the child, no other persons have such direct

---

17. *U.S. News and World Report,* "Now: Too Many Teachers," July 6, 1970, p. 23.

and enduring contact with youngsters. In some urban schools, youngsters come into more frequent contact with teachers than with parents.

Three general characteristics are likely to appear in a teacher whose influence is favorable on the students. First, the teacher has legitimate power. The teacher's behavior is in basic accord with the established professional norms of his profession. This is the power delegated to the teacher by virtue of his role as a teacher. Confidence in the fairness of the teacher is directly related to the exercising of this power adequately, evenly, and in a consistent manner.

Second, the teacher has expert power. The teacher is considered well-informed and is an expert who is competent in his subject matter area, as well as in the psychological nature of learning and adolescent behavior. The higher the perceived competence of the teacher, the greater the congruence between the level of aspiration and the student's capacity.

Third, the teacher has personality power, which means that a personal, humane influence can be exerted over pupils. Personality power must be the cohesion of legitimate power and expert power, as it really determines the successful or unsuccessful rapport between student and teacher. The greater the personality power, the greater the congruence between aspiration and capacity.[18]

Normally, an effective teacher is a consequence of six principle conditions.[19] They are:

1. Knowledge of the world and his subjects.

2. Sensitivity to people, the capacity for empathy.

3. Accurate and appropriate beliefs about people and their behavior.

---

18. See H. Rosenfeld and A. Zander, "Influence of Teachers on the Aspirations of Students," *Journal of Educational Psychology*, February, 1961. See also Solomon, Rosenberg, and Bezdek, "Teacher Behavior and Student Learning," *Journal of Educational Psychology*, January, 1964.

19. Arthur Combs et al., *The Professional Education of Teachers* (Boston: Allyn and Bacon, 1974): pp. 170–172.

4. Positive beliefs about self.

5. Appropriate and congruent beliefs about purposes, the goals of society, schools, the classroom, and the teacher's own goals of teaching.

6. The personal discovery of his or her own appropriate and authentic ways of teaching.

To be an effective teacher, one must have a realistic, positive self-image; thorough training and knowledge in the psychology of learning and group behavior; a thorough grounding in his or her subject matter so that valuable time is not wasted in researching content on the job; a realistic and workable methodology that is flexible, current, that has been tested through valid, relevant experiences to avoid future trial and error, and that has a social and philosophical value pattern consistent with social realities of the school, community, and the profession. In other words, a teacher must be prepared, for he cannot work through trial and error, particularly in urban classrooms where situations change rapidly and must be responded to accordingly.

To train urban teachers is to guide them in the acquisition of certain skills. They must be given theoretical background and then put in a situation where they can apply the skills they have learned. Performances need to be analyzed and assessed. Suggestions for changes must be made. Acceptable performance is reinforced by the trainer; opportunities for expansion and new roles are provided. The National Institute for Advanced Study in Teaching Disadvantaged Youth has suggested that the training process of urban teachers must include six elements.[20] They are:

1. Establishment of the practice situation.

2. Specification of the behavior.

3. Performance of the specified behavior.

4. Feedback of information about the performance.

5. Modification of the performance in light of the feedback.

---

20. *Teachers for the Real World,* National Institute for the Advanced Study in Teaching Disadvantaged Youth (Washington, D.C.: American Association of Colleges for Teacher Education, 1968), pp. 70–71.

6. A performance-feedback-correction-practice schedule that is continued until desirable skillfulness is achieved.

The report strongly asserts that "in order to train new teachers and to continue the training of those in service, it is necessary to design a program and sets of training materials that will incorporate each of the above elements."[21] The day of Competency-Based Education in teacher training is upon us.

The skills required of an urban teacher generally fall into three main divisions: (1) interpersonal skills (interacting with parents, fellow teachers, pupils, administrators, and self), (2) classroom-management skills (setting and maintaining classroom activities and an effective communication process), and (3) teaching-learning skills (the maintenance of a learning climate in the classroom).[22] Expanding on these three basic categories, the following list is a rather thorough comprehensive description of skills perceived by teachers as relating to accountability.[23] They consist of the ability to:

- Develop learners who are self-motivated and capable of taking a major responsibility for directing their own learning.
- Arouse student interest in subject material.
- Promote positive attitudes in students toward school and education.
- Diagnose individual learning difficulties.
- Organize material to promote student learning.
- Create awareness of and respect for fellow students.
- Organize classroom to promote student learning.
- Control disruptive situations effectively.
- Self-diagnose the instructional effectiveness of a lesson.
- Make the classroom an enjoyable place to spend time.

---

21. *Teachers for the Real World,* p. 71.
22. See Claude W. Fawcett, *The Skills of Teaching* (Los Angeles: University of California Teacher Education Project, 1965).
23. The list is taken from Thomas Good, Richard Coop, Myron Dembo, John Denton, and Philip Limbacker, "How Teachers View Accountability," *Phi Delta Kappan,* January, 1975, pp. 367–368.

- Communicate facts and information to students.
- Help students develop their creativity.
- Be perceived by students as warm and concerned.
- Construct valid teacher-made tests to assess student learning.
- Use a variety of instructional aids in class activity.
- Cooperate with colleagues.
- Cooperate with school administrative staff.
- Aid in the social adjustment of students.
- Plan remediation activities.
- Communicate general facts and information to parents.
- Counsel students who are having personal problems.
- Explain a child's test score to his parents.
- Improve pupil performance on teacher-constructed tests.
- Carry out programs initiated by the principal.
- Contribute to committee work (curriculum committees, program committees).
- Improve pupil performance on standardized tests.

Developing an effective teaching style is not easy, especially if the future teacher is a victim of a school of education that is still preparing future teachers to teach only in middle-class schools. Such schools are less and less likely to be available to tomorrow's teacher.

Teacher Training for Urban Schools
Almost all individuals change jobs sometime during their careers, and a large number of persons even change occupations. As indicated earlier, persons leave the teaching profession in comparatively large numbers regardless of the teacher surplus. There is still a tremendous professional mobility among teachers.

Several studies[24] have shown that teachers would tend to stay in the teaching profession if:

---

24. *Teachers for the Real World,* p. 30.

- They were adequately trained for the job they were expected to do.
- They were satisfied with the conditions under which they work.
- They were satisfied with the living conditions in the community where they work.
- They were able to make decisions about their occupational and instructional activities.
- The profession were self-respecting and had control over its own affairs.
- There were opportunities for advancement and fulfillment in their work.
- Financial incentives were requisite to the efforts and work put forth.

Any large urban school system experiences a large degree of teacher mobility, as does a large corporation. The largest degree of mobility, however, exists in inner-city schools. The retention of teachers in the ghettos would be increased if the above conditions were improved. In a recent study done by Sewell (1972),[25] who surveyed three southern California school districts, inner-city teachers indicated they would be happier and more willing to stay in their schools (others indicated they would be willing to transfer to an inner-city school) if the following priorities were given to urban teachers in the central city:

1. Reduced class size
2. Bonus salary
3. Larger raises for inner-city teachers
4. One less class to teach
5. Paraprofessional aides
6. Teacher personnel rotation
7. Opportunity to select grade level and subject
8. Right to depart from course of study

---

25. Orville Sewell, "Incentives for Inner City Teachers," *Phi Delta Kappan*, October, 1972, p. 129.

9. More competent administrators

10. Updated educational programs and materials

11. More staff specialists

12. Reduced counselor-pupil ratio

13. Teacher-selected administrators

14. Reduced administrator-student ratio

15. Extra retirement credit

16. More released time for staff

17. More supplies

18. Upgraded physical plants

19. Central office administrator interviewing teachers to teach in the inner city

20. Priority for sabbatical leave

A Los Angeles psychiatrist reported in the *Los Angeles Times* (December 15, 1975) that ghetto teachers suffer from "combat neurosis." Dr. Alfred Bloch, clinical professor of psychiatry at UCLA, described the battered teacher syndrome as having striking similarities to the combat fatigue of World War II. Having had some 200 inner-city teachers referred to him by their union or by their attorneys, Dr. Bloch noted that "teachers assigned to inner city areas must be able to function in an ongoing way with the Damoclesian reality that the incidents of school violence are usually directed at them. They are the target. And they are not prepared." These teachers suffer from anxiety and fear, stress, sleep disturbance, gastrointestinal upsets, high blood pressure, depression, headaches, fatigue, lowered self-esteem, irritability, and occasional psychotic collapse. Such feelings, according to Dr. Bloch, are caused by the constant exposure to "the threats of violence, actual assault and beatings, theft or arson of school and personal property, vandalism, rape and murder at the hands of students or non-students who wander on campus," and the general ineffectiveness of the school and the administration in coping with the unique characteristics of the inner-city school environment. Obviously, training for these realities will take some revolutionary changes in teacher training, and failure to do so only adds to the growing list of failed students and teachers.

The Problem Schools. The most difficult teaching adjustments must be made in the common-man and inner-city schools. These adjustments require skills above and beyond the aforementioned skills. To cope, to be effective, and to stay in the common-man and inner-city school situations in a large urban community, additional recognizable skills are not only necessary, but vital for survival. In a study by Haubrich (1965),[26] the following skills were considered essential for survival in an inner-city school at any grade level.

1. Ability to understand and use developmental and remedial reading procedures.

2. Ability to organize and make routine specific classroom procedures.

3. Ability to reconstruct syllabi, textbooks, and reading materials in terms of the backgrounds of students.

4. Ability to work effectively with small groups within the classroom and to know when to use such procedures.

5. Ability to adjust new entrants to the classroom situation quickly.

6. Ability to construct and use concrete materials for classroom work.

7. Ability to handle aggression and violence.

8. Ability to use individual and group procedures to promote classroom discipline.

9. Ability to know when a child should be referred for additional counseling or tutoring and to whom.

10. Knowledge of the language patterns in a community and the ability to correct such patterns.

11. Knowledge of neighborhoods and families to see the effect they have on classroom work and procedures.

12. Ability to translate whatever street knowledge children from depressed areas may have acquired into specific procedures for classroom use.

---

26. See Vernon Haubrich, "The Culturally Different: New Content for Teacher Education—The Culturally Disadvantaged and Teacher Education," *Reading Teacher,* March, 1965, pp. 502–503; see also Helen Rees, *Deprivation and Compensatory Education* (Boston: Houghton Mifflin, 1968), p. 134.

One component part of teacher training for urban schools is often overlooked: the multicultural realities of the urban classroom. Many states, notably California and Wisconsin, have mandated teacher education in this area and have set up a specialty in bilingual-bicultural education. Some states require all future teachers to have student teaching experience with culturally different youngsters. Asa Hilliard, Dean of the School of Education at San Francisco State University, stated that there are certain recognizable and essential skills for multicultural teacher education.[27] Among them are:

- The ability to communicate with students from other cultures.
- The ability to diagnose the knowledge and abilities of students from other cultures.
- Skill in the evaluation of professional literature bearing upon multicultural educational problems.
- Self-diagnosis regarding one's own behavior in a multicultural context.
- Recognition of cultural equivalencies such as nonstandard English and ethnic slang.
- Detection of conscious and unconscious negative signals in interpersonal interactions.
- Development of attitudes that are free of bias and open to continuing self-examination, that honor and recognize cultural alternatives such as language, beliefs, values and behaviors, as well as a feeling that a multicultural orientation is beneficial to them personally.
- Recognition that the teaching process is always a cross-cultural encounter.

American public education is a culturally diverse society. As such, its educational enterprise must prepare teachers for the demands of a culturally diverse society. Some 90 percent of our educational personnel

---

27. Asa Hilliard, "Restructuring Teacher Education for Multi-Cultural Imperatives," in William Hunter's, *Multi-Cultural Education Through Competency-Based Teacher Education* (Washington, D.C.: American Association of Colleges for Teacher Education, 1974), pp. 40–53.

trained in this country are trained by 860 education departments in universities and colleges. It is imperative that greater attention be paid to the preservation and encouragement of cultural pluralism in education.

Learning to Teach the Culturally Different

Educators have to recognize and identify different problems that exist in the inner-city communities. The problems are more acute, more intensified, more comprehensive, and more pervasive than they are in other sections of the urban community.

Students in inner-city schools have problems that cannot be divorced from their outside lives, since survival in one place is closely related to survival in another. Matters of survival that go virtually unnoticed by persons living in middle- or high-income areas become acute in the inner city. These include such things as buying or renting decent housing, maintaining that housing, fighting the overrun of insects and rodents, and managing landlord-tenant conflicts. Knowing when and how to use public transportation presents special problems to the ghetto dweller whose livelihood and education may be dependent on them. Frequently children must play in the streets, which presents obvious hazards. Physical self-defense is a real problem for many inner-city dwellers. Inner-city dwellers suffer from problems related to legal and consumer issues; because of their lack of education, they are often ill-informed of their rights, and because of the isolation of their neighborhoods, they often turn to inadequate sources of information for such things as obtaining credit or legal services.

Changing Values vs. Direct Action
Social scientists have long suggested that we approach the problem head-on by attacking the act, as in the case of prejudice and discrimination, before attacking the value behind the act. If we attack the values first, it will take years to change those values, assuming we have even correctly perceived the values. A case in point: a person may say that he strongly believes one thing (the value), but he may do something else behaviorally (the act). If we acted on the perceived value, we would be inaccurate. Behavior, not professed belief, is the key component social scientists watch for. As a social scientist, this

writer finds less validity in a person's protestations that he is opposed to pornography and more validity in his actual behavioral pattern: does he buy pornography, does he patronize pornographic establishments— in other words, what does he actually consume?

The same, then, is true for society's attack on social problems. Society must attack and label acts as wrong or illegal, rather than waiting and hoping to win over minds through value transformation. Much of the legislative action of recent decades has been predicated upon this course of action. People cannot sit back and wait for values to change and hope that, with change, improvements will be made in the living conditions of the urban core. Schools are no exception. We must identify what is wrong and correct it, regardless of the values and beliefs of those who would caution us to go slowly and to change feelings first.

Teachers are the catalysts in the struggle over social action, for they are the front-line fighters, the interveners between society and school. Yet, how can they be agents of change if they themselves are poorly trained and poorly informed? Such training is vital and necessary and should be mandated.

Training could have two component parts: (1) training for teachers about the culturally different child, and (2) the specific implementation of that training by teaching urban-core youth the essentials of survival, or as they are called, the coping skills. Let us briefly explore these two components and establish their perimeters.

**Component One: Training the Teacher
about the Culturally Different**
Skilled teachers should have knowledge about the following variables related to the culturally different, the minority, the urban core, and the visibly poor.[28]

---

28. Taken from Allen R. Sullivan, "Cultural Competence and Confidence: A Quest for Effective Teaching in a Pluralistic Society," in William Hunter's *Multi-Cultural Education Through Competency-Based Teacher Education,* pp. 56–71. Some modifications in his outline were made by me in terms of applicability. See also Madelon Stent et al., *Cultural Pluralism in Education: A Mandate for Change* (New York: Appleton-Century-Crofts, 1973); William Ryan, *Blaming the Victim* (New York: Vintage Books, 1972); Allen R. Sullivan, "Afro-American Communication in America: Some Educational Implications," *Pan African Journal,* Spring, 1972, pp. 231–37.

I. Making the culturally different visible
   A. Contributions to American society by minority groups
   B. Life-styles of minority groups
   C. Plight and prospects of minority groups
   D. Asian-Americans and their lifestyles
   E. Economics and U.S. minorities
   F. The rage of minorities: historically and currently
   G. Future options for minority groups in the U.S. society

II. Racism in society
   A. Racism defined and its strategies
   B. Subtleties of racist attitudes
   C. Effects of systemic racism
   D. Racism and its impact on education
   E. Ways of coping with the issue of racism
   F. Ways of changing racial attitudes

III. Language and the minorities
   A. The nature of language
   B. Dialects in the U.S.
   C. Diverse cultures and language
   D. Standard and nonstandard English
   E. Sociolinguistics
   F. Linguistics and the teaching of languages in schools

IV. Innovation and minority education
   A. Recent research: profile of the creative person
   B. Creativity tests and their possibilities
   C. The teacher as innovator
   D. Eliciting creativity in the classroom
   E. Creative needs in American business
   F. Creativity as a measure for occupational choice

V. Affirming minorities in education
   A. The negative connotation of compensatory education
   B. Evidence of the self-fulfilling prophecy
   C. Strengths of the survival culture
   D. A positive look at minority values
   E. Self-concept and ethnocentricity

VI. The community and the schools
   A. Minority parental interest in education
   B. The community's role in schools

C. The college role in the community
D. The school's role in the community
E. The issues of community control
F. Ways of obtaining community cooperation

VII. Curricular issues in minority education
A. Self-enhancement concept
B. Affective and cognitive domains
C. The "two cultures" controversy
D. The use of tracking systems
E. Grade levels, marks, and homogeneous groupings
F. Making subject matter relevant for the 1980s
G. Changes in curricular design; new curriculum methodologies
H. Intelligence testing

VIII. Preparing teachers for a polychromatic society
A. The human relations component
B. The liberal education component
C. Interaction analysis: theory and practice
D. Development of skills
E. Exposure to cultural diversity
F. Models of teacher preparation
G. The ideal teacher
H. Determining psychological predispositions regarding minority youngsters

Component Two: Needs Assessment for the Culturally Different: Instructional Objectives

Skilled inner-city teachers need to concentrate on certain basics in multicultural education that will improve the lives of youngsters as they cope with societal realities and still provide the basics for the fullest possible social and educational mobility. The following needs assessment outline[29] suggests several objectives for specific teaching directions for urban core youth.

---

29. Taken from Henry L. Anderson, "Urban Core Educational Needs," unpublished doctoral dissertation, UCLA, 1973. Significant modifications and changes were made by author in terms of applicability. See also, Henry L. Anderson, *Revolutionary Urban Teaching* (Inglewood, California: American University Publishers, 1973).

I. Coping Skills: Society
A. Survival and well-being, for urban core inhabitants depends on proficiencies related to:
1. How to get along with others. A knowledge of personality-dynamics needs of children relative to peer-related fears and anxieties.
2. How to think critically and creatively. A knowledge of inquiry methods and the processes of logic and the science of thinking.
3. How to express feelings and thoughts. The encouragement, development, and redirection of student expression in both peer and non-peer communications.
4. How to possess a dependable self-identity. Knowledge and use of experiences that are known to be successful in developing positive self-images.
5. How to be self-sustaining. Real-life, problem-solving skills making the student capable of dealing successfully with personal problems, community concerns, peer conflicts, adult encounters and income demands.
6. How to move about in society. Movement out of the urban core into a variety of planned encounters and creative exposures.
   a. Life-style modification for society. Knowledge of the wisdom of modifying ethnic or environmental life-styles to a level of compatibility with society.
   b. Life-style modifications by society. Diffusion of subcultural mores and culture into society so that society accepts the reality of racial and cultural differences.
7. How to function within capitalism and our economy. Knowledge of the realities of the business and vocational world so as to be a part of it rather than outside of it.
8. How to interpret legal rights. Against the background of a legal system hostile to poor people, students should be prepared in workable constructs through which they can realize concrete results from redress procedures.
9. How to work the system. Urban-core constituents need to know how the system works, legitimate ways provided for manipulating it, and the rewards of working through the system. Viable forms of free enterprise must

be introduced so that the attraction of such illegal enterprises as dice shooting, stolen goods traffic, or drug traffic will wane.

II. Coping Skills: School
A. Critical needs a school system can fulfill in the educational enterprise.
   1. Study skills.
   2. Vocational skills.
   3. Knowledge skills (subject matter).
   4. Self-adjustment skills.
   5. Social-adjustment skills.
B. Activities and programs designed to foster interaction skills as opposed to conformity behavior in the traditional sense.
C. Audio, visual, kinesthetic, imaginary, and empirical experiences in the social worlds of other-strata Americans (white, middle class, other minorities).
D. Strategies for developing higher cognitive and creative skills.

III. Coping Skills: Personal
A. Creatively constructed alternatives to traditional life-styles.
   1. Concerning the physical environment of the urban core.
   2. Concerning the occupational alternatives available in the urban core.
   3. Concerning entertainment, recreation, and leisure activities in the urban core.
B. Strategies that liberate inner dynamics.
   1. Understanding elementary psychology about the nature and character of inner thoughts, feelings, and personality.
   2. Understanding others' feelings.
   3. Respect for differing thoughts and feelings; understanding prejudice.
   4. Putting thoughts and feelings into language and action.
C. Strategies for improving the self-image.
   1. Systems that demonstrate how much classes of people have in common.
   2. Reconstruction and elimination of ghetto isolationism.

3. Multilevel exchange programs, crisscrossing geographical and economic stratification.
4. Guided experiences of varied public contacts.
5. Exposure to public agencies.

D. Strategies for coping with financial needs.
1. Dealing with collectors, door-to-door salesmen, etc.
2. Bargaining contacts with business establishments and credit agencies.
3. Banking and other vital services.
4. Fundamentals of self-employment.
5. Consumer protection; rent protection; buyer protection sources.

E. Vocational skills.
1. Entry-level job skills.
2. Specialty skills.
3. Paraprofessional skills.
4. Apprenticeship training.
5. Higher education and professional skills.
6. The civil employee.

F. Strategies of social mobility.
1. Toward public acceptance of minority life-styles.
2. Toward modification of antisocial characteristics of life-styles.
3. Strategies for manipulating a capitalist system.
4. Strategies for exercising legal rights and privileges.
5. Strategies for developing common ties across sociocultural barriers.
6. Legal and illegal activity.
7. Dynamics of police encounters.

G. Health considerations.
1. Disease and illness; community aid.
2. Foods and beverages—health needs.
3. Alcohol and medications.
4. Health services and treatment.
5. Hazards of neglect.
6. Psychological homicide.

IV. Strategies for Appropriate Teacher Training
A. Strategies for the effective recruitment and training of teachers for the urban core.

B. Strategies for effective inservice education for all front-line and in-school contact staff.

C. Strategies for effective paraprofessional training.

D. Strategies for total community, wider family, educational community (college and university), and general public involvement in the urban-core enterprise.

E. Strategies for accountability and competency-based training.

V. Strategies for the Assessment and Evaluation of School Programs as to Their Effectiveness in Teaching Urban-Core Youth.

Conclusion

To educate teachers to operate in the complex society of the 1980s requires programs addressed to national, state, community, and local needs. It is no longer realistic to assume that there is one approach to teacher education, one methodology, one culture, or one singular recruitment need for teachers. The only one clear assumption that can be made about teacher preparation is the reality that urban schools and their problems are going to get worse before they get better, and one of the fundamental reasons that urban schools will get worse before they get better is because teacher training for urban schools is also on that same cycle. The NDEA put it most succinctly when it concluded that "reforming teacher education is like rebuilding the wheels of a car in motion."[30] How true, and yet, how sad; delay means loss. Each day's delay means further deterioration in the entire educational enterprise. America can ill afford further delay. The strength of urban education rests with its teachers; a renaissance is sadly needed.

Exercises

1. Case Study

Teacher background. You are a substitute teacher assigned to an inner-city English class for one day only. Use your true background for this exercise.

---

30. *Teachers for the Real World*, p. 173.

School background. An inner-city junior-high school with a totally black enrollment. On the city-wide reading tests, the school scored at a scale that indicated most of the students are reading 3 to 4 years behind grade level. The school has its share of discipline problems.

Your schedule. You will be assigned four classes of English: two seventh-grade classes and two eighth-grade classes. The semester is only two weeks old; the study units are the library and the dictionary; and the teacher left no lesson plans. You have only the seating charts and the textbooks on the teacher's desk. Your schedule for the day is as follows:

> Period 1: 7B11 English
>
> Period 2: 7B12 English
>
> Period 3: Preparation
>
> Period 4: 8B10 English
>
> Period 5: Lunch
>
> Period 6: 8B12 English

(The numbers signify the number of sections of English and not ability groupings.)

Problem. Assume that you have not met your classes as yet. Prepare a lesson plan for the day and a structure for the day. What rules, regulations, and activities would you plan? What materials would you bring? What alternatives would you keep in mind? How would you use the day's schedule to best advantage? What would you do differently from a permanent teacher? List five things that you would *not* do.

Sociopsychological Situations
React to the following situations:

> 1. You are a new teacher just starting a sixth-grade teaching assignment. You will meet your 30 students for the first time tomorrow. The only knowledge you have of them is what other teachers have told you—and you are expecting a difficult class in terms of behavior and below-average abilities. What planning will you do and what procedures will you suggest for your first day?

2. Social studies to your students is a dull, tedious subject that they find irrelevant. Several students challenge you by asking "Why do we have to study social studies?" How do you respond?

3. You are faced with a class of students who are negatively inclined and collectively organized against school, your subject, and teachers. They are in school and your class because they have to be. How do you handle your first meeting with them?

4. You teach in a working-class school that has a mixture of problem kids, mostly low achievers whose first language is Spanish and who have a different cultural orientation than yours. What adjustments must you or they make?

5. George is a student with limited ability and little inner motivation. He has recognizable and seemingly irreversible language deficiencies. He wants to quit school early and take up auto mechanics at which he is good. His parents want him to go to college. Whose side should you take?

6. You are a substitute taking over a new class for the first time. You know you will be there only one day, two at the most. What structures and procedures will you impose? For an average middle-class school? For a ghetto school?

Socioeconomic Dimensions of Inequality

Chapter 5

Upon completion of this chapter, you should be able to do the following tasks.

1. Name the primary factors that influence the fulfillment of equal educational opportunity.

2. Explain the differences between *race* and *culture* and state several social scientific conclusions about race.

3. Tell what the neighborhood school attempts to accomplish.

4. Describe the extent of segregation in America's schools today; describe the various historical periods leading up to the present state of events.

5. State specific conclusions about recent results of desegregation.

6. Cite some basic assumptions about integration in urban communities; describe several examples of school systems and what they have done to integrate.

7. Name the special problems and challenges that integration poses for the urban teacher.

8. Analyze the differences between community-impact strategies that school districts use for desegregation with those of school-district impact strategies.

9. Describe and summarize the potency of social class in determining educational opportunity and educational achievement.

10. Define what is meant by the "culture of poverty" and describe the type persons who fit that description.

To talk about urban education is to talk about the unprecedented threat posed to the continuance of public education. The problems can no longer be constrained by the forces of conservatism, nor can they be laughed off as figments of the imaginations of liberal educators. City school systems are faced with the same major cleavage as are social systems, namely, the great distance socially, economically, and educationally between the haves and the have-nots, between the socially and educationally advantaged and disadvantaged. Urban schools have not paid adequate attention to the have-nots. The equality lag in city systems becomes more glaring each year, as documentary evidence about class inequities in education piles up. City planners seem all too preoccupied with urban renewal—to the detriment of educational renewal.

Equal educational opportunity has been a dream of American educators since the inception of the public school movement. Although it has broad appeal as a concept, its practice has been limited. Relatively fixed structures perpetuate an educational system that has an uneven distribution of educational services. The consequence of these structures has been a minimal education for thousands of poor and ethnic children. Factors that can influence the education of children are described below.

1. *Ethnicity*. Nonwhites are clearly and systematically discriminated against in all facets of social living; schooling is no exception. Being black or brown often brings restrictions to a black or brown school, supposedly equal, but, in fact, one that only serves to limit access to opportunity in our society and restrict social mobility. Education is the one key force promoting social mobility and occupational improvement. Deny a person an optimum education, restrict his housing pattern, control his occupational opportunities, and you doom him to an inferior status socially, economically, and educationally. Minority children today have by no means achieved equal educational opportunity.

2. *Social class*. Upper- or middle-class status has come to mean unlimited educational opportunity, unlimited social mobility, and consistently higher achievement in schools. Studies

have shown with great regularity the correlation between high income and good education. Children born to relatively well-to-do parents who are engaged in high-status occupations are more likely to have better educational opportunities. The American ideal of an open-class society, one in which all citizens have an equal opportunity for social mobility, is a well-established myth that our culture seemingly perpetuates in theory and denies in practice. European systems make no pretense about social tracking, but the American tracking system is more subtle in application, which, in turn, leads to raised expectations.

3. *Geographic background.* Persons born in rural rather than urban areas, from the South, or foreign countries, tend to come from poorer educational systems, lessening the probabilities of successful mobility.

4. *Culture.* Persons who are considered apart from the mainstream of commonly accepted traditional values in life-style, language, cultural and historical heritage, and in customs have extreme difficulty in realizing equal economic, social, and educational opportunities.

Numerous socioeconomic hypotheses have been advanced to explain the educational gap between the haves and the have-nots. While sociologists have been preoccupied with the societal factors that have produced this gap, educators have become concerned with the problems of the disadvantaged, and a new wave of interest and scholarship has led to the introduction of the term *cultural deprivation.* Most of the materials dealing with the socially disadvantaged have been produced in the last ten years. While the problem is not new, it is more visible as city slums continue to fester and expand. Designating certain pupils or schools as disadvantaged remains a problem for educators. But the primary problem of how to educate those so designated constitutes a greater challenge for educators and society.

Desegregation remains as another of the crucial problems confronting urban schools. The rationale for school desegregation is the simple reality that separate schooling, equal or not, is unfair and undemocratic to both minority and majority children. Few would dispute the academic and psychological damage done to both groups. Such damage erodes the social order, making democracy a shallow ideal. Americans suffer a profound conflict between the democratic ideals they profess to and the actions or social arrangements that they practice. For present-day educators, the task of desegregating the urban schools throughout the country is monumental.

The Questions of Race and Culture

Race is unanimously regarded by anthropologists as a classification device that provides a framework within which the various groups of people can be arranged, as well as a means by which studies of evolutionary processes can be facilitated. From a purely anthropological sense, the word *race* should be reserved for groups possessing well-developed and primarily heritable physical differences.[1]

Humans can be and have been classified in varying ways by anthropologists. Most agree to classify people into at least three large units, which may be called major groups. Such a classification does not depend on any single physical characteristic, for example, skin color by itself does necessarily distinguish one major group from another. Furthermore, so far as it has been possible to analyze them, the differences in physical structure that distinguish one major group from another give no support to popular notions of superiority or inferiority that is sometimes implied in referring to these groups.[2]

Most anthropologists do not include mental characteristics in their classification of humans. Studies within a single group have shown that both innate capacity *and* environmental opportunity determine the results of tests of intelligence and temperament, although their relative importance is disputed. When intelligence tests, even nonverbal, are made on a group of nonliterate people, their scores are usually lower than those of more civilized people. It has been recorded that different groups of the same race occupying similarly high levels of civilization may yield

1. Taken from the UNESCO Statement on Race and Racial Prejudice, Paris Conference, June, 1951.
2. See UNESCO, *Race and Science* (New York: Columbia University Press, 1961).

considerable differences in intelligence tests. When the two groups have been brought up from childhood in similar environments, however, the differences are usually very slight. Moreover, there is evidence that, given similar opportunities, the average performance (that is to say, the performance of an individual who is representative because he is surpassed by as many as he surpasses) does not differ appreciably from one group to another.

Even those psychologists who claim to have found great differences in intelligence between groups of different racial origin, and who have contended that such differences are hereditary, report that some members of the group of inferior performance surpass not merely the lowest ranking member of the superior group, but also the average of its members. In any case, it has never been possible to separate members of two groups on the basis of mental capacity. It is possible, though not proven, that some types of innate capacity for intellectual and emotional responses are commoner in one human group than in another, but it is certain that, within a single group, innate capacities vary as much as, if not more, than they do between different groups.

The scientific material available at present does not justify the conclusion that inherited genetic differences are a major factor in producing the differences between the cultures and cultural achievements of different peoples or groups. It does indicate, to the contrary, that a major factor in explaining such differences is the cultural experience that each group has undergone.[3]

Generally speaking, several clear-cut statements can be made about race and racial prejudice based upon overwhelming scientific evidence.[4]

---

3. See the following: Robert Kuttner, *Race and Modern Science* (New York: Social Science Press, 1967); Ashley Montagu, *Race, Science and Humanity* (New York: Van Nostrand Company, 1963); Ashley Montagu, *The Idea of Race* (Lincoln: The University of Nebraska Press, 1965); Melvin Tunin, *Race and Intelligence* (New York: Anti-Defamation League of B'nai B'rith, 1963); UNESCO, *What Is Race? Evidence From Scientists* (Paris, 1952). See also Charles Tesconi, *Schooling in America* (Houghton Mifflin, 1975): Chapter 14.

4. *Statement on Race and Racial Prejudice,* UNESCO, Paris, September, 1967. See also Gertrude Noar, *The Teacher and Integration* (Washington, D.C.: NEA, 1974), pp. 68–72.

1. All living persons belong to the same species and descend from the same stock.

2. The division of the human species into groups is partly conventional and partly arbitrary and does not imply any hierarchy whatsoever.

3. Current biological knowledge does not permit us to impute cultural achievements to differences in genetic potential. Differences in the achievement of different peoples should be attributed solely to their cultural history. Racism grossly falsifies the knowledge of human biology.

4. The human problems arising from "race relations" are social rather than biological in origin.

5. Racism tends to be cumulative. Discrimination deprives a group of equal treatment and presents that group as a problem. The group then tends to be blamed for its own condition, leading to further elaboration of racist theory.

Important changes in the social structure of any society that may lead to the elimination of racial prejudice and discrimination require decisions of a political, social, economic, and educational nature. Agencies of enlightenment, such as the schools, can be effective agents for the advancement of broadened understanding about the potentialities of people. To that end, the schools must ensure that the curriculum contains scientific understandings about race and cultures and that invidious, unscientific, ethnocentric distinctions about peoples and cultures are not made in textbooks and classrooms. Most important, the resources of the schools and communities should be fully available to all parts of the population with neither restriction nor discrimination. In the case of American history and tradition, where, for historical reasons, certain groups have a lower educational and economic standing, it is the responsibility of society and the schools to take corrective measures.

Teachers are most important in any educational program and special attention should be given to their training. Teachers should be made conscious of the degree to which they reflect the prejudices current in their society, the degree to which they stereotype youngsters according to these prejudicial preconceptions, and the degree to which they contribute to a self-fulfilling prophecy, in their relations with some students in their classrooms.

Teachers should be encouraged to avoid such prejudices. Through the study of the psychology of intercultural relations, teachers would come to understand basic facts regarding the inter-relationship of race and culture. Twelve of these facts are described below.[5]

1. *All people of the earth are a single family and have a common origin: Homo sapiens.*

2. *Biological differences of skin, color, hair, eyes, and cultural differences do not denote superiority or inferiority.* All of us are too accustomed to thinking that if a society or a person is different than us, it is inferior.

3. *Race is purely a biological term.* It describes people only according to physical characteristics. Most people of the world fall into one of three groups, according to shape of nose, hair, skin color. Variations within any of these groups are greater than those between groups.

4. *All human blood is the same.*

5. *There are no pure races.* People have mixed and produced children from the beginning. All people are members of the same species.

6. *Race means nothing in terms of psychological or intellectual functioning.* After classifying races, anthropologists ask what race means, an issue that has been the subject of scientific experiments over the last 50 years. Results to date have been completely negative. It has nothing to do with intellectual quotient, personality, aggressiveness, introversion or extraversion.

---

5. Teachers should look through the following materials related to this topic and its concerns: John Baker, *Race* (New York: Oxford University Press, 1974); James A. Banks, *Teaching Ethnic Studies* (Washington, D.C.: National Council for the Social Studies, 1974); Foundations for Change, Inc., *Fact Sheets on Institutional Racism* (New York: The Foundation for Change, 1974); Herbert Ginsberg, *The Myth of the Deprived Child* (Englewood Cliffs: Prentice-Hall, 1972); NEA, *School Desegregation Guidelines for Local and State Education Associations* (Washington, D.C., NEA, 1974); NEA, *Understanding Intergroup Relations* (Washington, D.C.: NEA, 1973); Gertrude Noar, *Sensitizing Teachers to Ethnic Groups* (Rockleigh, New Jersey: Allyn and Bacon, 1975); Francis Sussna, "Human Relations in the Classroom," *Today's Education,* January, 1973, pp. 30–43; Foundations for Change, Inc., "Definitions of Racism." *Viewpoint—Newsletter Series for Classroom Use,* March, 1974.

7. *There is the same wide range in every group.* There are individual differences in children, but these seem to have nothing to do with race.

8. *There are no pure cultures,* just as there are no pure races. People have been wandering over the face of the earth for a long time. Culture refers to everything one gets from society.
We do not get our language from the germ plasm.
We do not get our religion from our germ plasm.

9. *Culture has nothing to do with race.* It is a historical development, not a biological one. Degree of development depends on geographical factors. All cultures tend to be ethnocentric. Dominant cultures assimilate subcultures. Few cultures allow total cultural pluralism.

10. *There is no group that cannot take on the culture of another group.* There is nothing in one's physical make-up that prevents people from taking a culture and making a contribution to it.

11. Race does not determine emotion. If you are interested in butterflies, you might classify them as yellow, black, or yellow with black spots. You would hesitate to say which is most beautiful. Markings have no more meaning than do the physical characteristics called race.

12. Racial inferiority is taught in our society and reinforced by major social institutions. Feelings of hate or superiority or inferiority must be learned.

Segregation and Integration in the Schools
The courts have a formidable responsibility to eliminate prejudice and discrimination in our society. In addition, most Americans have an interest in preserving the concept of the neighborhood school. But before moves can be made by the courts, the school system has to focus attention on the opposing forces within its own house. A school system is responsive to community norms and standards, and community views on segregation and racism largely determine the shape of local schools. The responsibility for reallocating school resources to facilitate desegregation stems from its original control and organization over those resources. Without question, some school segregation, such as societal

segregation, is de facto, that is, caused by social and economic factors that determine neighborhood patterns. On the other hand, many school boards, as legally constituted authorities, compound the problem with de jure segregation policies. By setting attendance zone boundaries, deciding on the geographic locations of schools, providing easy transfer for whites, discouraging majority to minority transfers, employing only minority teachers and administrators in minority schools, setting teacher and administrator standards that favor whites, and by manipulating educators and the public in ways that support white control of curriculum and services, schools add their approval to local community norms and openly support both de facto and de jure forms of segregation.[6]

Whether through de jure segregation (by legal means) or de facto segregation (due to circumstances), schools have become increasingly segregated over the years. At the base of many of the questions regarding desegregation is the principle of the neighborhood school system. As mentioned, local community norms largely determine the various facets of de facto segregation. People move and live in areas because of the schools in that area. School boards determine school boundary lines. The argument has often arisen that, because school boards determine the neighborhood school boundary lines, this is, in effect, allowing school boards the discretionary power of de jure decisions relative to segregation since people move to areas because of the schools. The entire question of the neighborhood school policy is under fire.

Basically, what are the purposes of the most traditional of school system practices, the neighborhood school? The neighborhood school attempts to achieve four key goals.[7] They are:

> 1. The neighborhood school provides the cheapest, safest and fastest means of transporting the child from home to school. The farther a school is from a home, the greater the amount

---

6. See *Desegregation/Integration: Planning for School Change,* Kathleen Smith, ed. (Washington, D.C.: NEA, 1974), pp. 10–16.
7. See Allan Blackman, "Planning and the Neighborhood School," in *Integrated Education: A Reader,* Meyer Weinberg, ed. (Beverly Hills, California: Glencoe Press, 1968), p. 142; see also Fred Hechinger, "Neighborhood School Concept," *The New York Times,* June 26, 1963.

of time spent in the transportation process, the more streets (especially major ones) that must be crossed by the walking child, and the more the public feels obliged to transport the child with expensive public transportation.

2. Many educators believe schools should be small. The neighborhood form of organization helps keep them small.

3. Educators believe that young children benefit from the security that comes from learning and living in a familiar environment. They feel that children should be able to have their classmates as after-school playmates and that they should be able to return to or remain at school for after-school classes and programs.

4. This major purpose is quite complex but best summarized by saying that educators want a close relationship between the school and the family. The neighborhood school should, and often does, serve as an invitation to parents to know, confide in, and work with its staff. This offers a good chance for constructive community pressures on the central school administration and on the political authorities for local school improvements. Thus, the neighborhood school can reflect the values and goals of the community it serves and can gain that community's loyalty and support. Stated from a different perspective, the neighborhood school is a reflection of the belief that education should be locally controlled.

Obviously, the neighborhood school concept has contributed effectively to both de jure and de facto segregation. The *Brown* vs. *the Board of Education* decision in 1954 made de jure segregation unconstitutional, thereby overturning the long-standing *Plessy* vs. *Ferguson* in 1896.[8] In so doing, it struck down the separate but equal doctrine that had dominated public education since the Civil War. The battle centering around de facto segregation began to materialize and has monopolized American education ever since. The *Gittelson* decision (1971) in Los Angeles is a case where the distinctions between de jure and de facto

---

8. *Brown* v. *Board of Education*, 347 U.S. 483, in *The Supreme Court and Education*, David Fellman, ed. (New York: Teacher's College, Columbia University, 1960).

segregation were clearly dealt away with in determining that the Los Angeles Board of Education had pursued a policy of segregation. Step by step, the neighborhood school system has come under direct attack.

Extent of Segregation in Schools

To cite statistics that are accurate and up-to-date is almost impossible. Most figures change and have been changing yearly. Even the Coleman Report has been revised based on newer interpretations of the data by Coleman. Perhaps the best way to examine this topic is to review the statistics and related facts over a period of several years.

Early and Mid-1960s. A study by the U.S. Commission on Civil Rights and the Office of Education, *Equality of Educational Opportunity*[9] (called the Coleman Report) generalized that "the great majority of American children attend schools that are largely segregated, that is, almost all of their fellow students are of the same racial background as they are." It cited such specifics as:

1. 65 percent of all first-grade black students (in 1965) attended schools that had an enrollment of 90 percent or more black students; 77 percent of all first grade white students attended schools that were 90 percent or more white.

2. In large urban areas, 80 percent of the non-whites attended central city schools, while almost 70 percent of the white enrollment attended suburban schools.

3. Within the 75 central cities in the U.S., 75 percent of the black elementary students were in schools that were almost all black; 83 percent of the whites were in nearly all white schools.

4. In the South, most students attended schools that were 100 percent white or black.

---

9. *Equality of Educational Opportunity* (U.S. Office of Health, Education, and Welfare, 1966–67), pp. 10–13; *Racial Isolation in the Public Schools* (U.S. Commission on Civil Rights, 1967); see Summary Report of *Equality of Educational Opportunity*, pp. 3, 8, 9, 14, 20, 21, 22, 24, 27, 28, 32, 33. See also Harry L. Miller and Roger Woock, *Social Foundations of Urban Education* (Hinsdale, Illinois: Dryden Press, 1973), pp. 411–418.

The Early 1970s. In fall, 1970, the Office of Education studies revealed several trends.[10] They were:

> 1. The percentage of black students attending majority white schools had increased from 23 percent to 33 percent nationwide. Almost all of that increase was due to changes in the South; the northern and western states remained steady.
>
> 2. During the late 1960s and early 1970s, the number of larger cities with a majority of black students in their school population increased.
>
> 3. An awareness of the segregation of other minority groups such as Chicanos, Asian-Americans, and the American Indian became more visible. Forty-five percent of Mexican-Americans in the Southwest went to predominately Mexican-American schools.

Figure 5–1 illustrates the changes in the early seventies.[11]

Mid- to Late 1970s. Studies in the mid- to late 1970s showed that segregation was increasing in the schools. Whereas the southern and border states showed some decrease, the northeastern and western states showed a steady increase. Perhaps the biggest stir over the impact of desegregation were the recent conclusions of sociologist James Coleman, author of the Coleman Report. Coleman concluded that, between 1908 and 1973 in 22 of the nation's largest cities, there was a sizable decrease in the white student population, largely due to school desegregation. He defined desegregation as any change in the racial composition of schools that increased contact between white and black students.[12]

In his study, Coleman separated the 22 districts into two categories: (1) those that had undergone little or no change in the five-year period, and (2) those that had undergone more pronounced racial change.

10. *New York Times,* June 17, 1971; *The Condition of Education: A Statistical Report on the Condition of American Education, 1975* (U.S. Dept. of Health, Education, and Welfare, 1975, National Center for Education Statistics), pages 70–71; Miller and Woock, *Social Foundations,* p. 412.

11. *The Condition of Education,* p. 70, Chart 4.14.

12. James S. Coleman, "Racial Segregation in the Schools: New Research With New Policy Implications," *Phi Delta Kappan,* October, 1975, pp. 75–78.

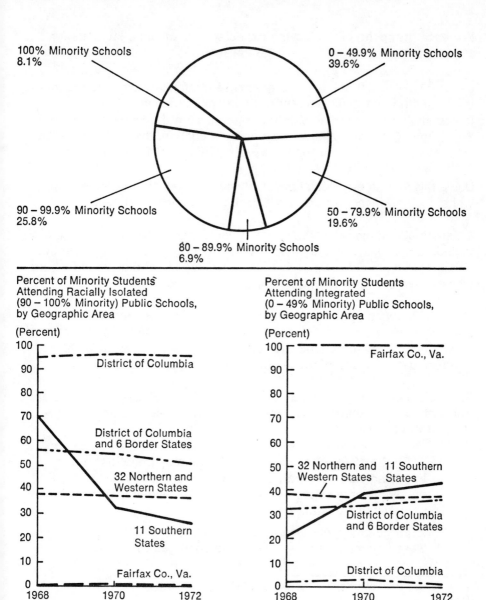

100% Minority Schools
8.1%

0 – 49.9% Minority Schools
39.6%

90 – 99.9% Minority Schools
25.8%

50 – 79.9% Minority Schools
19.6%

80 – 89.9% Minority Schools
6.9%

Percent of Minority Students
Attending Racially Isolated
(90 – 100% Minority) Public Schools,
by Geographic Area

(Percent)

District of Columbia

District of Columbia
and 6 Border States

32 Northern and
Western States

11 Southern
States

Fairfax Co., Va.

1968   1970   1972

Percent of Minority Students
Attending Integrated
(0 – 49% Minority) Public Schools,
by Geographic Area

(Percent)

Fairfax Co., Va.

32 Northern and   11 Southern
Western States   States

District of Columbia
and 6 Border States

District of Columbia

1968   1970   1972

Figure 5-1. Percent of Minority Students Attending Public
Schools With Different Racial Composition: 1972

Source: *The Condition of Education: A Statistical Report on the Condition of American
Education, 1975* (U.S. Dept. of Health, Education and Welfare, National Center for
Educational Statistics, 1975): 70 – 71.

For each group, he projected the expected loss of white students for 1968–73 based on losses in the 1968–69 year.

Of the 12 districts that had undergone little change, Coleman found that the projected loss of 17 percent of their white students was approximately the same as the actual 20 percent loss in the five-year period. But in the 10 districts that did experience change, the actual loss was 26 percent—much higher than the projected loss of 10 percent.

Using this and other calculations, Coleman concluded that more black-white contact in schools causes a decline in white enrollment.

Coleman added many qualifications to the conclusions of his study, including his observation that white flight occurs rapidly with or without desegregation in cities that have high percentages of blacks and where whites have convenient white suburbs to move to.

His qualifications, unfortunately, have been rarely mentioned in his statements before a Senate committee and in court affidavits, where he blamed school desegregation for sharply accelerating white flight and, in effect, defeating the purpose behind desegregation in the large cities.[13]

The Coleman findings caused controversy, critics accused Coleman of political bias and questionable research.[14] Nonetheless, statistics[15] indicated the following:

> 1. By the 1974–75 school year, Hispanic segregation trends indicated that 67.4 percent of youngsters attended predominately minority schools and 30 percent attended intensely segregated schools.
>
> 2. Large-city school systems in the Northeast and in the West were becoming increasingly more segregated.

---

13. Coleman, *Phi Delta Kappan,* October, 1975, pp. 75–78. See also *Los Angeles Times,* December 17, 1975.

14. See Robert Green and Thomas Pettigrew, "Urban Desegregation and White Flight: A Response to Coleman," *Phi Delta Kappan,* February, 1976, pp. 399–402; Gregg Jackson, "Some Limitations in Coleman's Recent Segregation Research," *Phi Delta Kappan,* December, 1975, p. 274.

15. *Los Angeles Times,* June 20, 1976; *Los Angeles Times,* August 10, 1976; *Statistical Report on Education* (Washington, D.C.: HEW, 1976).

3. Regardless of the increasing segregation index, more than half of all American school children are bused to school currently, the largest figure in the nation's history.

4. Statistics from HEW show that 51.5 percent of public elementary and secondary students were bused in 1973–74 compared with 48 percent ten years earlier.

5. Large school systems such as New York, Chicago, Detroit, Los Angeles, and San Francisco were becoming more segregated.

Conclusions Regarding Desegregation Figures

Recently Green and Pettigrew[16] analyzed all the recent studies and statistics regarding segregation and white flight. In spite of the discrepancies among the many studies, all of which were based on HEW data, they have suggested six trends that are consistent with all the analyses:

1. There has been a long-term trend of whites leaving the central cities and of blacks migrating into these areas.

2. All the studies agree that desegregation and white flight are not related to each other in the smaller cities.

3. In large metropolitan school districts, desegregation has little or no effect on white flight.

4. Court-ordered desegregation has not had effects on white flight that are different from desegregation resulting from other factors, such as residential or neighborhood transition.

5. The loss of white and black students from large central-city districts is related to the proportion of black students attending those districts. In part, the proportion of blacks variable is a surrogate for a range of other variables, from eroding tax bases to old housing stocks.

6. While extensive school desegregation may hasten the white flight phenomenon, particularly in the largest, nonurban districts in the South, the effect, if it obtains at all, may only

---

16. Green and Pettigrew, "Urban Desegregation," *Phi Delta Kappan,* February 1976, p. 401.

be observed temporarily during the first year of desegregation, and then only for those families that have already made plans to move.

Desegregation Effects

What does research tell us about the effects of desegregation? In 1954 in conjunction with the *Brown* decision, social scientists provided the Supreme Court with the summarized findings of over 500 social scientists regarding the detrimental effects of segregation upon minority children.[17] The findings noted that minority children were characterized by feelings of frustration, inferiority, submissiveness, aggressiveness, withdrawal tendencies, unrealistic self-images and self-concepts, distortion in reality, and poor social and academic development. The findings also concluded that white children felt a deterioration in moral values, a hardening of social sensitivity, inner conflicts and guilt feelings, unrealistic self-images, and disturbances in their sense of reality. The research on race relations supported the propositions that:

- Black youngsters become aware of their skin color before they reach school age.
- Black children are taught to feel that their schools and education are poor and inadequate.
- Black children come to realize that black and white teachers look upon them as inferior and maintain lower standards of expectation for them.

There is no question that segregated schools are unequal. Given the simple reality that the U.S. spends approximately 15–20 percent more per year on the average white child than on the average black child, one can see certain built-in inequalities.[18] Not everyone, however, would agree with this assessment. The Coleman Report concluded that unequal facilities and materials had little, if anything, to do with measurable differences. He also concluded that the socioeconomic level of a student's school had more effect on his achievement than any other measurable factor except the socioeconomic level of his

---

17. See footnote 8, 1954, *Brown* vs. *Board of Education.*
18. See Christopher Jencks, *Inequality in the Schools* (New York: Basic Books, 1972), p. 28.

home. Jencks wrote that "effectively, this meant that both blacks and whites were better off in predominately white schools, since these schools were more likely to be middle class."[19]

More recent research from the National Institute of Education produced a comprehensive, 22-point summary of desegregation research.[20] Based upon what NIE Director Harold Hodgkinson said was "about 60 pounds" of substantiating documents, studies, and data, the principle conclusions of NIE were the following:

1. Desegregation does not reduce achievement scores of whites.

2. Desegregation, on the average, does slightly increase the achievement scores of blacks; the increase is probably due to an increase in the quality of services and instruction.

3. White flight from the central city is a common phenomenon of the last 20 years; no one knows what factors help control white flight.

4. Some compensatory school intervention can change short-term achievement scores in a dramatic fashion, but within the limits of natural variation, differences in educational expenditure have little relationship to achievement.

5. Achievement scores bear little relation to success in later life, measured by factors such as income and occupational status; some achievement scores are dropping while others are rising. The situation is confusing.

6. Hypotheses of genetic racial differences in intelligence and achievement have no basis in data.

7. The urban school environment is entangled with lots of other problems in urban areas such as poverty, level of resources of cities, racial tension, and overcrowding.

Overall, the NIE report concluded that the mood today was such that, while Americans believe in desegregation and do not mind school

---

19. Jencks, *Inequality in the Schools*, p. 100.
20. NIE Report, *Phil Delta Kappan*, December, 1975, pp. 289–290.

busing, they do not favor busing for purposes of school desegregation.[21] An earlier study[22] regarding busing results in seven urban communities, yielded the information on Chart 5-1.

Basic Assumptions About Integration

One assumption stems from the moral and legal requirements that different ethnic groups should be represented in equal proportions in various aspects of social living: jobs, social services, neighborhoods, and schools. This assumption has led to affirmative action policies in employment and controversial quota systems based on the moral argument that America is a land of equal opportunity and the legal argument that the Constitution guarantees equal rights to all citizens. A second assumption regards educational benefits and stems from the belief that, if two unequally performing groups are brought together, the poorer performing group will be influenced by the better performing group to the extent that the end results will include a more equal achievement level, improved academic performance, and increased motivation.

A third assumption, which social scientists like to call the contact theory, is based on the theoretical works of Gordon Allport, who found that prejudice and discrimination will be improved if different groups come into interpersonal contact, particularly at early stages, and grow up together.[23] It is based on the hypotheses that the more numerous the social interactions of a person, the greater will be the learning and motivation of the person. Conversely, a person with more restricted social interactions will learn less and be less motivated. Regarding self-image, the more multiple the social interactions of people, the more realistic will be their self-image, while the more restricted the social interactions of people, the more unrealistic the self-images.

From the 1960s to the present, school systems have struggled with the questions of integration. Many have conscientiously taken up the

21. NIE Report, *Phi Delta Kappan*, December, 1975, pp. 289–290.

22. See Kenneth Goodall, "The Anti-Busing Paper: Wayward and Wrong," *Psychology Today*, November, 1972, pp.41-43 (Ziff-Davis Publishing Company, 1972).

23. See Norene Harris and Nathaniel Jackson, "An Interview With David Armor," in *The Integration of American Schools* (Boston: Allyn and Bacon, 1975), pp. 142–150.

Chart 5–1. Busing and Desegregation Results

Place	Grade Level	Achievement Results for Black Children	For White Children (if tested)
Goldsboro, N.C.	7 – 11	statistically significant gains in reading, closing black-white differential; gains in math scores do not close racial gap; gains greatest for initially high achievers	both reading and math gains; gains greatest for high achievers
Newark-Verona, N.J.	1 – 2	statistically significantly greater total achievement gains for desegregated in both grades	no negative effects (only difference favors the desegregated)
Rochester-West Irondequoit, N.Y.	K – 2	statistically significantly greater verbal, reading and math achievement gains on 13 of 27 tests for desegregated	no negative effects (only differences favor the desegregated)
Buffalo, N.Y.	5 – 7	two and a half months greater achievement gain for desegregated	no negative effects
New York, N.Y.	4	statistically significantly greater math achievement gains, and somewhat greater reading gains for desegregated	no negative effects
Philadelphia, Pa.	4 – 6	statistically significantly greater reading and somewhat greater math achievement gains for desegregated in fourth and fifth grades	
Sacramento, Calif.	2 – 6	statistically significantly greater gains on three of 10 tests and greater gains on six more for desegregated	

Source: See Kenneth Goodall, "The Anti-Busing Paper: Wayward and Wrong," *Psychology Today*, November, 1972, pp. 41-43 (Ziff-Davis Publishing Company, 1972).

challenges that desegregation poses. The New Haven Public Schools[24] began the desegregation of their system in 1964, declaring that it made its decision to desegregate for three fundamental reasons:

1. A moral decision: "The courts had decided and the educational leaders had concurred that racially imbalanced schools perpetuated the problems of unequal educational opportunities. . . ."

2. An educational decision: "The New Haven Board of Education concurs in the principle that racially imbalanced schools are educationally unsound. . . ."

3. A timely decision: ". . . the time has come to face the issue of imbalances . . . squarely . . . to work out a sound local solution to a pressing national problem. . . . Integration is now an idea whose time has come."

More recently, the Milwaukee Public Schools[25] adopted the following declaration regarding the desegregation of its schools before it unveiled its far-reaching, innovative integration proposal.

Respect for the dignity and worth of each individual is paramount in the establishment of all policies by the Milwaukee Board of School Directors and in the administration of those policies by staff members in the Milwaukee Public Schools. The Constitution of the United States of America and the State of Wisconsin, pertinent legislation enacted at those two levels of government, as well as the judicial interpretation regarding citizens' rights and responsibilities, undergird this statement on education and human rights.

An examination of relevant conditions as they currently exist in the Greater Milwaukee area indicates that not all persons are recipients of the rights and benefits afforded them as citizens of our state and nation. For children particularly, who are the primary concern of each area school district, this has resulted in situations of socioeconomic, racial, and ethnic separation due to housing patterns and economic conditions which are handicapping to the growth and development of these children. Our multi-ethnic population is potentially one of the richest resources available to our schools. However,

---

24. New Haven Public Schools, "Proposals for Promoting Equality of Educational Opportunity and Dealing With the Problems of Racial Imbalance" (New Haven, Board of Education, June 8, 1964); see also *Integration of American Schools*, p. 94.

25. Milwaukee Public Schools Information Sheet, "Planning for September, 1976" (Milwaukee: Board of Education, March 12, 1976); see also *Milwaukee Journal*, "Milwaukee Public Schools Supplement," March 12, 1976.

if barriers exist and communication breaks down, difficult problems develop both for the schools which must function in this setting and for the children who are most affected by it. Such situations are beyond the capacity of the schools to conquer on their own; all of society is responsible for and must participate in their solutions. Nevertheless, all school districts have the responsibility to overcome within their capabilities any barriers that may exist and to maximize the achievement potential of the children in their care.

Many educators, social scientists, and community leaders have advanced arguments against integration and in favor of segregated schools They argue that integrated schools cause psychological damage to blacks because such schools tend to (1) emphasize black pupils' low achievement as opposed to whites and thus create black feelings of inferiority in school achievement evident to black students, (2) emphasize and suggest the superiority of white culture and deemphasize the culture and heritage of blacks in equal proportion, (3) cause blacks social isolation and rejection by whites or force blacks to engage in resegregation in school facilities to protect their own identities, (4) fail to provide black models of achievement and authority and decrease the number of adult role models for blacks, (5) make impotent black local community input and control over their schools and what is taught in them, and (6) impede the educational and social processes by facilitating a situation of unrest that often spills over into violence, gang warfare, and peer-group competition. Some groups even argue forcefully about the teachers and their lack of preparation for integrated classrooms.

Integration poses special challenges to the teacher. Prejudices surface and are challenged; problems of classroom management become more acute; the process of instruction itself enters a new context; and the greater complexities of organizational reorientation become more difficult with administrators, teachers, and community often going in different directions. Problems that arise often breed overreactions to new situations. Even if integration is handled smoothly, the problems arising from the prejudices and stereotypes of teachers are monumental. As far back as 1968, the American Association of Colleges for Teacher Education[26] anticipated the problems that would arise in the transition from segregation to integration. Among the problems they considered were:

---

26. B. Othanel Smith, ed., *Teachers for the Real World* (Washington, D.C.: American Association of Colleges for Teacher Education, 1968), pp. 159–161.

1. How to be fair in an integrated class: the questions of classroom instruction and self-fulfilling prophecies, being overly lenient or overly severe.

2. How to establish and maintain an atmosphere in which each child feels liked and respected; the questions of classroom atmosphere and psychology, the verbal and body language responses of teachers and pupils, the fairness or unfairness of decisions.

3. How to handle social events: the questions of teacher interaction on a social level, the social mingling at school and in the community, where biases and animosities of the community itself are involved.

4. How to handle routine classroom matters such as seating, distribution of materials, and grading. The questions of classroom management and the use of individualizing as opposed to grouping.

5. How to handle disruptive behavior: the questions of classroom discipline and the questions of fairness, consistency, flexibility, and rapport in the teacher-pupil exchange.

6. How to maintain sound intergroup relations and establish communications between different groups: the questions of social sensitivities and peer group interactions.

Obviously, these are matters that will determine the success or failure of any integration project. The best intentions of the community, the school board, and the administration rest solely on the best intentions of the teacher in the classroom. Once the classroom door closes in any school room, the teacher is the sole agent for change, good or bad, regardless of the pious platitudes of curriculum guides, school board directives, or community sermons.

School Desegregation Plans
Since 1954, thousands of plans have been proposed to remedy the problems of racially imbalanced school districts.[27] A detailed analysis

27. To give the reader some idea of the vastness of this particular topic, I would refer you to the following: Meyer Weinberg (ed.), *Desegregation Research: An Appraisal* (Bloomington, Indiana: *Phi Delta Kappan*, 1970); NEA *Combating Discrimination in the Schools: Legal Remedies and Guidelines* (Washington, D.C.: NEA, 1973); NEA, Project 1975: *Educational Neglect* (Washington, D.C.: NEA, 1975).

of every proposed plan would be virtually impossible. Generally speaking, and for the convenience of our brief discussion, this section will deal basically with two areas of remedy, the legal and compensatory approach and the school desegregation strategies.

The legal and compensatory approach refers to the numerous legal and constitutional decisions or pieces of legislation enacted that have required substantial changes in the educational framework. The compensatory approach refers to the efforts by agencies to use state and federal funds and other means of assistance to compensate for marked deficiencies in schools. These programs are often remedial programs that concentrate on individual student skills. Individuals with problems are chosen and provided with intensive remedial help. Compensatory education has a twofold task: remediation for those identified as disadvantaged and reduction in the number of future cases of disadvantaged persons by early detection and help.

The legal and constitutional framework of this approach stems from a succession of court decisions continuing even now starting with the *Brown* decision and with the hundreds of local, district, and state court decisions that pertain to equality in education. The legislative framework stems from the Civil Rights Act of 1964 (especially Title VII), the Elementary and Secondary Education Act of 1965, the Equal Pay Act of 1963, the Higher Education Act of 1972, the Public Health Act of 1971, the current rulings of HEW, the rulings of the U.S. Commission on Civil Rights, and executive decrees emanating from the Executive Branch and the Justice Department, such as Executive Order 11246.[28] To go into detail on these enactments and decisions would necessitate the writing of another text. The reader should merely be aware that they were the seminal influence for present actions and views.

School Desegregation Strategies
Of more importance are school desegregation strategies. Unlike compensatory education, school desegregation strategies are based on the assumption that local districts must make immediate efforts at racial mixing to achieve equality of opportunity essential for success in schooling. Such strategies underscore group practices and community

---

28. For a discussion of some of the relevant cases, see NEA *Legal Remedies and Guidelines;* publications from the *U.S. Commission on Civil Rights* and the *American Civil Liberties Union;* see also David Fellman, *The Supreme Court and Education.*

standards rather than individual programs. They involve and stress movement, planning, and change in fundamental structures within the school and community. As mentioned earlier, such strategies are numerous and have involved hundreds of school systems—some successful, some unsuccessful. These strategies have not necessarily been successful; they merely have been or are being tried. They are by no means an exhaustive listing of solutions.

The strategies can be grouped into two main categories: (1) those involving great impact upon the total community and (2) those involving more immediate impact upon the school district itself. One is external because it involves community involvement and acceptance; the other is internal because it involves only the school district per se and causes fewer community-relations problems.

Community-Impact Strategies

The simplest and most economical approach to racially balanced schools is to redraw the boundary lines of the school district to update population shifts. By redrawing boundary lines on a continuous basis, systems account for neighborhood changes and make some attempt to control those changes. There is, of course, the danger of racial gerrymandering, but this can be avoided by frequent boundary line changes. In some cases, simple boundary line changes would affect a minimal number of students for busing purposes.

A more complicated procedure that involves complete community co-operation would be the abolition of the neighborhood school concept and the substitution of other devices that will be mentioned in the next category. Such changes would rest, by and large, upon voluntary student movement programs attuned to the specialized needs of the students and the schools they selected to attend.

Another complicated and frustrating alternative for many systems has been the decentralization of the school system into smaller school districts, which allows for more direct local community control. This entails, however, more administrative bureaucracy since it involves more school boards, more committees, and more top-level administrators. An immediate danger in local community control is the degree of provincialism of the district, which is related to the possibility of reseg-regation. Decentralization, by and large, depends greatly upon compensatory aid programs, especially in districts that tend to be overly segregated.

The most controversial community strategy is busing, the forced movement of pupils from one school to another to achieve racial balance at the schools involved. Most citizens grow upset at the vision of their youngsters being bused out of their neighborhood into a strange neighborhood where the possibility of physical and academic harm may come to them. Yet, as previously mentioned, 51 percent of all children are currently being bused (see note 16). The busing controversy is still the most intense, yet educators generally agree that few solutions to desegregation can avoid some form of busing. The public still largely opposes busing (see Chart 5–2), and this creates intense political pressures for school board officials.

Chart 5–2. Opinions of the Public on Interdistrict Busing: 1972, 1974, 1975

Question item and possible responses	Percent distribution		
	1972	1974	1975
In general do you favor or oppose the busing of Black and White school children from one school district to another?			
Total	100.0	100.0	100.0
Favor	19.5	20.1	17.2
Oppose	76.6	76.2	78.1
Don't know	3.9	3.7	4.7

Source: National Opinion Research Center, University of Chicago, 6030 South Ellis Avenue, Chicago, Illinois, 60637, *General Social Survey,* 1972, 1974, 1975.

The Educational Park Complex is the most radical and expensive of strategies involving the community because it involves a tremendous financial investment to build a new educational park complex. Under this proposal, a new educational park structure would be constructed, and all of the students in the district would attend that structure. Such a structure might look like the following, with each building containing all the students at that grade level.

In a more realistic sense, without building a special complex, a group of adjacent school buildings are brought together as a small school system within a larger system (as in Figure 5–3) or a particular school in

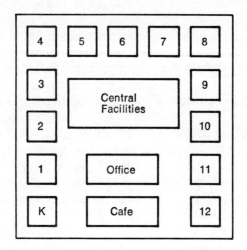

Figure 5-2. Educational Park Complex

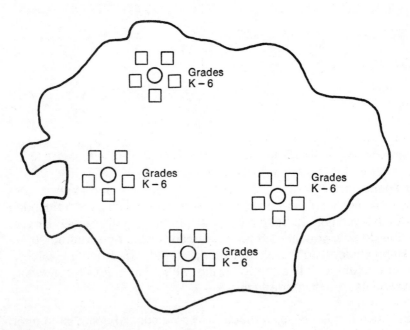

Figure 5-3. Syracuse Campus Plan
24 Elementary Schools Closed

a district could be designated a seventh-grade building and all seventh-grade students in that district would be based at that school (as in Figure 5–4).

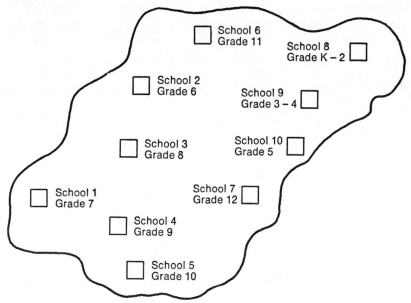

Figure 5-4. Pasadena Plan

School District Impact Strategies

Voluntary transfer is one means districts use to shift students around. If a school is not overcrowded and can take additional youngsters, any student from any other school can volunteer to be bused to the receiver school. On the whole, however, less than 5 percent of pupils in large urban districts volunteer to go to another school, and even then, the departure is usually from an inner-city school rather than into an inner-city school.

Site selection is yet another means a district can use to equalize racial balance. When the need for new buildings arises, the schools should not be placed in geographic areas that automatically guarantee their segregation; instead, they should be placed at crucial locations that insure maximum integration. One difficulty is the white flight to the suburbs; however, it can be noted that the middle-class population in the suburbs is declining while central-city enrollments have become stabilized.

The Princeton Plan, or school pairing, is another device that can be used internally in a school system. It merges two neighborhood schools into paired schools. One school takes all youngsters in K–3 and the other takes all students in 4–6. After pairing, students of both the attendance areas enroll in the two schools according to the grade offered at the receiving school. It is a modified educational park concept (see Figure 5–5).[29]

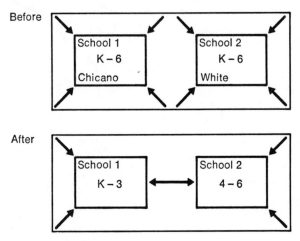

Figure 5-5. Modified Educational Park

Source: U.S. Commission on Civil Rights, "Racial Isolation in the Public Schools," Vol. 1, p. 141.

Magnet or specialized alternative schools within regular school systems are based on inducing pupils to select schools that offer special programs. These Satellite Specialization Centers, as the Milwaukee Public School system calls them, offer specialized curricula dealing with science, the arts, social sciences, vocational studies, or the basic fundamentals. Students select the schools on a part-time or full-time basis and attend them regardless of where they live. In fall 1977, the

---

29. U.S. Commission on Civil Rights, "Racial Isolation in the Public Schools," Vol. 1, p. 141. See also Charles Kniker, "The Search for Equal Educational Opportunities," in Kniker's *Myth and Reality* (Boston: Allyn and Bacon, 1975) p. 219.

Milwaukee Public School system[30] offered the citizens of that community the following specialty schools.

Open-Education School. Pupils are organized into flexible, multiaged family-like groups in an informal educational setting. They are given the freedom to initiate or select their own learning activities, and each pupil advances at his or her own rate of learning. Children in K–4 are eligible.

Montessori School. Montessori education develops a child's mental, physical, and psychological powers through freedom to explore learning materials and apparatus in a prepared, orderly manner under the guidance of a trained Montessori teacher. Four and five-year-olds with or without preschool experience are eligible.

Basic Fundamental School. Instruction focuses on basic skills, particularly in reading, mathematics, and English, in a strict disciplinary environment. Homework is required, and promotion and failure depends solely on academic achievement. Open to pupils in K–6.

Second-Language Proficiency School. In addition to the regular elementary school program, in this school, classes are taught by bilingual (English-German) speaking teachers so that pupils can acquire language skills in English and German. Children also receive 20 to 30 minutes of formal German language instruction daily. Enrollment is limited to pupils in K–3.

Schools for the Gifted and Talented. This school offers a challenging curriculum for pupils who are screened for intellectual ability, creative ability, and qualities of leadership. Its program for study prepares pupils for higher education. It is open to pupils in grades 4–6.

Continuous Progress School. This ungraded school provides an individual program of instruction to accommodate each child's learning needs. Pupils learn at their own rates in flexible, multi-age groups, commensurate with their instructional level. The ungraded organization permits

---

30. Milwaukee Public Schools, "Planning for September, 1976" (Milwaukee: Board of Education, March 12, 1976).

continuous movement of children to match their rate of achievement. It will be open to pupils in K–6.

Multi-Age, Multi-Unit School. Pupils are organized into units of 120 to 150, with each unit having four to five teachers, a unit leader, and two sides working as a team. Instruction is conducted in large groups, small groups, and paired situations. Independent study also is encouraged. The instructional program allows for differences in children's rates of achievement, levels of motivation, and styles of learning.

The application of a variety of the aforementioned tactics and strategies applied in a systematic way has succeeded in some school districts, but it has failed in others. One of the basic reasons for failure in the large urban school districts is the fact that there still remain larger concentrations of minority youngsters. They constitute such sizable majorities of the school population that any plan, including busing, will not materially change the overall racial mix in most schools. What does one do with such systems as Atlanta, which has a school population reaching 80 percent minority, Detroit with a school population that is 75 percent minority, or Washington, D.C., with a black population approaching 95 percent? And what can be done with a system such as Los Angeles, which is so spread out geographically that any of the proposals such as busing, specialized schools, or the educational park concept are not feasible? The battle for racial balance and equality of educational opportunity will be even more savage in the 1980s, and, this writer predicts, no closer to solution than in the 1970s.

Let us now turn our attention to another, more demanding problem: the potency of social class in determining educational opportunity. As mentioned earlier, James Coleman and his colleagues concluded that socioeconomic level was far more potent than race or any other singular factor in determining who gets educated well. Most follow-up studies have supported the Coleman Report on this basic conclusion.

The Effect of Social Class in Public Education

All societies, large or small, primitive or modern, urban or agricultural, show some overall hierarchical structure based upon socioeconomic status. Each society can be identified by its intricate pattern of interrelationships between persons and groups. The phenomenon of rank is a characteristic of every social community.

American democracy has characteristics of rank, along with every other organized society. People are ranked on a scale that divides them into three conceptualized positions: the top, the intermediate position, and the bottom. Social stratification, as a concept, refers to the identifiable social structure that exists in society, that ranks people into appropriate position, and that carries with that ranking certain social characteristics that impart prestige, power and role playing. Joseph Kahl, in his classic book, *The American Class Structure,* delineated these major dimensions as prestige, group or class consciousness and cohesiveness, value orientations, and power. These dimensions interact, thus forming the basis and holding power of the social-class structure. People can be stratified according to any quality that is recognized and enforced by other members of the society. Social stratification is the primary means of social differentiation in organized society.

Using Kahl's major dimensions, social class becomes an important factor in education and schooling. To a large extent, an individual's socioeconomic status determines his peer group relations, his schooling and educational opportunities, as well as his community contacts and successes, whether they be political, social, or occupational. As a broad concept, social-class affiliation describes a fairly consistent pattern of life, behavior, and opportunity. In the educational sphere, social class affects the kind of education received, the quality as well as the quantity of that education, and, to a very large extent, the academic performance correlated to that education.

Social class is significant to education in several ways. First, the relationship between social class and academic performance has been demonstrated by a number of studies. Such studies have concluded that, the higher a person's social class, the higher will be his or her level of academic performance and attainment.

Second, a child's social class is defined by the position his or her parents hold in society, which suggests a value orientation and a class consciousness that must be recognized in educating children if education is truly a value-oriented enterprise. Socioeconomic status determines where a family lives and where a child will go to school, whether that be a ghetto school, a suburban school, or a private school. Financing of higher education is also determined by socioeconomic status.

Third, social class is important because the school system and the educational establishment represent, reflect, and seek to inculcate certain social-class values and attitudes consistent with a dominant cultural orientation. This middle-class psychology operates as a conditioning process that subsequently divides and treats children from different social classes in different ways. Teachers, administrators, curricula, textbooks, school activities, standardized tests, structural and organizational patterns, discipline, and numerous other evidences of middle-class operations set the stage upon which the child acts, provide him or her with the ways of acting, and the means of defining the action.

Fourth, education has become the main road to occupational and professional success. The amount of education, in most cases, is a good indicator of a person's potential for achieving a sought-for socioeconomic status. In other words, education is of major concern in social mobility. It can restrict or enhance social position. As a variable, it affects other factors such as choice of vocation, choice of spouse, place of residence, and choice of possessions. Hence, the amount and kind of education received by an individual affect the class rank, position, and prestige he or she will secure. It is the most potent force affecting social mobility.

The American public school system has been hailed by educators as the single most significant social institution with reference to changing the social-class position of members of the lower class. It has been suggested by many egalitarians that the public school has been the most influential factor in creating a free, open-class society, by affording equal opportunity for all segments of society. Such a position presupposes that all children receive the same quality of education, as well as the same quantity. It further presupposes that equal educational opportunity exists in our public schools, and that all citizens can avail themselves of these opportunities. Are such suppositions accurate? Are our public schools the epitome of the democratic philosophy of equality? Many persons—this writer included—cannot agree that the public schools are the showcase of the democratic ethic.

Educational Inequities and Social Class

One of the most persistent themes in the long history of public education in America has been the ideology of equal educational opportunity.
As a philosophic ideal, few would offer alternatives or profess strong
disagreement. Yet in actual practice, this theme tends to be a shallow
echo of an ideal that everyone desires but realistically knows is not
practiced in our schools. As one surveys the social foundations of
education and views the inequities that exist in the schools, one cannot
but realize the potency of social-class membership in determining and
setting these inequities.

Social class is a sociological concept that refers to a significant number
of people who hold similar positions of respect within their society, who
perform in roles that reflect beliefs and values held in common, and
who are willing to accept others within their aggregate as equals. The
concept, more precisely renamed "socioeconomic level," has been
recently used by scholars to mean a statistical aggregate of people in
the same income bracket or occupational level who are identified almost
exclusively in terms of their material accumulations and life-styles.[31]
Sociologists have long tried to identify status characteristics, as well
as the number and size of social classes. The Warner study, Hollings-
head's study, Lynd's study, and more recently, Havighurst's study,[32]
have all attempted to estimate the distribution of social class. Havighurst
estimated the following:

Class	Percent
Upper	1–3
Upper Middle	7–12
Lower Middle	20–35
Upper Lower	25–40
Lower Lower	15–25

---

31. Milton Gordon, *Social Class in American Sociology* (Durham, N.C.: Duke University
Press 1958), Ch. 8; Grace Graham, *The Public School in the New Society* (New
York: Harper and Row, 1970), p. 45. See also Tesconi, *Schooling in America*, 1975,
Ch. 11 & 13.

32. Robert Havighurst, "Social Class Influences in American Education," National
Society for the Study of Education, 16th Yearbook, 1961, p. 121. Havighurst's current
figures are in *Society and Education* (Boston: Allyn and Bacon, 1975), p. 25. See also
Miller and Woock, *Social Foundations of Urban Education*, 1973, pp. 66–73.

Although percentages change, these figures are probably as accurate as any and will serve our purpose for analysis. As one looks over the figures, certain things become apparent: (1) the upper class in American society is a definite minority and probably has always been; (2) the middle class, which dominates the culture and its orientation, represents approximately 38 percent of the population, yet exploits the mainstream of social interaction; (3) the lower class represents about 60 percent or more of the population, is clearly the dominant group statistically, but is the weakest group in terms of power and social influence.

Delineated class formations yield certain benefits for the student of sociology. First, they are a valuable service in describing life-styles within society. Second, they help us understand the patterns of thought and behavior as possessed by a person's family, job, neighborhood, or peer group. Third, they help to identify the track of education that a child will experience as he passes through the socialization process. It is this third dimension that is important for our purposes. Since any cultural pattern associated with a distinct class dominates the interaction and mobility within that class, it is only logical to suggest that, as a result of these distinct class orientations, certain cultural inconsistencies between classes in the whole culture will arise. Consequently, a pattern or patterns emerges as dominant, while others are subordinate and subcultural patterns of less importance. Differences in patterns from different social classes and their consequent motivations, values, and social environments, have significant implications for education and for teachers. Any analysis of the influences of social class upon children should increase our insight into the complexities of human interaction in the schools.

Sociologists have generally concluded that social class is an important factor in educational achievement and social mobility. From first impressions of social class, it seems there should exist a tri-level system of education, one based on each of the three classes as they form a subculture within the whole culture. Such is not the case. In actuality, the social structure, as well as the educational structure, is subsumed under and dominated by the middle-class culture and its respective representatives. The schools are almost completely oriented toward middle- or upper-class values. If one were to look at the social class structure of the American school, it would look something like this:

School Board	94% Upper Middle
Administrators	90% Upper Middle, Middle
Teachers	94% Middle
Taxpayers	80% Middle
Students	10% Upper (Private Schools)
	10% Upper Middle (Private and Parochial)
	30% Lower Middle (Public)
	50% Lower Class (Public)

Significant, then, to our concerns are the several observations:

1. Education is run by a dominant middle class, which operates a "system" based upon a social environment that is often foreign to the lower class.

2. The system tends to perpetuate itself because of a formal set of expectations.

3. The major characteristics of the American public school that can be identified in our school are functions of the value systems of the middle class.

4. Since the family and the pre-school social environment of a child are important, it is obvious that the child in a middle-class family receives a more abling background than does the child from the lower-class family.

5. The lower-class child is at a continued disadvantage when he or she enters school because, more often than not, the teachers' judgment of children and their performance is based on middle-class values and middle-class culture. Even standardized tests are based on middle-class values.

Several tentative conclusions about the influence of social class upon education are in order. These conclusions are drawn from the many classic studies[33] made in the field.

---

33. See Allison Davis, *Social Class Influences Upon Learning* (Cambridge: Harvard University Press, 1948); Frank Riesman, *The Culturally Deprived Child* (New York: Harper and Row, 1962); Carl Bereiter, *Teaching Disadvantaged Children in the Pre-School* (Englewood Cliffs, N.J.: Prentice-Hall, 1966); Fred Stodtbeck, "Family Interaction, Values, and Achievement," in *Talent and Society* (New York: Van Nostrand, 1958). 181–184. See Tesconi, *Schooling in America,* 1975, Ch. 15.

1. Attitudes towards education held by parents and children vary from class to class with the middle class having the highest regard for education and the lower class having the lowest.

2. Social-class membership largely determines where a family lives and the public school that the children will attend.

3. Social class determines income and thus the financing of further education.

4. Social class and family background determine to a large extent the language skills of children.

5. The higher a person's social class, the higher his or her academic performance and level of aspiration.

6. Social classes provide experiences upon which education depends: the narrower one's range of cultural experiences, the narrower the range of experience one can use to relate to and draw upon for school work.

7. Social class determines to a large extent the degree of social interaction within families. Interaction between child and parent is reduced in poverty homes because of the family size or the relative instability of the home.

8. Since middle-class culture dominates schools, the elaborate code of communication (formal language), the dominant value pattern (competition, punctuality, hard work, cleanliness), and the external determinants of ability grouping for special education (middle-class standardized tests), as well as the instructional programs and techniques children are exposed to, testifies to the recognition that the children of the lower class will in all likelihood become increasingly disadvantaged in their present school environments.

9. If the conclusion in point 8 is correct, the only means the lower class has of escaping this disadvantage, namely, social mobility, is closed. An impoverished social environment, added to an inferior education, produces a person inadequately prepared for a good job and income, one who is doomed to a caste-like status for the rest of his life. Sociologists call this the "cumulative deficit hypothesis."[34]

---

34. See Nat Hentoff, "Making Public Schools Accountable: A Case Study of P.S. 201 in Harlem," *Phi Delta Kappan,* March, 1967; James B. Conant, *Slums and Suburbs*

There exists a consensus that, generally, those students comprising what is called the culturally deprived or the socially disadvantaged group come from the lower class; their numbers are growing due to the urbanism in our society. The socially disadvantaged can be identified and described in terms in their family characteristics, personal characteristics, and their social group characteristics.[35] They represent approximately 30 percent of the pupils in urban schools; they come from a culture of poverty, and they are often the most recent immigrants to our cities.[36] They have certain personality and learning characteristics directly related to their class membership.[37] These include:

1. Weak ego development, lack of self-confidence, and a negative self-concept.

2. A cognitive style that responds better to visual and kinesthetic signals than to oral or written ones.

3. The ability to learn more readily by induction than deduction.

4. The ability to work better at a single activity than at multiple activities.

5. A short attention span.

6. Significant gaps in knowledge and uneven learning.

7. Deficiencies in word precision and a lack of basic skills in language and reading development.

8. Little experience with success in life and school.

Consequently, lower-class membership and cultural disadvantagement are somewhat coterminous.

(New York: McGraw-Hill, 1961); M. Eddy, *Walk the White Line: A Profile of Urban Education* (Garden City, N.Y.: Doubleday, 1967); G.A. Moore, *Realities of the Urban Classroom* (Garden City, N.Y.: Doubleday, 1964); Kenneth Clark, "Clash of Cultures," *Integrated Education*, 1964.

35. See Robert Havighurst, "Who Are the Socially Disadvantaged?" *Journal of Negro Education*, Summer 1964; also in Alfred Lightfoot, *The Culturally Disadvantaged: Perspectives in Urban Education* (New York: SAR, Simon and Schuster, 1970). See also Arthur Davis, *Racial Crisis in Public Education* (New York: Vantage Press, 1975).

36. Havighurst, "Who Are the Socially Disadvantaged?" *Journal of Negro Education*, 1964.

37. See Newton Metfessel's study, *Project Potential*, University of Southern California, October, 1965, "Conclusions." See research and conclusions in Chapter 7. See also Davis, *Social Class Influences*, 1975.

What is known of the culturally disadvantaged child has only been learned very recently. Research on poverty is a very new field. It is now commonly recognized that these children are in need of special attention from society and the schools. Much more work remains to be done in analyzing and understanding the variable of social class and its influence upon educational achievement.

Exercises

I. *Desegregation*
Read the attached case study for Community X.
Given:

> 1. A medium-sized urban community having: (a) a population of about half a million, (b) de facto conditions of segregation in all aspects of the community, and (c) a well-defined neighborhood housing and school pattern.

> 2. A well-defined neighborhood school pattern with the following districts:

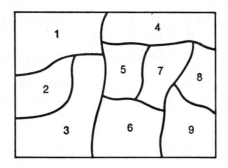

> 3. District analysis is as follows:
> a. Each district has approximately four elementary schools, two junior high schools, and one high school. There are sixty-three schools in all.
> b. Districts 5, 7, 3, 9 are minority districts, while the others are not. The distribution is as follows:

No. 5: Blacks, 95 percent; whites, 5 percent; solid lower class

No. 7: Blacks, 90 percent; whites, 5 percent; Chicano, 5 percent

No. 3: Blacks, 100 percent

No. 9: Chicano, 80 percent; blacks, 10 percent; whites, 10 percent

No. 1: Blacks, 33 percent; whites, 33 percent; Chicano, 33 percent

No. 4: All white

No. 6: All white

No. 2: All white, solid middle class

No. 8: All white, solid middle class

4. A federal court order to desegregate by the following term, with little hope of reversal.

5. Limited financial resources, the failure of several bond issues, militant minority-group pressures for local control over their own schools, and a divided school board.

Problem
Assume that you are on the Board of Education. Use this information to develop a specific working program of desegregation that would be in compliance with the law and realistic. Think in terms of:

1. Short-term solutions to take effect the following term.

2. Long-term measures to be instituted following the short-term period.

The short-term guidelines should be specific in terms of changes in each district and should detail what should be done. The long-term guidelines need not be that specific, but in all cases, short term or long term, explanations and justifications must be given. Whenever possible, refer to pertinent scholarly sources to reinforce your suggestions.

Note: You have not successfully completed this exercise if you merely list solutions and do not analytically apply them to the districts by showing specific changes, e.g., if you select the educational park concept, you must show its implementation.

II. *Questions on Desegregation*

1. Have schools become more or less segregated? Give evidence to support your answer. Describe the specific area.

2. Is integration of schools and classrooms the answer?

3. Is segregated education detrimental to youth?

4. What has been done in the past to provide for racial balance? How did this work?

5. What solutions should be tried? Why? Should we have a set percentage for an integrated classroom or school?

6. How does the general public feel about desegregation? How do teachers feel about it?

7. Is there educational value in segregated education when it is coterminous with local control, e.g., black controls black schools?

8. Is there any evidence that segregated education has been educationally and psychologically damaging to minority and majority children?

9. What have been the prime obstacles to desegregation, both outside and inside the profession?

10. What is the present administration's position on desegregation? (Federal administration) Do you agree?

11. How can large city systems tackle the problems of desegregating their schools?

12. Is integration basically a school problem, or does it have a larger base? Should the schools be in the forefront in the battle for integration?

Sociopsychological Dimensions of Inequality in Education

Chapter 6

When you have finished this chapter, you should be able to perform the following tasks.

1. Define the term *classroom interaction* and describe how the classroom teacher analyzes behavior in the classroom by examining the social setting of the classroom.

2. State the determinants of sound mental health in the classroom.

3. Define *self-concept* and *self-image* and state the variables affecting them.

4. List several characteristics of self-accepting individuals.

5. List the most common educational deficiencies of the urban child who is economically poor.

6. Define and describe the teacher's role in setting the sociopsychological climate of the classroom.

7. List the influences that the home has upon the child's psychological health and some specific effects of the absence of a father role model.

8. State the relationship between self-image and segregation.

9. Explain the Mercer model as it characterizes an integrated school setting.

Learning is a complex process by which human beings change their ideas and behavior patterns. To a very large extent, the behavior of individuals is influenced by the social interactions they engage in. Human beings are influenced by the actual or implied presence of other human beings. Thus, the social nature of an individual is a primary concern in determining the behavior patterns of human beings. Learning is not only individual, but social in origin. Any change in individual behavior is largely determined by considerations that have their origin in social interaction or in the social environment. No human being learns entirely in isolation; interpersonal interaction defines, molds, and reinforces behavior. Hence, a study of the organized social environment of a child is as important as the study of an individual child.

Schooling is carried on functionally in an organized social environment in which all human beings are interacting in interpersonal processes. Response mechanisms of the learner are largely based upon his reaction to such factors as the organization, structure, climate-culture, norms, procedures, and value patterns within the classroom, as well as the stereotypes he thinks his peers, parents, and teachers will have of his behavior. In this social world of multiple interactions, education and goal setting take place. No child learns in isolation or in a vacuum; classroom, school, group, and societal circumstances mold his behavior and form his value patterns. His behavior is differentiated as acceptable or not acceptable through his ability to comprehend these interactions, interpret them successfully, and adjust to the demands made upon him by these forces.

Since the school, as well as the classroom, is a social system operating with a specific social organization, learning can be analyzed in terms of the interpersonal processes taking place among individuals in such a social setting. If the classroom teacher is to be successful in teaching, each teacher must be able to identify the various roles that students are playing, the norms to which they have subscribed in their role behavior, the values in which the norms are embedded, and the reasons that such a behavioral pattern has emerged in the first place. To understand this, and to maximize productive learning in the classroom, the effective teacher must be able to reduce the variability of human behavior and to produce stable patterns of activity based upon a realistic conceptualization of the operating social system. In other words, appropriate member behavior (in a class, school, club, or family) rests upon a realistic picture of self, which has been formed through the numerous social expectations of others. The good teacher recognizes why Johnny is acting up and sanctions or corrects role behavior so that it is realistic to the social circumstances. The self-actualizing learner is also a socialized learner; his input, transformation, and output of behavior are as much social as individual in origin.

Classroom interactions operate largely on four planes. All the interacting parties take their role clues from the circumstances inherent in these interactions:

> teacher to student, or student to teacher (individual super-ordinate or subordinate interaction)
>
> student to student (individual peer interaction)
>
> student to students (student to group interaction)
>
> students to students (group interaction)

A student may react one way to a peer in one situation and in a completely different way with another interacting partner in the same situation. Teachers must recognize this and be able to channel the energy of the various social systems into acceptable stable patterns of activity. Obviously, the teacher must be aware that the psychological functions of peer association are the most potent forces restricting or enhancing learning. The socialization function of peer-group affiliation is just as important in learning as is the educational function of the school and classroom. If one were isolated from the other, or if they were polarized, formal learning would be minimal. Class productivity and individual achievement increase when the school situation is relevant to and coterminous with peer-group cohesiveness and solidarity within a conceptual framework.

The effective classroom teacher analyzes behavior in the classroom by determining what problems beset the individuals and the class and to what extent the relationships discussed above produced the problems. By looking to the social nature of learning and the social setting of the classroom, the teacher is better able to resolve some of the problems induced by the social structure of the class. With such an awareness, the teacher can achieve a higher degree of class productivity and co-hesiveness, as well as a higher degree of individual productivity.

Mental Health in the Classroom

The child lives a good portion of his life in the classroom and in the school environment. The teacher and the child's peers are the two most important relationships affecting the mental health of the child. As the child discovers the social structures of the classroom, peer groups, and society, he also begins to seek his position in each of these categories. His position in these groups bears directly on his mental health.

Mental health is largely determined by his attitude toward himself, his perception of reality, his mastery of his environment, and his attempts at the actualization of his potential. Student's feelings about people, tasks in the classroom environment and his relationships to that environment, and the positiveness of his feelings about himself constitute the grounds for sound mental health in the classroom.[1]

Every child has a set of judgments, conclusions, thoughts, evaluations, and feelings about himself. These combined thoughts are known as the *self* or *self-concept.* These judgments are largely based upon interaction and communication with other persons, frequently called significant others. The person perceives how he is judged by other persons around him; sociologists call this the concept of the looking-glass self.[2]

Also part of self-concept is the standard or set of expectations that he and others hold. The child compares his concept of self against a standard or set of expectations that he and others hold as to how one should behave and act and what features one should have. Obviously, as a child assesses his self-concept, he is likely to feel proud if he

---

1. See Cole Brembeck, *Social Foundations of Education* (New York: Wiley and Sons, 1971): pp. 62–64; Richard Schmuck et al., "Interpersonal Relations and Mental Health in the Classroom" *Mental Hygiene,* Vol. 2, 1963, p. 290.
2. See the classic sociological study, C.H. Cooley, *Human Nature and the Social Order* (New York: Scribner's, 1902). Also see Carl Backman and Paul Secord, *A Social Psychological View of Education* (New York: Harcourt, Brace and World, 1968): Chapter 2.

exceeds his standard and ashamed if he falls below his standard. The process is largely the same for all persons.

A child that has a backlog of successful encounters will, in all likelihood, believe that he is valuable and worthy. An occasional defeat or failure will merely be interpreted as a belief that "I have failed" rather than the conclusion that "I am a failure." The inner forces of self-concept that guide behavior are different for all youngsters because their experiences vary greatly. A healthy self-concept or a poor self-concept depends upon the quality of the experiences that the youngster undergoes and the influence of other people.[3]

George Herbert Mead (1934),[4] known as the father of social psychology, stated the following about self-concept:

> The self arises in conflict when the individual becomes a social object in experience to himself. This takes place when the individual assumes that attitude or uses that gesture which another individual would use and responds to it himself or tends to so respond. . . . The child gradually becomes a social being in his own experience, and he acts toward himself in a manner analogous to that in which he acts towards others.

Cooley (1902),[5] in developing his looking-glass self, noted:

> As we see our face, figure, and dress in the glass, and are interested in them because they are ours, and pleased or otherwise with them . . . as, in imagination we perceive in another's mind some thought of our appearance, manners, aims, deeds, character, friends, and so on, and are variously affected by it.

Kinch (1963) introduced the symbolic interactionist theory, in which the self is formalized and defined as the "organization of qualities that the

---

3. An excellent treatment of the entire question of self-concept can be found in Wallace LaBenne and Bert Greene, *Educational Implications of Self-Concept Theory* (Pacific Palisades, California: Goodyear, 1969). Also see A.W. Combs, *Perceiving, Behaving, Becoming* (Washington, D.C.: Association for Supervision and Curriculum Development, 1962).

4. George Herbert Mead, *Mind, Self, and Society* (Chicago: University of Chicago Press, 1934).

5. Cooley, *Human Nature*, p. 184.

person attributes to himself." Such a definition, according to theorists,[6] yields the following basic postulates:

1. The individual's self-concept is based on his perception of the way others are responding to him.

2. The individual's self-concept functions to direct his behavior.

3. The individual's perception of the responses of others toward him reflects the actual responses of others toward him.

4. The way the individual perceives the responses of others toward him influences his behavior.

5. The actual responses of others to the individual will determine the way he sees himself.

6. The actual responses of others toward the individual will affect the behavior of the individual.

The implications of such postulates for education are far-reaching, especially as they involve the self-fulfilling prophecy. If a child believes that he cannot comprehend social studies, he will tend to ignore the lessons, the work, and the classroom discussions. As a result, he fails social studies. The failure will reinforce his attitude that he cannot really comprehend this subject. Thus a student's self-attitudes can lead to a self-fulfilling prophecy for himself. The student who thinks he cannot learn or do a particular thing may fulfill his own prophecy. This is also true for groups as well as teachers. Teachers who look at a class as low achievers and then teach in a perfunctory way will be reaffirmed in their belief when, indeed, the class performs poorly. The teacher has structured the lesson so that the performance is self-fulfilling.[7]

The educational implications for minority students in urban schools is even more startling. If the self-fulfilling prophecy is at work in urban

---

6. See J.W. Kinch, "A Formalized Theory of the Self-Concept," *The American Journal of Sociology,* 1963, pp. 481–486. For an excellent treatment of these postulates, see David W. Johnson, *The Social Psychology of Education* (New York: Holt, Rinehart, and Winston, 1970), pp. 82–99. The postulates are taken from Johnson, pp. 84–85.

7. The classic study of the self-fulfilling prophecy is Robert Rosenthal and Lenore Jacobson, *Pygmalion in the Classroom* (New York: Holt, Rinehart, and Winston, 1968).

schools, then minority students who are low achievers are victims of a self-fulfilling prophecy. After repeated failures the child gives up, and so does the school. The level of aspiration may remain high, but the level of expectation is no longer closely correlated, as information on Chart 6-1[8] suggests. It was taken from a study of Detroit youth.

Variables Affecting Self-Image and Acceptance

A school child's concept of himself and his place among his peers and teachers is influenced by many significant variables. Among them are his family's socioeconomic status, the type of family structural organization, the value and norm orientations and behavioral expectations of the subcultural group with which he identifies, the educational background and language skill of his family, his racial and ethnic identification, his sex-role identity, his knowledge of the value orientations and behavioral expectations of his peer group and teachers, his degree of social acceptance and adaptability, and, as mentioned earlier, his own experiences with success or failure socially and academically.[9]

From these variables, one can divide the self-image influences into two basic components: (1) the personal adjustment component and (2) the social adjustment component. The personal adjustment component measures self-image according to one's sense of self-reliance, personal worth, personal freedom, feeling of belonging, withdrawal tendencies, and the reactions of one's body to these variables. The social adjustment component measures self-image according to one's adjustment to social standards, acquiring of social skills, antisocial tendencies, and family, peer, and community relations.[10]

Social scientists have found that the peer group as a socializing agency has an important influence upon the child. Peer groups mold self-images in a number of ways, and consequently, have important functions in

---

8. William Ragan and George Henderson, *Foundations of American Education* (New York: Harper and Row, 1970), p. 206.

9. Sandra Worden, *The Leftouts* (New York: Holt, Rinehart, and Winston, 1968): pp. 121–122.

10. See *The California Test of Personality* (Sacramento, California, Department of Education, 1975).

Chart 6-1. Ideal and Real Levels of Occupational Aspirations of Target Area Youths (in percentages)

| | Aspiration | | | | | |
| Occupational Aspiration | Ideal | | | Real (expected) | | |
	Lower class (N = 150)	Middle class (N = 50)	Total (N = 200)	Lower class (N = 150)	Middle class (N = 50)	Total (N = 200)
I. Professional and managerial	78.0	82.0	79.0	13.3	72.0	28.0
II. Clerical and sales	13.3	16.0	14.0	44.7	20.0	38.5
III. Skilled	1.3	2.0	1.5	3.3	8.0	4.5
IV. Semiskilled	6.6	0.0	5.0	31.3	0.0	23.5
V. Unskilled	0.8	0.0	0.5	7.4	0.0	5.5
Total	100.0	100.0	100.0	100.0	100.0	100.0

Note: N signifies number of respondents.
Source: William Ragan and George Henderson, Foundations of American Education (New York: Harper and Row, 1970), p. 206.

the overall socialization process. Peer groups as subcultures have values of their own, some of which reflect adult society and some of which reflect the organizational structure of the group itself. The child learns from his peer group a set of values and norms relative to competition, cooperation, honesty, responsibility, and achievement. As a child grows older, these values and orientations mature.

In conjunction with the teachings of the family, church, and school, the peer group is a major force in teaching children sex roles. The peer group is also an important source of information in other social areas as well. Since the peer group considers what knowledge is important and what is not, information takes on value only to the extent that a peer group is willing to consider it relevant. Social systems of an ethnic, religious, regional, racial, or socioeconomic nature are transmitted through the peer group. The distinct characteristics of a particular peer group reinforce values and induct the child into his society and into the broader society.

The peer group provides opportunities for new role behavior and for trying out behavior on an experimental basis without fear of failure or rejection. Members learn new roles and the differentiation of roles. The group allows for a wide range of experimentation not often allowed in family, school, or church relations. As such, the child experiments and finds his level of expectation and reality.

Readjustment and reconciliation become necessary when two sets of expectations are in conflict: a set from the world of one's peers and a set from the world of adults. Unfortunately, this conflict can bring added confusion to the child. Adults often expect children to act as adults, yet the very objectives that adults expect of youngsters are denied because adults insist upon treating them as children. Peer groups are often supportive in such an instance because the expectations of peer groups are often more realistic than those of adult groups.

In the peer group, a child is not automatically in a subordinate role as he is with adults. Further, the child is in a less emotionally charged environment with peers than with adults, which aids learning. Teachers and adults lack emotional investment in the outcome of learning, while youngsters in a peer setting can offer each other reinforcement. This reinforcement is important because our schools and adult society tend to prolong adolescence. As the child is continuously excluded from participation in the adult society, he turns more and more to the peer group for recognition. In this sense, the peer group also helps the child in his attempts to achieve independence from adults; it helps the child in dealing with adults by giving him feelings of support with others like himself; and it provides him with new models of behavior with whom he can identify in terms of age and experience. The peer group is basic in the molding of self-identity and can have a positive or negative influence upon the child's learning and self-image.

Successful teachers understand that they must work with and through peer groups to accomplish their goals. Unsuccessful teachers exclude the child's peer group or declare open war on the group in the attempt to make all youngsters conform. Negative and unrealistic self-image and self-esteem occur when a peer group itself has taken on a negative self-fulfilling prophecy that is reinforced by the teacher. For example, if some peer groups believe it is useless to achieve success in the classroom because members of the group are not going anywhere anyway, and the teacher has the same notion, this self-fulfilling prophecy would tend to be confirmed.

This process is presently going on in many ghetto schools today. An attitude of defeatism prevails, with reinforcement offered by peer group, teacher, school, and community.

Self-Expression, Self-Esteem, and Schooling

Self-expression responses related to self-esteem and self-image follow a bipolar response scale. Although this scale has bipolar opposites, most normal behavior falls in the middle of the scale, rather than at the two extremes. A variety of behavior responses on this scale are described in the following paragraphs.[11]

Role Dispositions
Ascendance (social timidity). Defends his rights; does not mind being conspicuous; not self-reticent; self-assured; forcefully puts self forward.

---

11. Taken from David Krech et al., *Individual in Society* (New York: McGraw-Hill Book Company, 1962). Also see David Alloway and Francesco Cordasco, *Minorities and the American City* (New York: David McKay Company, 1970), pp. 60–61.

Dominance (submissiveness). Assertive; self-confident; power-oriented; tough; strong-willed; order-giving or directive leader.

Social initiative (social passivity). Organizes groups; does not stay in background; makes suggestions at meetings; takes over leadership.

Independence (dependence). Prefers to do own planning, to work things out in own way; does not seek support or advice; emotionally self-sufficient.

Sociometric Dispositions

Accepting of others (rejecting of others). Nonjudgmental in attitude toward others; permissive, believing and trustful; overlooks weaknesses and sees best in others.

Sociability (unsociability). Participates in social affairs; likes to be with people; outgoing.

Friendliness (unfriendliness). Genial, warm, open, and approachable; approaches other persons easily; forms many social relationships.

Sympathetic (unsympathetic.) Concerned with the feelings and wants of others; displays kindly, generous behavior and defends underdogs.

Expressive Dispositions

Competitiveness (noncompetitiveness). Sees every relationship as a contest—others are rivals to be defeated; self-aggrandizing; noncooperative.

Aggressiveness (nonaggressiveness). Attacks others directly or indirectly; shows defiant resentment of authority; quarrelsome; negativistic.

Self-consciousness (social poise). Embarrassed when entering a room after others are seated; suffers excessively from stage fright; hesitates to volunteer in group discussions; bothered by people watching him at work; feels uncomfortable if different from others.

Exhibitionistic (self-effacing). Is given to excess and ostentation in behavior and dress; seeks recognition and applause; shows off and behaves outrageously to attract attention.

According to psychologists, what would be the characteristics of self-accepting individuals? The behavioral picture[12] for a self-accepting individual looks something like this:

---

12. David Johnson, *Reaching Out: Interpersonal Effectiveness and Self-Actualization* (Englewood Cliffs, New Jersey: Prentice-Hall, 1972), pp. 144–145. See also D.E. Hamachek, *Encounters With Self* (New York: Holt, Rinehart and Winston, 1971).

- He believes strongly in certain values and norms and is willing to defend them even in the face of strong group disagreement.

- He is capable of acting without feeling guilty or regretting his actions if others disapprove of what he has done.

- He has confidence in his ability to deal with problems, even in the face of failure and setbacks.

- He feels equal to others as a person, not inferior, irrespective of the differences in abilities, family backgrounds, and attitudes of others toward him.

- He is inclined to resist the efforts of others to dominate him.

- He is sensitive to the needs of others and to accepted social customs.

- He is able to accept the idea and admit to others that he is capable of feeling a variety of impulses and desires, ranging from being angry to being loving, from being sad to being happy, from feeling deep resentment to feeling deep acceptance.

In the context of this chapter, one of our main concerns is the effect the school has upon sociopsychological health of the child, namely the building or destroying of self-identity, self-image, and self-esteem. The school's role, the family's role, and peer group's role in viewing education is an essential element of the child's performance in school and an essential element in shaping the child's self-image. Critics such as Jonathon Kozol, Herbert Kohl, Ivan Illich, James Conant, Patricia Sexton, Elizabeth Eddy, and Christopher Jencks have written about the schools and their impact on youth. In doing so, they have led us to believe that the schools are failing miserably in their objectives.

In an interview in Chicago, Kozol remarked that the "school was perhaps the single most destructive agency in a child's life." With condemnations such as these, one wonders what the effects upon minority youth are in schools that are located in slum areas, taught by inadequately prepared teachers, struggling with the problems of financial insecurity, drug traffic and violence, vandalism and gang warfare, and battling the forces of bigotry and prejudice that permeate a society that expounds equal educational opportunity but does not practice it.

There is no question that the school plays a significant role in retarding the lower socioeconomic child's ability to display intelligence and achievement as well as do children from higher socioeconomic levels. This, in turn, retards the self-image and self-concept of these youngsters and contributes to the development of self-destructive and antisocial behavior.

The school must realistically deal with all youngsters, but has failed to come to grips with those youngsters who are socially deprived, disadvantaged, and underprivileged. The attributes of these youngsters are described below.[13] They are direct challenges to our schools as they try to improve the sociopsychological climate.

> 1. *Impaired intellectual functioning.* A large proportion of the lower-status segment of the population is intellectually impaired. Typically, lower-status persons score much lower on intelligence tests than those higher on the socioeconomic ladder. A high proportion of lower-status children perform poorly in school and are educationally retarded. In general, lower-status persons find mind activity arduous and have little energy for, or interest in, new thoughts and ideas.
>
> 2. *Deficient conceptual abilities.* Lower-status persons are dependent on, or prefer, concrete modes of problem solving. Conceptual performance is restricted. They are poor at handling abstractions, relationships, and categories.
>
> 3. *Inadequate verbal skills.* Lower-status persons have various language handicaps. Reading and writing abilities are defective. General linguistic retardation is common. The lack in verbal facility is manifested by problems in ordering and connecting sentences, a restricted vocabulary, and a near-absence of qualifying nuances. These deficiencies restrict verbal expansion of thought.

---

13. Taken from Elizabeth Eddy, *Walk the White Line* (New York: Doubleday, 1967), pp. 52–55 and Orville R. Gursslin and Jack Roach, "Some Issues in Training the Unemployed," *Social Problems* (Summer, 1964), pp. 91–93. See also Christopher Hale, "Educational Deficiencies Upon the Urban Poor of Los Angeles," Master's Project, 1976, Loyola Marymount University.

4. *Cognitive restriction.* The cognitive process of lower-status persons is relatively unstructured. Ideas of what the "outside world" is like are garbled and hazy. There is negligible comprehension of the implications or possible alternatives to critical choices made (e.g., the job) during the life-span.

5. *Defective self-system and low self-esteem.* The self-system of lower-status persons tends to be unintegrated and characterized by poor ego controls. Their self-concepts are only minimally shaped by social structures. They are not inclined toward introspection and appear to have defects in self-conceptualization ability. Lower-status persons commonly suffer from a severe degree of low self-esteem.

6. *Limited role repertory.* The lack of role models in the lower-status world results in a restricted role repertory, impeding articulation with the social system. Further limitations stem from inadequate role behavior skills. Lower-status persons appear restricted in the ability to take the role of the other. Complex role-playing may be beyond the capacities of most lower-status persons in view of their lack of subtleties in role-playing and difficulties in shifting perspectives.

7. *Minimal motivation.* The conditions of life of lower-status persons make planning and concern for the future unrealistic. They are preoccupied with a struggle to obtain the basic necessities of life. In general, aspirations are geared to the exigencies of day-to-day living. The psychological state of the lower-status person—particularly the chronically unemployed—is characterized by hopelessness and apathy.

Teacher's Role in Setting the Sociopsychological Climate

As one reviews the literature about inner-city education, one wonders how experienced, credentialed teachers can so inadequately and negatively influence the personal lives of students, so poorly judge the needs of youth, and so incompetently judge the students' abilities. Corwin and Schmit (1972) in their classic study of teachers in inner-city schools concluded that teachers in the lower socioeconomic schools rate students lower on academic motivation as well as on ability. This sets up a self-perpetuating self-fulfilling prophecy. In support of data originally researched by Kenneth Clark and by Rosenthal and Jacobson, Corwin and Schmit noted that "children tend to achieve at the level expected of them by their teachers. If teachers hold their pupils in low esteem and have little hope for them . . . they will teach in a perfunctory way and convey their attitudes in a variety of ways; the children will sense this and gauge their own expectations and performance accordingly."[14]

Classic studies such as that by Howard Becker (1952), as well as more recent studies, seem to suggest that, within lower socioeconomic schools, there is a "lack of faith and optimism in the motivations and abilities of pupils, and a tendency to disclaim responsibility for the educational problems that exist."[15] This has an immediate and direct effect upon the sociopsychological climate in these schools. Consequently, the role of the classroom teacher is the most significant variable operating for the success or failure of lower socioeconomic class children.

In a recent study by John Branan (1974), an educational psychologist, students were asked to rate the two most negative experiences in their lives, experiences that made their lives worse or hindered their development. Over 300 experiences were listed as nonpersonal or interpersonal. The interpersonal experiences were the most numerous and involved experiences with teachers at all grade levels. These negative experiences far outweighed any interpersonal experiences with significant others such as parents or friends. Branan reports that the students related numerous instances in which teachers had humiliated them in front of the class, evaluated them unfairly, and destroyed their self-confidence or openly embarrassed them. Branan concluded that "those who are concerned as much with the psychological development of students as

14. Ronald G. Corwin and Sister Marilyn Schmit, "Teachers in Inner City Schools," in *Inquiries Into the Social Foundations of Education*, Alfred Lightfoot, ed. (Chicago Rand McNally, 1972), pp. 219–240.

15. Ibid. See also Howard Becker, "Social Class Variations in the Teacher-Pupil Relationship," *Journal of Educational Sociology* (Vol. 52, 1952), pp. 451–65. See also recent studies that discuss this issue, such as Lawrence Hynson, "Teacher Preferences of Children's Qualities," *Urban Education* (April, 1976), pp. 49–58; B.J. Andrews, "Relationships Between Selected Community Variables and School Atmosphere," doctoral dissertation, Rutgers University, 1973; Shirley Hyman, "Measured Self-Esteem of Inner City Secondary Students in Relation to Scholastic Achievement and Occupational Aspiration and Expectation," doctoral dissertation, Fordham University, 1975; Geraldine Johnson, "White Achievement in a Mainly Black School," *Integrated Education* (Sept.–Oct., 1976), pp. 27–29; Herman Witkin and John Berry, "Psychological Differentiation in Cross-Cultural Perspective," *Journal of Cross-Cultural Psychology* (March, 1975), pp. 4–87.

human beings as with their cognitive development are likely to find such findings disquieting."[16]

Smith (1968) has listed the disapproving behaviors that are injurious to the child's self-concept and psychological growth.[17]

1. *Physical disapproval.* Shaking, slapping, ear-pulling, spanking, corporal punishment administered by several teachers.

2. *Physical restraint.* Isolation, exclusion, banishment, sending child to the office, removing the child's desk to the corner of the room, not allowing the child to participate in activities he enjoys.

3. *Negative evaluation.* Direct contradiction of the opinion of the child; qualifying a child's response negatively; assigning a low grade; defining the response of the child in a negative way; belittling a child's culture, background, or friends.

4. *Social shaming.* Belittling, ridiculing, using sarcasm or public castigation, singling out a child in front of his peers and berating him, using racial, ethnic, or cultural slurs.

5. *Academic stereotyping.* Labelling and assigning the child according to a preconceived tracking system; allowing the child to do only rote, simple, and concrete work; demanding complete conformity to structures and standards that thwart the child's curiosity and creativity.

Studies have generally supported the hypothesis that there is a positive correlation between the child's perception of their teacher's feelings towards them and the child's perceptions of themselves. Thus, the more positive the child's perception of his teacher's feelings toward him the more favorable a child's perception of himself. Also correlated would be a relationship between the child's perception of teacher's feelings

---

16. See *Psychology Today,* "A Dillar, A Dollar, A Traumatized Scholar," July, 1974. The Branan Report is also in the *Journal of Counseling Psychology* (Summer, 1974).

17. Modified from the suggestions given in B. Othanel Smith *et al., Teachers for the Real World* (Washington, D.C.: The American Association of Colleges for Teacher Education, 1968), p. 60. .

and his classroom behavior and performance. A study by Davidson and Lang (1960)[18] that is generally sustained by current research yielded several conclusions.

> 1. Children's perception of their teacher's feelings toward them was correlated positively and significantly with their own self-perception. The child with the more favorable self-image was the one who more likely than not perceived his teacher's feelings toward him more favorably.
>
> 2. The more positive the children's perception of their teacher's feelings, the better was their academic achievement and the more desirable their classroom behavior as rated by the teachers.
>
> 3. Children in the upper and middle social class groups perceived their teacher's feelings toward them more favorably than did the children in the lower social class group.
>
> 4. Not surprisingly, social class position was also found to be positively related to achievement in school.

Home Influences on the Child's Psychological Health

The home environment provides many variables that are relevant to educational achievement and sound mental health. Variables in the home, such as child-rearing methods, parent's occupation status, parent's attitude toward education, size of the family (and child's position), absence of a father or mother, racial and cultural background, and the sociopsychological pressures, provide us with clues as to the strengths or weaknesses that a child is going to bring to school. The home provides in a positive or negative sense achievement pressures, language and

---

18. Helen Davidson and Gerhard Lang, "Children's Perceptions of Their Teacher's Feelings Toward Them Related to Self-Perception, School Achievement and Behavior," *Journal of Experimental Education* (December, 1960), pp. 107–118. Summation taken from Harry Miller and Roger Woock, *Social Foundations of Urban Education* (Hinsdale, Illinois: The Dryden Press, 1970), pp. 174–75. See also Shirley Hyman, *Measured Self-Esteem,* 1975; Edgar Epps, "The Impact of School Desegregation on Aspirations, Self-Concepts and Other Aspects of Personality," *Law and Contemporary Problems* (Spring, 1975), pp. 300–313; Barak Rosenshine, "Experimental Classroom Studies of Teacher Training, Teacher Behavior, and Student Achievement," *Review of Educational Research* (Summer, 1974); Thomas Sowell, *Black Education: Myths and Tragedies* (New York: McKay and Co., 1973); Peggy Sanday, "On the Causes of I.Q. Differences Between Groups and Implications For Social Policy," in Ashley Montagu, *Race and I.Q.* (New York: Oxford University Press, 1975), pp. 220–249.

behavior models, academic and social guidance, materials and opportunities to explore various aspects of the total environment, basic value patterns, and the degree of conformity to mores and folkways. The work habits and value patterns emphasized and practiced in the home are brought with the child to the urban classroom. These habits and patterns can be a distinct advantage or disadvantage to the child. They are advantageous when the patterns and values are closely associated with middle-class orientations to which the school is closely attuned; they are disadvantageous when the patterns and values are in conflict with the orientations of the school.

For example, the Puerto Rican youngster is taught by his home and culture that when an adult is speaking or reprimanding him, he should lower his head out of respect. On the other hand, the school, with its middle-class orientation, expects the child to look one in the eye when being reprimanded. Given this conflict, the child cannot easily make the adjustments required in both situations and will, in all likelihood, adopt avoidance tendencies that will eventually endanger the interpersonal communication process.

Because of the limitations of space, it is impossible to go into all of the home environment variables that operate upon a child, but instead, one, the absence of a father figure, has been selected for more detailed analysis.[19]

Adolescent boys who grow up without their fathers are supposed to develop all sorts of problems—poor self-esteem, trouble getting along with others, low aspirations for their lives. Black males, in particular, are supposed to suffer without fathers. According to the Moynihan (1972) report,[20] boys who come from the disorganized, matriarchal families of the ghetto get trapped in a jungle of delinquency and deprivation.

Sociologists Larry and Janet Hunt (1976) of the University of Maryland wanted to see just what happens to boys without fathers and to find

19. The analysis was taken from an editorial, "Effect of Lack of Father In Home on Black Teens and White Teens" that appeared in *Stimulus* (March–April, 1976), pp. 1–3.
20. Daniel P. Moynihan, "Education of the Urban Poor," *Harvard Graduate School of Education Bulletin*, Vol. 12, pp. 3–13; Daniel P. Moynihan and Frederick Mosteller, *On Equality of Educational Opportunity* (New York: Randam House, 1972).

out if the effects of father absence are stronger for blacks or whites, lower-class boys or middle-class boys. They looked at data on 445 junior and senior high school students in Baltimore. As expected, they found more fatherless boys among the blacks (46 percent) than among the whites (24 percent), and the percentage of absent fathers rose as social class declined.[21]

The researchers found that white adolescents without fathers had poorer grades and lower educational aspirations than did white boys who had fathers, and fewer of the fatherless boys expected to marry. They also showed lower self-esteem and greater insecurity about being male. These results held true for white boys of all social classes, though lower-class boys without fathers had the lowest self-esteem.

Black adolescents, however, did not have the same bad effects from living without their fathers. They scored slightly higher on all achievement and self-esteem measures than did black boys who had fathers, again among all social classes.

The Hunts explain this strikingly different set of results in terms of the status that black and white fathers have in our society. The white father is usually the breadwinner, a respected member of the family who serves as a positive model of achievement for his son. Many black fathers, hampered by discrimination and lack of work, serve as models of failure. The Hunts draw the poignant conclusion that black adolescent boys are no worse off, and indeed may be better off, if their fathers are not around to set a discouraging example of what they can look forward to.

But there is another interpretation of these findings. In the black community, say the Hunts, where father absence is more common, boys have a measure of insulation against any negative consequences. They suffer no special stigma or handicap; they do not learn to view the intact family as a route to success; and they learn to identify racism and discrimination, not parental failure, as reasons for their lesser achievement. By contrast, white boys without fathers may feel the lack more acutely, and attribute any personal problems to the lack of a father rather than to poverty or other economic reasons. A boy's reaction to the loss of

---

21. *Stimulus,* pp. 1–3.

a parent, say the Hunts, has as much to do with the social world that directs his perceptions as with any psychological matters of identification with the lost person. And the social realities of blacks and whites are still far apart.

Self-Image and Segregation

The Dimensions of Self-Image
There are two important aspects of self-image. The first is referred to as self-esteem, that is, a person's feeling of individual worth and dignity. It exists when one feels positively about himself and is able to accept himself as no less than any other person in terms of his own humanity.

The second aspect of self-image is that of self-concept of ability, one's perception of his potential to perform, interact, and achieve in a social environment.

It is important, in discussing the development of self-image, to make this distinction, and it is especially important in this section since we will be dealing specifically with the effects of segregated education on the development of self-image.

Carl Rogers (1951) and Abraham Maslow (1954), in their theories of personality, make clear their belief that the maintenance and enhancement of self-esteem is a fundamental motive.[22] The growing infant, for example, is completely dependent for his existence not only on the physical assistance of others, but also on their love and approval. The importance of such acceptance to the development of a healthy personality has been shown in many studies. The Marasmus phenomena is a term originally used to describe the pathology in infants where "for no apparent reason," they become weak and lethargic. It has since been discovered to be a condition that is caused from the lack of physical contact, affection, and other forms of caretaking from a human being.

In intensive studies of 158 children, Langdon and Stout (1951) concluded that the most important single factor in the development of

22. Abraham Maslow, *Motivation and Personality* (New York: Harper and Row, 1954); Carl Rogers, *Client-Centered Therapy* (Boston: Houghton Mifflin Company, 1951).

a healthy personality—in fact, the only factor common to all cases studied—was the satisfying of the child's need for love and acceptance.[23]

This need for recognition and acceptance by others applies not only to infants and children but also to each person throughout his or her life. Rohrer (1961)[24] indicated:

> Eloquent testimony to man's need for social approval, acceptance, and relatedness was provided by the experience of small groups of scientists, officers, and enlisted personnel who voluntarily subjected themselves to isolated antarctic living for the better part of a year. During this period, troublesome individuals were occasionally given the "silent treatment"—the man was completely ignored by the group as if he did not exist. This "isolation" procedure resulted in a syndrome called the "long eye," which was characterized by varying combinations of sleeplessness, spontaneous bursts of crying, hallucinations, a deterioration in habits of personal hygiene, and a tendency for the man to move aimlessly about or lie in his bunk staring into space. These symptoms cleared up when he was again accepted by the group and permitted to interact with others in it.

Acceptance by others seems to be causally related to feelings of positive self-esteem, at least until one's personality is developed and strong enough to provide some self-support. But even self-support will only sustain a person within certain limits. At any rate, it seems that the child is at the mercy of others in his early stages of development, and if he is rejected and isolated in serious ways, he will not develop a sense of self-worth, and this, in turn, will affect his psychological growth in every way.

To speak of the need for self-esteem, however, is only to consider a basic, underlying requirement for sound psychological growth. There is also the area of a properly developed self-concept of ability to be considered if one is to understand a child's growth and achievement. An excellent model for viewing the dynamics of a developing self-concept

---

23. G. Langdon and J. Stout, *These Well Adjusted Children* (New York: John Day, 1951). See also Wallace LaBenne and Bert Greene, *Educational Implications of Self-Concept Theory* (Pacific Palisades, California: Goodyear Publishing Company, 1969).

24. J.H. Rohrer, "Interpersonal Relations in Isolated Small Groups," in B.E. Flaherty, *Psychological Aspects of Space Flight* (New York: Columbia University Press, 1961), p. 263.

is called Johari's Window, the name *Johari* honoring the two originators, Joe Luft and Harry Ingham.[25]

	Known to Self	Not Known to Self
Known to Others	I. Area of Free Activity (Public Self)	II. Blind Area (Bad Breath Area)
Not Known to Others	III. Avoided or Hidden Area (Private Self)	IV. Area of Unknown Activity

Figure 6-1. Johari's Window for Adult Self

Source: Reprinted with permission from J. Luft, *Of Human Interaction* (Palo Alto, California: National Press, 1969).

This model divides the self into four areas. Quadrant I represents the public self, which is known by the individual as well as by others. Quadrant II is the blind area, which is seen by others but not by the individual and is sometimes referred to as the "bad breath area." Quadrant III is the area of self that is known to the individual but which he keeps hidden from others. Finally, Quadrant IV is the area of activity that is unknown to both the individual and others.

The structure of an infant's self might look something like Figure 6–2.

At this point, there is not much self-concept. Although a very young child may experience a satisfying sense of acceptance and approval, his activities are for the most part unconscious or observed consciously only by others. As he begins to grow, he trys out various types of behavior. As others give him feedback about his behavior, his private and public self begins to form and expand, as shown in Figure 6–3.

25. J.W. Pfeiffer and J.E. Jones, *Structured Experiences for Human Relations Training* (Iowa: University Association Press, 1969), p. 66.

Not Known to Self

Known to Others	I.	II. Blind Area
	III.	IV. Area of Unknown Activity

Figure 6-2. Infant's Self

Source: J.W. Pfeiffer and J.E. Jones, Structured Experiences for Human Relations Training (Iowa: University Association Press, 1969): 66.

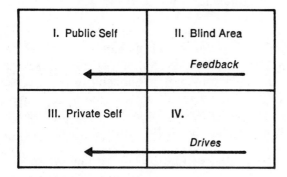

I. Public Self	II. Blind Area
	Feedback
III. Private Self	IV.
	Drives

Figure 6-3. Self of Young Child

Source: Pfeiffer and Jones, Structured Experiences for Human Relations Training, p. 66.

Under conditions of continuous feedback and self-disclosure, the public self expands into a healthy, socially functional and acceptable personality.

In this ideal manner, a person continues to learn about himself and develops an accurate and congruent self-concept. He will learn about his inner drives, instincts, and capabilities; he will experiment with behavior; he will benefit from the objective observations of others. Most important, he will be able to satisfy his needs and develop his potential

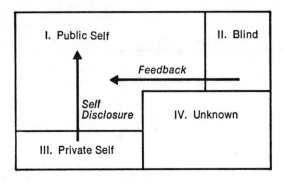

Figure 6-4. Functioning Adult Self

Source: Pfeiffer and Jones, Structured Experiences for Human Relations Training, p. 66.

without any conflict with the "other," who provides him with recognition and acceptance and who attempts to help him develop a concept of himself that is accurate and realistic in terms of his potential.

Unfortunately, this ideal does not always exist, and, in fact, sometimes this relationship between the individual and his significant other can become quite perverted. This writer believes that it is the breakdown and distortion of this vital developmental relationship and feedback process that most seriously and adversely affects the development of self-concept, especially when the breakdown is spawned by a racially segregated environment and the attitudes that exist therein.

The child rapidly learns that, when he behaves in socially approved ways, he is rewarded, whereas socially disapproved behavior brings punishment. His behavior may not be looked upon objectively by family, friends, and society, but it will be seen through the filters of stereotyped attitudes.[26]

Kurt Lewin (1948) was one of the first psychologists to believe in the self-concept as the central construct (drive) of personality. He also pointed out that, in forming self-concept, an individual does not respond

---

26. See the following: Sylvia Scribner and Michael Cole, "Cognitive Consequences of Formal and Informal Education," *Science,* Vol. 182, 1973, pp. 552–559; James S. Coleman et al., *Youth: Transition to Adulthood. Report of the Panel on Youth of the President's Science Advisory Committee* (Chicago: University of Chicago Press, 1974).

to the objective environment but rather, he responds to the environment as he sees it or as it is presented to him, regardless of how distorted this perception may be.[27]

Because of the demand for acceptance, and given the group-oriented society in which we live, we learn to strive for positive regard from esteemed groups of others. If our behavior is not acceptable, we change it to conform to the values and standards of that group. If we can measure up to the standards, whether they be physical appearance, life-style, achievement, or economic status, we can approve of ourselves and feel worthwhile. If we see ourselves as falling short, we tend to feel guilty, inferior, and insecure.

Leon Festinger (1966), in his theory of cognitive dissonance explains this dynamic further by showing that, when an expected behavior (a standard) is at odds with an individual's established attitude, a change is demanded. This change, he points out, usually takes the form of altering the established attitude to conform with the actual behavior. Accordingly, when a person behaves differently, he will also change his attitude about himself, once again, regardless of the distortion or compromise that may be involved in his own thought processes.[28]

Therefore, in the process of growth and development of personality and potential, it is important to understand the crucial nature of the proper feelings of self-esteem, the necessity of arriving at an accurate, reality-based self-concept. To thwart either of these is to thwart personality development.

Schooling, Segregation, and Self-Image
Prior to school, the child grows, experiences, and develops to a great extent, but schooling is often his first significant work experience, and for many, it will be the longest continuous work experience of their lives. It represents the period of life where one develops a set of attitudes about himself that are largely based on the manner in which he is accepted

---

27. Kurt Lewin, *Resolving Social Conflicts* (New York: Harper and Row, 1948); see also Richard Lazarus, *Patterns of Adjustment and Human Effectiveness* (New York: McGraw-Hill, 1961), pp. 104–106.
28. Leon Festinger, "Cognitive Dissonance," in S. Coppersmith, *Frontiers of Psychological Research* (San Francisco: W.H. Freeman, 1966).

and the ability he has to succeed. Conversely, his acceptance and success will be dependent on his individual self-concept.

William Glasser (1969) is correct when he describes the child as coming to school with expectations of being recognized, loved, and respected by his teachers and classmates. He and many others feel that the shattering of this optimistic outlook is the most serious problem of elementary schools.[29]

The school period is also the critical time in one's life when one begins to sort out and select behavioral patterns. In school, the child searches for a unifying concept of self, and in doing so, constantly perceives and is responsive to the behavior of reference groups. These significant others become, through the mechanisms of social imitation and social reinforcement, the models by which one selects, enacts, appraises, and continually adapts one's several life roles.

The effects of segregation and racism on self-concept are readily observable. Segregation and racism create feelings among minority communities that are quickly communicated to their children, even as early as kindergarten and first grade. Early experiences—the value placed on the color of skin, where the lighter-skinned child is favored by the parents—were realities to most blacks living today except perhaps for those born most recently.[30] There are many other realities of life in a segregated community that become a part of the child's perception of the world and engender in him free-floating anxieties and insecurities. The realities of poverty, unstable and impoverished home environments, dysfunctional patterns of child rearing, prenatal malnutrition, retarded reading and language skills, may not all be conscious experiences, but they all are, nonetheless, experiences that become a part of the child's self—unknown by the self, perhaps, but still opera-

29. William Glasser, *Schools Without Failure* (New York: Harper and Row, 1969).

30. See the following: James Banks and Jean Grambs, *Black Self-Concept* (New York: McGraw-Hill, 1972); Martin Deutsch, Irwin Katz, and Arthur Jensen, *Social Class, Race, and Psychological Development* (New York: Holt, Rinehart, and Winston, 1968); Norene Harris, Nathaniel Jackson, and Carl Rydingsword, *The Integration of American Schools* (Boston: Allyn and Bacon, 1975). A classic study is Mary Ellen Goodman, *Race Awareness in Young Children* (Cambridge: Addison-Wesley Press, 1952). See also H.B. Pinkney, "Urban Educational Problems," *Today's Education* (March–April, 1976), p. 71.

tional in the developmental process (see Chart 6–2, Area IV of Johari's Window).[31]

Evidence of the effect of these early experiences was dramatically shown by the classic studies of Clark (1958), which revealed that black children have a harder time than white children have in identifying themselves correctly in terms of race. Also, Moreland (1963) has reported on a series of tests on race awareness and race identification involving nursery school children.[32] A group of whites and a group of blacks were asked, "Are you white or are you colored?" Chart 6–2 shows how the children responded.

Chart 6–2. Race Identification by Nursery School Children

Response	Blacks (%)	Whites (%)
Said they were white	31.4	98.3
Said they were colored	57.1	1.7
Not sure	11.4	0.0

Source: Kenneth Moreland, "Racial Self-Identification: A Study of Nursery School Children," *American Catholic Sociological Review* (Fall, 1963), pp. 231–242.

Moreland's explanation was that the black child's identification with the white race is related to the white's higher status in the community at large. The black child sees the superior position of whites on television, movies, magazines, books, and pictures on the nursery school walls. His limited contact with whites shows him that those of power and wealth are predominantly white. Therefore, it is logical to believe that the black child unconsciously identifies with the more privileged race. Other studies bear this out.

31. Another classic that the reader should be aware of is Urie Bronfenbrenner, "The Psychological Costs of Quality and Equality in Education," *Child Development* (December, 1967): pp. 909–925.

32. Kenneth Clark, "Racial Identification and Performance in Negro Children," in *Readings in Social Psychology,* Eleanor Macoby, ed. (New York: Holt, Rinehart, and Winston, 1958); see also Clark's *Prejudice and Your Child* (Boston: Beacon Press, 1963) and *Dark Ghetto* (New York: Harper and Row, 1965). Kenneth Moreland, "Racial Self-Identification: A Study of Nursery School Children," *American Catholic Sociological Review* (Fall, 1963), pp. 231–242. See more recent studies such as Dorothy Holden, "Academic Achievement of Black Students: A Black Parent's View," *Integrated Education* (July–August, 1976), pp. 39–43; Azinnia Nwafor, "History and the Intelligence of the Disinherited," *Review of Political Economics* (Fall, 1975), pp. 43–54.

It is understandable that, in these early years, the home, if it is strong and positive enough and has resources, can furnish the child with positive reenforcement in what Abraham Citron (1971) calls a subculture of equality, where life-style and values are considered good and are not stacked up against those of the larger society. In this situation, the child's position is more solid and secure, since he can enter into satisfying relationships as a matter of course without facing racist attitudes and the frequently accompanying experiences of self-degradation.[33]

Problems of self-esteem begin to surface when the child becomes more aware of the larger society, which becomes an influence in Area II of Johari's Window (see Chart 6–2). He then learns that his public self (Area I) is no longer adequate or acceptable. He gradually becomes aware of the social significance of racial membership and begins to form a perception of himself as an object of less status than others. This may all suddenly come together as he enters the educational system, particularly one that is segregated.

On the other hand, several studies indicate that integration actually lessens the black child's view of himself. Blacks growing up in segregated communities and attending segregated schools tend to have a higher appraisal of themselves in general. Based on the theory of subcultures of equality this certainly may be true. Certainly the effects of integration on the development of self-image is a major area of additional concern. The existence of segregated communities, however, is an admission to the reality that two societies exist side-by-side and that segregation in education, regardless of how it is brought about, simply isolates children from one another by race and, as such, generates and perpetuates a sense of rejection and inferiority that is bitter enough to kill a child's spirit.[34] The existence of a dual school system reflects the value judgment of the society at large,

---

33. Abraham Citron, *The Rightness of Whiteness* (Detroit: Wayne State University Press, 1971), p. 16.

34. See Joshua Tishman, "Childhood Indoctrination for Minority Group Membership," *Daedalus* (Spring, 1961): pp. 329–349; John Caughey, *To Kill a Child's Spirit* (Chicago: F.E. Peacock and Company, 1973); David Johnson, "Treating Black Students Like White Students," *Urban Education* (April, 1976), pp. 95–114; Eric Winston, "Advising Minority Students," *Integrated Education* (July–August, 1976), pp. 22–24; Witkin and Berry, *op. cit.,* 1975.

and there is really no question as to which system carries the negative stigma.

Escalated Problems of Self-Esteem

The problems of gaining self-esteem, if they are not already serious, become compounded when the child enters the school. From the classroom to the PTA, minority children discover that the school does not understand them, does not respond to them, does not appreciate their culture, and does not think they can learn. A new standard of behavior is being demanded—one that conflicts with attitudes about oneself. The dynamic that Festinger spoke of then becomes functional. Does the attitude remain the same, or does the behavior that has the support of the powerful segment of society prevail? Distorted perceptions of the child are fed to him at a time when his self-concept is extremely malleable and his need for acceptance is greatest.

The inner conflicts that result are intensified due to the fact that the distorted feedback is coming from a very significant other—the teacher. As stated before, studies show that children may be greatly affected by what their teachers believe they can accomplish. Kenneth Clark (1965) summarized it succinctly: "Stimulation and teaching based on positive expectation seems to play an even more important role in a child's performance in school than does the community environment from which he comes." Children desire the positive esteem of their teachers perhaps more than anything else in the world, at that time.[35]

Instead of positive feelings, the child begins to receive information about himself that is confusing, to say the least. The teacher views the minority student as a potential middle-class person. Little consideration is given to his distinct culture and style of life. Some educators even insist that black children be educated out of their blackness.[36] Many are taught that their speech, dress, food, customs, and values are not worthwhile, that they, therefore, are not worthwhile.

---

35. Clark, *Dark Ghetto*, p. 132.
36. See Louis Knowles, *Institutional Racism in America* (Englewood Cliffs, New Jersey: Prentice-Hall, 1969); Paul and Ouida Lindsay, *Breaking the Bonds of Racism* (Homewood, Illinois: ETC Publications, 1974).

The negative feedback about blacks and other minorities comes not only from individual teachers but from all directions in an institution that is shot through with subtle and overt racist attitudes and values—all of which are presented as real and necessary for the welfare of the minority child.

In the minority segregated school, the average curriculum has little relation to the realities of life in a city slum—the reality of poverty, the sharpness of class distinctions, or other facts of life that are daily ignored in the classroom. Too often, slum life is thought of as an unpleasant subject and in our society, unpleasant subjects are not discussed.

Books, films, and other study materials, although far better than they were a few years ago, still perpetrate middle-class values. Several studies of history books and other texts showed that, while race is now covered, the authors rarely take a moral stand on discrimination. Most sections on blacks consisted of selected black heroes to be celebrated.[37]

The general atmosphere and curriculum in the classroom reinforces the sense of superiority of the white middle-class student and the inferiority of the minority and lower-class students. Further, segregation, when viewed as a normal procedure, gives rise to the expectation that the minority child will fill subordinate positions for the rest of his life. The foundation of the self-fulfilling prophecy is firmly laid. The teacher has decided that the student cannot learn and declines, in turn, to even try to educate. Having no compelling reason for not accepting this officially sanctioned, negative evaluation of himself, the student develops ingrained feelings of inferiority and indifference and too frequently joins the growing list of school dropouts at the first opportunity.

Self-confidence and self-esteem can become such negative and threatening factors that an individual can learn to be terrified even of

---

37. See James A. Banks and William Joyce, *Teaching Social Studies to Culturally Different Children* (Addison-Wesley Publishing Company, 1971); Barbara Glancy, "Why Good Interracial Books Are Hard to Find," in Jean Grambs and John Carr's *Black Image: Education Copes with Color* (Dubuque, Iowa: William Brown Company, 1972), pp. 44–57; Juel Janis, "Their Own Thing: A Review of Seven Black History Guides Produced by School Systems," in Grambs and Carr's *Black Image*, pp. 97–115; Rafael Cortada, *Black Studies* (Toronto, Canada: Xerox, 1974).

opportunity itself, which he sees only as another test—and another occasion for failure. To be defeated by daily experiences is to destroy self-worth and positive self-concept and to create a situation where one's worst fears become a confirmed reality.

The view that one can realize his full potential presupposes a view of society in which there are many possibilities. But segregation and segregated education create a view of a society with very limited opportunities and with little or no role flexibility. Self-actualization under these conditions is meaningless. Rather, a sense of determinism prevails, especially when youngsters can see that others, like themselves, have not risen even one or two rungs on the social ladder, that there are few models to emulate that are actually within the realm of possible achievement.

Prevailing over the entire situation of segregation in education is the feeling of powerlessness—the lack of leverage required to bring about any change in the school system or in a life situation. The Coleman Report found that the degree of faith students have in their school's ability to help them shape their futures has a stronger relationship to achievement than do all the other school factors. If school administrators, teachers, parents, and the students themselves regard ghetto schools as inferior, they will be inferior. Reflecting this attitude, students attending such schools lose confidence in their ability to shape their future.[38]

Not only has segregation in education brought about a situation where schools have failed to provide the educational experiences that could help minority children to overcome deprivation, but it has actively fostered and maintained that deprivation by starving such children of their need for self-esteem and by devastating their self-concept of ability. Educational systems have become major pillars of racism.

Segregation and the Self-Image of Whites
The effect of segregation and segregated education on the development of self-image is most malicious in the case of minority group members, but damage is done also to the self-image of whites. The problem is the same, but it moves in a different direction. The white child is

---

38. Coleman, *Report,* p. 23 and p. 427; H.B. Pinkney, "Urban School Problems," *Today's Education* (March–April, 1976), pp. 70–72.

subjected to a similar feedback process involving distorted perceptions of minority group members as well as himself.

The white child grows up in a white environment in which he usually does not experience any break in reinforcement patterns related to his race. Within his personality, he slowly builds a feeling and belief in the rightness of whiteness. He is led to believe that whiteness, the way he is, is natural, standard, and dominant.[39]

At the same time, the feedback process from his significant others (the powerful majority of society) includes the same distorted perceptions about other groups of people who are different in a negative and inferior way. The effectiveness of this feedback process represents no mean feat. Clark (1963)[40] reveals an interesting characteristic of the communication of such stereotypes.

> When white children in urban and rural sections of Georgia and urban areas of Tennessee were compared with children attending all-white schools in New York City, their basic attitudes were found to be the same. Students of the problem now generally accept the view that the children's attitudes toward Negroes are determined chiefly not by contact with Negroes but by contacts with prevailing attitudes toward Negroes. It is not the Negro child, but the idea of the Negro child, that influences children.

This whole process is what Knowles (1969) refers to as the miseducation of white children. He points out that the same dynamics of racist textbooks and teachers and institutional policies and procedures that adversely affect the minority child also adversely affect the white child in terms of his perceptions about himself and others. In addition, he emphasizes that other false attitudes, such as the optimistic view, are fostered in terms of racial segregation and discrimination. The optimistic view is that "things aren't really so bad" and "everything will work out."[41]

Conclusion: An Integration Model
Personal growth comes from one's own activities. Through them, one discovers how to do what previously was outside one's own boundaries.

---

39. Citron, *Rightness of Whiteness*, p. 3.

40. Clark, *Racial Identification*, p. 25; Pinkney, *Today's Education*, pp. 70–72.

41. Knowles, *Institutional Racism*, pp. 46–57. See also James Edler, "White on White: An Anti-Racism Manual for White Educators in the Process of Becoming," doctoral dissertation, University of Massachusetts, 1974; "Success Story of An Inner City School," *Today's Education* (Sept.–Oct., 1976), pp. 43–46.

In the matter of segregation and self-image, this is precisely the core issue. Segregation represents the placing of boundaries around a person —an object that wants and needs to grow and expand. These boundaries are in one sense imposed, monitored, and reinforced by an external force, and yet, on the other hand, they are transformed by the personality into one's own boundaries. It is not that people cannot find the resources to step beyond these boundaries, but rather, that given the nature of people, with their critical and pressing needs for self-esteem and acceptance by others, they simply find it difficult to risk the loss of acceptance by what appears to be society—the main body of others. And so, one's first inclination is to believe and trust in that body and to move toward its demands. The same reasoning is followed in our schools.

As a means of integrating the materials and concepts presented in chapters 4 and 5, what does characterize the ideally integrated school? Mercer (1975) has given us the most comprehensive model to date. She suggests the following design as one that a truly integrated, multicultural school might look like in its attempts at integrated education. Her design identifies six types of educational outcomes which characterize an integrated school. She then suggests measures developed to assess these six outcomes. Although a theoretical model, the Mercer model is sound and comprehensive.[42] It is shown in Figure 6–5.

1. Self-concepts and attitudes: Student's responses to self and school are equally positive for students of all ethnic groups.

2. Academic achievement: The performance of students from all ethnic groups matches or exceeds the national norms for standardized achievement tests.

3. Multiethnic environment: Curriculum materials, teacher attitudes, and teaching procedures provide all students with an opportunity to understand and to develop pride in their own ethnic heritage and to understand and respect the ethnic heritage of other groups.

42. Taken intact from Jane R. Mercer, "The Role of the School Sociologist: System Assessment, Feedback, and Intervention as a Possible Role Model," in *Proceedings of the National Invitational Conference on School Sociologists,* May 1–3, 1975. Printed by the University of Southern California, pp. 115–143.

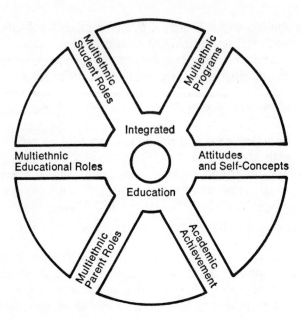

Multiethnic
Student Roles

Multiethnic
Programs

Integrated

Multiethnic
Educational Roles

Attitudes
and Self-Concepts

Education

Multiethnic
Parent Roles

Academic
Achievement

Figure 6-5. The Mercer Model

Source: Jane R. Mercer, "The Role of the School Sociologist: System Assessment, Feedback, and Intervention as a Possible Role Model," from *Proceedings of the National Invitational Conference on School Sociologists,* May 1 – 3, 1975. (Printed by the University of Southern California, Los Angeles, pp. 115 – 143.)

4. Peer relations and roles: Students of all ethnic groups hold comparable statuses and play comparable roles in the school so that the distribution of valued statuses and roles in the school is similar for all groups and children of all ethnic groups perceive each other as friends.

5. Multiethnic educator roles: The opportunity structure is open to educators of all ethnic groups so that educators from all ethnic groups are recruited, hold statuses, and play roles at all levels of the school hierarchy.

6. Multiethnic parent roles: Parents of all ethnic groups are involved in the life of the school community so that they hold comparable statuses and play comparable roles in school related organizations.

The Mercer Model incorporates all the role models needed for the attainment of a workable, plausible, and innovative strategy for desegre-

Table 6–1. Measures Developed to Assess Each of the Six Types of Outcomes Described in the Theoretical Model

Self-Concepts and Attitudes

        Self-esteem

        Reflected self

        Attitude toward school

        School anxiety

        Status anxiety

Academic Achievement

        Reading—Used standardized tests given by the schools themselves

        Word Knowledge—Subtest of Metropolitan Achievement Test

Multiethnic Environment

        Teacher educational expectations for students

        Teacher occupational expectations for students

        Teacher ratings of student sociability

        Teacher ratings of student competence

        Teacher ratings of student emotional stability

        Teacher report of multiethnic programs

Peer Relations and Roles: Student Sociometrics

        Choosing Anglo-American students

        Choosing Mexican-American students

        Choosing black students

        Choosing Asian-American students

Multiethnic Educator Roles

        Staff sociability with black staff

        Staff sociability with Anglo staff

        Staff sociability with Mexican-American staff

        Staff sociability with Asian-American staff

Multiethnic Parent Roles

        Teacher report of parental participation

        Teacher rating parental achievement motivation

        Teacher rating parental power

        Teacher rating parental attitude toward desegregation

        Teacher rating parental support for school program

gated schools. All aspects of educational growth are considered: self-concept, academic achievement, multicultural experiences, peer relations, and parents. If only the reality were such that a school of this nature were pragmatically possible at this time. If it were possible, chapters 4 and 5 would be unnecessary, and we could be talking about the equal educational opportunity that every child would be enjoying.

Education in the Inner City

Chapter 7

When you have finished this chapter, you should be able to perform the following skills.

1. Define some specific characteristics of the ghetto.

2. Describe and state some characteristics of inner-city schools.

3. Identify several pressing school, educational, and sociopsychological problems found in the inner-city school.

4. List several component parts of sound teacher training for inner-city schools and several factors that determine teacher success in the inner city.

5. Explain the correlation between teacher attitude and instructional success in the inner city.

6. Explain the reasons that some teachers fail in the inner-city while others succeed.

7. Analyze your attitudes regarding inner-city children after taking the Inner-City Attitude Questionnaire in this chapter.

The failures of inner-city schools reflect a large and persistent failure of American society to fulfill its promise of equal opportunity for all citizens. Urban miseducation encompasses social and political institutions, economic realities, and psychological devices that define, organize, limit, and cripple the aspirations of minorities in society. Racism, poverty, miseducation, and segregation have taken their toll upon millions of youngsters in the urban ghettos of America. Gentry et al., (1972) have written of this problem.[1]

> The magnitude of inner-city education is startling. Three-quarters of all Americans live in metropolitan areas; one-third live in inner cities. The population of Brooklyn, one of the five boroughs of New York City, is larger than that of any one of the twenty-five smallest states in the United States. The combined population of New York, Chicago, Los Angeles, Philadelphia and Detroit (the nation's five largest cities) is greater than the combined population of the nineteen smallest states of the nation. Further, if all Americans lived as densely as in some blocks of East Harlem, the nation's entire population could live in three boroughs of New York City.

The ghetto as a sociocultural phenomenon has had little importance in the organizational, philosophical, and curricular makeup of public schools. As a singular phenomenon, it must be understood, appreciated, and remediated if urban education is going to have any success or relevancy. Demographers and social scientists have long studied the ghetto, but few of these studies have had any effect or produced any real changes in urban education. Bennett (1971)[2] derived the following facts from his study of the ghetto:

1. The size of ghettos is related to city size, i.e., the large ghettos generally are found in the large cities.

2. The ratio of whites to blacks in a city varies considerably, both regionally and locally.

3. The rate of growth of ghettos is related to city size and ghetto size. Growth is faster in the large cities and where there are existing large ghettos.

In addition to examining a formula for computing an index of segregation that students can apply to their own urban areas, Bennett examines phenomena that are generally associated with the ghetto—and thus

---

1. Atron Gentry, Byrd Jones, Carolyn Peele, Royce Phillips, John Woodbury, Robert Woodbury, *Urban Education: The Hope Factor* (Philadelphia: A.B. Saunders Co., 1972), p. 2.

2. Don C. Bennett, "The American Black Ghetto: A Geographic Appraisal" in *The Social Sciences and Geographic Education: A Reader,* John Ball, John Steinbrunk, and Joseph Stoetman, eds. (New York: Wiley and Sons, 1971), pp. 298–306.

have tremendous importance on the kind of education received by ghetto youngsters. The following demographic characteristics are common to most ghettos.[3]

1. High population densities

2. High birth rates

3. High death rates, especially infant mortality rates

4. Low levels of educational attainment

5. High rates of unemployment

6. Low incomes

7. High incidence of substandard housing

8. High numbers of persons on welfare

9. High crime rates

10. Low availability of social service and institutional services

These phenomena, in turn, provide negative stereotypes for educators. Since a teacher's own background seems to have a great deal to do with his or her attitude toward ghetto youngsters, and since most teachers are products of a middle-class upbringing, it is reasonable to assume that most teachers of inner-city youngsters represent a cultural bias against those youngsters. Numerous studies[4] have pointed up the stereotypes that inner-city teachers use to set up self-fulfilling prophecies. There is a feeling that ghetto youth:

1. Score low on I.Q. and other standardized tests.

2. Read and speak poorly and perform below grade level on other tasks.

---

3. Ibid. See also Anna Ochoa and Rodney Allen, "Creative Teacher-Student Learning Experiences About the City," pp. 103–104, in *Teaching About Life in the City,* Richard Wisniewski, ed. (Washington, D.C.: National Council for the Social Studies, 1972).

4. See David Gottlieb, "Teaching and Students: The Views of Negro and White Teachers," *Sociology of Education,* Summer, 1964, 345–53; Patrick Groff, "Dissatisfactions in Teaching the Culturally Different Child," *Phi Delta Kappan,* November 1963; Research Committee of the Coordinating Council on Human Relations, Detroit, "The Challenge to Education in the Multi-Problem Neighborhoods" (mimeographed report, Detroit, April 20, 1961); David Gottlieb and Charles Ramsey, *Understanding Children of Poverty* (Chicago: SRA, 1967), pp. 54–55.

3. Are not motivated toward the traditional academic goals teachers hold, such as completing high school or going to college.

4. Are not well-disciplined or taught good manners in their homes.

5. Are not clean.

6. Are not interested in school or in the future.

7. Cannot or will not learn.

8. Tend toward toughness, violence, listlessness, dishonesty, a perverted sense of humor, anomie, and sexual license.

It only stands to reason that teachers who hold such stereotypes will tend to be less understanding of the differentness of minority youngsters.

On the other hand, it does not follow that the best teachers for minority youngsters are minority teachers. It is also unwise to assume that only blacks can teach blacks or only Chicanos can teach Chicanos; ethnicity, race, or subcultural affiliation are not primary factors in successful teaching. There is no substitute for competency and professionalism. Joyce and Harootunian (1967) have noted that "a teacher who has known poverty may deliberately seek the education of poor children but may make the mistake of being too hard on them in an effort to drive them into seeking status themselves."[5] Brottman (1965) has also noted: "It may be that when an individual [from the lower class] has become a teacher with its attendant high status, he might not care to be reminded of his class origin. His origin might be denied by insisting on perfection in class or by being more middle class in expectations of students than a teacher from a middle-class environment."[6] Gottlieb (1964) has noted that there are instances when teachers from a middle-class environment try to avoid teaching in inner-city schools because it reminds them too much of the social setting that they entered teaching to escape.[7]

---

5. Bruce R. Joyce and Berj Harootunian, *The Structure of Teaching* (Chicago: Science Research Associates, 1967), p. 215.

6. Marvin Brottman, "Dimensions of the Problem of the Disadvantaged Pupil," in John Beck and Richard Saxes' *Teaching the Culturally Disadvantaged Pupil* (Springfield, Illinois: Charles C. Thomas, 1965), p. 23.

7. Gottlieb, "Teaching and Students: The Views of Negro and White Teachers," p. 350.

Characteristics of Inner-City Schools

What, then, can we piece together from the volumes of research done by social scientists about the characteristics of inner-city schools? Since many inner-city youngsters suffer from a poverty syndrome unknown to middle-class children, the inner-city child has been given many labels, such as ghetto child, culturally disadvantaged, culturally different, slum child, underprivileged, educationally handicapped, and socially deprived. Despite the numerous titles, some constant characteristics tend to emerge. Social scientists have assigned identities to the inner-city school by grouping common characteristics of students into five principle areas.

1. Who attends these schools?

2. What kind of socioeconomic background do the students have?

3. What are school facilities like?

4. What are the most pressing school and educational problems?

5. What are some sociopsychological problems?

Who Attends These Schools?

Inner-city schools are largely attended by minority populations. Demographically, the middle class has been fleeing the city in increasing numbers since the 1960s. In the 1960 Census, twelve of the largest cities in the United States showed a decrease in population from 1950 to 1960, and the decline is continuing into the 1970s. Metropolitan areas, which include a central city and the surrounding areas, did not decrease in population but actually gained. Minority populations continued to increase in all major urban centers.[8] The National Advisory Commission's Report of 1968 summarized the following:

> Almost all Negro population growth is occurring within metropolitan areas, primarily within central cities. From 1950 to 1966, the U.S. Negro population rose 6.5 million. Over 98% of that increase took place in metropolitan areas—86% within central cities, 12% in the urban fringe.

---

8. Philip Vairo and William Perel, *Urban Education: Problems and Prospects* (New York: McKay Company, 1969), pp. 8–25.

The vast majority of white population growth is occurring in suburban portions of metropolitan areas. From 1950 to 1966, 77.8% of the white population increase of 35.6 million took place in the suburbs. Central cities received only 2.5% of this total white increase. Since 1960, white central-city population has actually declined by 1.3 million.

As a result, central cities are steadily becoming more heavily Negro, while the urban fringes around them remain almost entirely white. The proportion of Negroes in all central cities rose steadily from 12 percent in 1950, to 17 percent in 1960, to 20 percent in 1966. Meanwhile, metropolitan areas outside of central cities remained 95 percent white from 1950 to 1960, and became 96 percent white by 1966.

The Negro population is growing faster, both absolutely and relatively, in the larger metropolitan areas than in the smaller ones. From 1950 to 1966, the proportion of nonwhites in the central cities of metropolitan areas with one million or more persons doubled, reaching 26 percent, as compared with 20 percent in the central cities of metropolitan areas containing from 250,000 to one million persons, and 12 percent in the central cities of metropolitan areas containing under 250,000 persons.

The 12 largest central cities (New York, Chicago, Los Angeles, Philadelphia, Detroit, Baltimore, Houston, Cleveland, Washington, D.C., St. Louis, Milwaukee, and San Francisco) now contain over two-thirds of the Negro population outside the South, and one-third of the Negro total in the United States. All these cities have experienced rapid increases in Negro population since 1950. In six (Chicago, Detroit, Cleveland, St. Louis, Milwaukee, and San Francisco), the proportion of Negroes at least doubled. In two others (New York and Los Angeles), it probably doubled. In 1968, seven of these cities are over 30 percent Negro, and one (Washington, D.C.) is two-thirds Negro.[9]

Currently more than 50 percent of enrollments are minority in major urban school systems such as Chicago, Detroit, Atlanta, New York, Los Angeles, Newark, and Washington, D.C. The largest percentage of minority enrollment, 75 percent, occurs in the inner-city schools. Estimates run as high as 99 percent for Washington, D.C., 65 percent for Detroit, 60 percent for Chicago, and 64 percent for Los Angeles. One out of every ten students in public schools come from homes where English is not the primary language.

Although minority enrollments are high in most large urban school systems, percentages vary by their level of isolation in these urban schools. The following chart gives some idea of the minority isolation scale in different geographic regions of the country.

9. Report of the National Advisory Commission on Civil Disorders (New York: Bantam Books, Inc. 1968); Harry Miller and Roger Woock, Social Foundations of Urban Education (Hinsdale, Illinois: Dryden Press, 1973): pp. 106–107.

Chart 7–1. Number and Percent of Minority Students Attending Public Schools with Different Racial Composition, by Geographic Area: Fall 1968, Fall 1970, and Fall 1972

	Continental United States[1]			32 northern and western states[2]			6 border states and D.C.[3]			11 southern states[4]		
	1968	1970	1972	1968	1970	1972	1968	1970	1972	1968	1970	1972
Total enrollment	43,353,568	44,910,403	44,646,625	28,579,766	30,131,132	29,916,241	3,730,317	3,724,867	3,742,703	11,043,485	11,054,403	10,987,680
Minority enrollment:												
Number	8,656,434	9,394,184	9,676,373	4,441,516	5,143,639	5,350,300	674,289	690,553	710,818	3,540,629	3,559,992	3,615,255
Percent of total	20.0	20.9	21.7	15.5	17.1	17.9	18.1	18.5	19.0	32.1	32.2	32.9
Minorities, by level of isolation:												
Attending 0–49.9% minority schools:												
Number	2,623,820	3,510,200	3,833,062	1,675,779	1,906,966	2,001,674	217,166	230,621	262,348	730,874	1,372,612	1,569,040
Percent	30.3	37.4	39.6	37.7	37.1	37.4	32.2	33.4	36.9	20.6	38.6	43.4
Attending 50–100% minority schools:												
Number	6,032,615	5,883,983	5,843,309	2,765,737	3,236,670	3,348,625	457,123	459,932	448,471	2,809,755	2,187,377	2,046,213
Percent	69.7	62.6	60.4	62.3	62.9	62.6	67.8	66.6	63.1	79.4	61.4	56.6
Attending 80–100% minority schools:												
Number	4,987,778	4,137,476	3,948,269	2,002,321	2,324,858	2,374,971	406,894	396,939	390,013	2,578,563	1,415,679	1,183,286
Percent	57.6	44.0	40.8	45.1	45.2	44.4	60.3	57.5	54.9	72.8	39.8	32.7
Attending 90–100% minority schools:												
Number	4,561,768	3,475,215	3,282,961	1,686,488	1,930,722	1,985,659	383,693	375,011	364,648	2,491,587	1,169,482	932,654
Percent	52.7	37.0	33.9	38.0	37.5	37.1	56.9	54.3	51.3	70.4	32.9	25.8
Attending 95–100% minority schools:												
Number	4,202,903	2,959,569	2,781,893	1,410,141	1,611,069	1,669,409	368,671	350,967	345,211	2,424,090	997,533	767,273
Percent	48.6	31.5	28.7	31.7	31.3	31.2	54.7	50.8	48.6	68.5	28.0	21.2
Attending 99–100% minority schools:												
Number	3,472,072	2,015,414	1,835,957	907,426	1,018,398	1,057,764	294,963	293,191	278,380	2,269,683	703,825	499,813
Percent	40.1	21.5	19.0	20.4	19.8	19.8	43.7	42.5	39.2	64.1	19.8	13.8
Attending 100% minority schools:												
Number	2,542,805	986,532	787,791	348,320	398,625	369,139	160,552	154,657	153,768	2,033,933	433,250	264,884
Percent	29.4	10.5	8.1	7.8	7.7	6.9	23.8	22.4	21.6	57.4	12.2	7.3

1. 49 states and the District of Columbia. Excludes Hawaii.
2. Alaska, Arizona, California, Colorado, Connecticut, Idaho, Illinois, Indiana, Iowa, Kansas, Maine, Massachusetts, Michigan, Minnesota, Montana, Nebraska, Nevada, New Hampshire, New Jersey, New Mexico, New York, North Dakota, Ohio, Oregon, Pennsylvania, Rhode Island, South Dakota, Utah, Vermont, Washington, Wisconsin, and Wyoming.
3. Delaware, District of Columbia, Kentucky, Maryland, Missouri, Oklahoma, and West Virginia.
4. Alabama, Arkansas, Florida, Georgia, Louisiana, Mississippi, North Carolina, South Carolina, Tennessee, Texas, and Virginia.
Notes: Chart includes American Indians, Orientals, and students with Spanish surnames. Data are based on surveys of all school districts enrolling 3,000 or more students and a sample of smaller districts enrolling 300 or more students. Because of computer rounding, detail may not add to totals.
Source: U.S. Department of Health, Education, and Welfare, National Center for Education Statistics, *Digest of Educational Statistics,* 1974 edition.

Socioeconomic Background of Students

Children attending inner-city schools tend to come from lower-class families. Since public education is largely based upon a neighborhood school pattern, the neighborhoods feeding inner-city schools are made up mainly of lower-socioeconomic groups of people. Neighborhoods with a lower socioeconomic population tend to be characterized by high unemployment, a large number of families on welfare, dense population, and numerous communication problems with agencies such as the police, school, social welfare, health, and family services. Crime is always a problem. In many cities, a vast amount of police manpower and services are used in central sections of the community. It is only natural to assume that, in large congested ghetto or barrio areas where unemployment is high, discrimination widespread, and human beings more vitally concerned about survival on a day-to-day basis, there will be more alienation and frustration with the system than there is in rich communities. There is also a higher dropout rate among minority youngsters in inner-city schools than in other public schools, which adds to the intensity of the community situation, a situation that Conant (1964) once termed "social dynamite."[10] He stated: "In a heavily urbanized and industrialized free society, the educational experiences of youth should fit their subsequent employment."[11] Unfortunately, this is not the case. Others, more recently, might disagree with the direct role the school plays in occupational success. Jencks (1972), for example, concludes in his massive study, *Inequality: An Assessment of the Effect of Family and Schooling in America:* "Anyone who thinks that a man's family background, test scores, and educational credentials are the only things that determine the kind of work he can do in America is fooling himself. At most, these characteristics explain about half the variation in men's occupational statuses. This leaves at least half the variation in men's occupational statuses to be explained by factors that have nothing to do with family background, test scores, or educational attainment."[12]

Nonetheless, statistics tend to substantiate the fact that unemployment is greater among the minorities, the unskilled, and the school dropout than

---

10. James B. Conant, *Slums and Suburbs* (New York: McGraw-Hill, 1964).

11. Conant, *Slums and Suburbs,* p. 38.

12. Christopher Jencks, *Inequality: An Assessment of the Effect of Family and Schooling in America* (New York: Basic Books, 1972), p. 192.

among other groups. That is not to say that high unemployment does not exist among those with college degrees and high academic qualifications, witness the teacher surplus, but there is no question that the forces of social and economic discrimination still strike the minority man and woman first.

What Are Facilities Like?

Numerous studies have been conducted about the differences in school facilities and programs offered to minority youngsters in inner-city schools versus those of public schools. Unquestionably, the educational enterprise for minority youngsters is over-taxed, unequal, and basically nonproductive when compared to the inner-city schools' counterparts. Also, the inner-city schools have the greatest needs since they have the greatest problems. The following compilation merely scratches the surface, but inner-city schools are characterized by these realities.

Inner-city schools have the highest teacher turnover rates, although the teacher surplus has changed this somewhat. In some inner-city schools, the turnover rate by the end of the first semester may be as high as 40 percent. In some cases, at the opening of the new school year, a principal might save time if he or she introduced the old faculty members to the new faculty members.

Inner-city schools have the highest administrative turnovers. Many larger urban systems reward principals after two years in an inner-city school with a transfer to a higher status school. In particular, the greatest toll seems to be with the position of vice-principal, especially if he or she is exclusively in charge of discipline for the school.

Inner-city schools have the most segregated teaching and administrative staffs. Until the courts stepped in, many urban school systems, as a matter of routine, simply put black teachers and administrators in black schools. In some cases, they were yielding to community pressures, but in other cases, they were misguided in the belief that only black teachers could teach black youngsters, or that only Chicano teachers teach Chicano youngsters. Competency, not race, was the issue.

Inner-city schools have the highest number of substitute teachers working in them. Placement offices confirm the fact that the largest requests and use of short-term and long-term substitute teachers come from inner-city schools. As Jonathon Kozol pointed out in *Death At An Early Age,* his fourth grade students had not had a permanent teacher since kindergarten.

Inner-city schools tend to have the youngest, least experienced, non-tenured teachers, and in some cases, even with the teacher surplus, they have semi- or noncertified personnel. Since there is less teacher mobility, and since teachers are staying put in high-status schools, most newly opened or available teaching positions tend to be in inner-city schools. In addition, transfer requests are greater in inner-city schools than in others, thus creating a highly mobile situation with few built-in opportunities for school stability. The younger and mostly inexperienced teachers have the most difficulty adjusting to the realities of teaching in these schools, and a critical and valuable amount of time is lost educationally to children as their teachers seek to adjust.

Inner-city schools tend to have the poorest facilities and equipment. In some communities, this is because the central city schools are older, more dilapidated, and in need of maintenance and repair. Many are overcrowded and do not have proper medical, social, or remedial facilities. Vandalism is also high in inner-city schools.

Inner-city schools tend to make the greatest demands upon teaching staff in terms of time, commitment, responsibilities, and accountability. Teachers in inner-city schools tend to have large classes, great problems with discipline, less released planning time, and great demands on them to spend time in supervision, patrol, or the simple takeover of another's class.

What Are the Most Pressing Problems?

The problems and complexities of inner-city teaching are numerous. It is estimated that an inner-city teacher, during an average school day, spends 80 percent of the time in supervision and disciplinary functions and only 20 percent of the time on instructional functions. The percentages are reversed in other schools, especially the high-status schools. Inner-city schools have by far the most pressing academic problems.

Reading and achievement scores are usually lower than in other schools in the system. They tend to show inner-city youngsters reading on the average of three to four years behind the other schools. The Los Angeles city schools are a case in point, as Figure 7–1 shows.[13] Generally, schools in which 90 percent or more of the students are Anglo scored near the seventieth percentile, while the minority schools had percentile scores below the fortieth percentile. At one senior high school in a black ghetto, twelfth graders scored in the ninth percentile.

Inner-city schools have the highest dropout rates and statistics. Educators estimate that, in some school districts, dropout statistics are as high as 50 percent for certain minority groups. Without question, transient rates are highest among inner-city schools, where students are especially mobile.

Inner-city schools have greater attendance and truancy problems. Absenteeism is such that it seriously interferes with teaching. As a case in point, on a particular rainy day in the Los Angeles public school system, an inner-city school might have a 40 percent absentee rate for that day. Absenteeism is attributed to peer pressure and family obligations or problems.

Discipline problems are more frequent, more intense, and more typified by extension into the community in inner-city schools. Gangs and gang warfare is more prevalent. Some experts say this is because peer group pressures are greater. There are more teacher assaults and confrontations in inner-city schools because, in many circumstances, teachers are unskilled in cross-cultural education. Greater security measures must be adopted in inner-city schools than are used in others, and many schools have resorted to electronic devices, police patrols, guard dogs, and parental involvement to help maintain order.

Curriculum offerings seem more limited in inner-city schools. Many of these schools offer few electives beyond the required courses for graduation. Few schools offer the full range of foreign languages, math, or social sciences, and some schools are bound to a policy of required minimum enrollment before a class is offered, which often lowers the

---

13. Adapted from the *Los Angeles Times*, July 24, 1975.

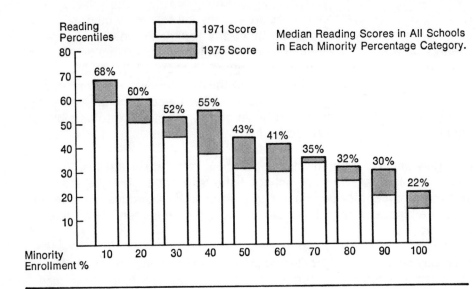

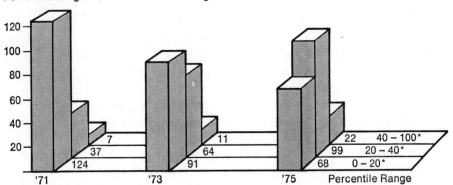

Figure 7-1. A Comparison of 1971 and 1975 Sixth Grade Reading Achievement in Los Angeles City Schools

Note: The higher the percentile score, the better the school's reading achievement. A score of 50 is considered the national average. Schools with 70% or more minority enrollment are classified as "Minority Schools" for this study. Minority scores are better in integrated schools.

Source: Adapted from the Los Angeles Times, July 24, 1975.

chances of offering interesting electives. Remedial classes such as reading are overcrowded and understaffed.

Bilingual/bicultural programs are either weak, nonexistent, or too slow in getting started. Many districts still maintain that they are operating bilingual/bicultural programs, but in practice, few are doing so with any measurable degree of effectiveness. Any bilingual/bicultural program requires sophisticated teacher inservice work, which few districts are providing.

Teaching is still largely unimaginative, uncreative, nondirected, and based on trial and error. The rigors of teaching in an inner-city school are such that they provide little opportunity for a teacher to be creative and imaginative. Teachers largely, albeit unconsciously, contribute to the self-fulfilling prophecy and are ill-prepared for the cultural differentness of the students. Class sizes are still much larger in inner-city schools than in others, and a large class size only magnifies a teacher's problems. Few teacher training institutions offer any training specifically related to the realities of the inner-city classroom. Loyola Marymount University in California is at this writing the only school that offers a program leading to a master's degree in inner-city education.

What Are Some Sociophysiological Problems?

Most minority youth bring problems to school, and many may act out their problems in the classroom. These problems may take one of several forms.

> 1. Lack of support or reinforcement from the home that serves to mitigate the efforts of the teachers. This frequently leads to lack of initiative and curiosity necessary for serious learning to occur.
>
> 2. Feelings of antagonism and rebellion that result from family environment in which there is tension, fighting and a feeling of hopelessness.
>
> 3. Crime caused by youthful loyalty to gangs that meet young peoples' needs for peer-group identification.

4. A social and emotional outlet from unbearable home or life situations that occurs in several forms in school: (a) noisy exuberance, (b) comic role playing as a way of compensating for feelings of discouragement from experiences of low achievement, (c) defiance of authority and the satisfaction it brings.

5. A lower level of aspiration in regard to current school expectations and future occupational plans.

6. An unrealistic self-image and view of the outside world as a result of the forces of segregation in housing, schooling, and employment.

Generally, lower-class youth suffer from the absence of positive external group controls that could help implement successful adjustment. Lower-class people tend simply to withdraw from middle-class competition because they feel that they cannot compete. By withdrawing, they set up correlative norms that tend to reinforce lower-class or peer-group conformity; this, in turn, creates a high degree of social disorganization within the school that is trying to assimilate youngsters culturally. Inner-city youngsters become disconnected from the school and eventually are dysfunctional in broader society.

Several important sociopsychological principles should be remembered when talking about the sociopsychological facets of inner-city youth:

1. Individuals who try to function only as members of their own cultural group are less likely to experience adjustment problems when interacting within their group. However, an identity and adjustment problem arises when the individual has to function outside of his own culture or peer group.

2. The lack of role models may impede individuals from interacting beyond their own cultural group. This frequently hinders the student's ability to communicate with others and weakens his reality base.

3. The more numerous the social interactions of a person, the greater will be the learning, the more realistic will be the interaction, and the more positive the self-image. In reverse, the

more restricted the social interactions of a person, the less will be the learning, the more unrealistic will be the interaction in the outside world, and the more limited will be the self-image. This hypothesis alone is a strong argument for desegregation of the schools.

Teacher Training

The only certain, nonvariable in education is the classroom teacher and his or her effectiveness in communicating. Effectiveness is critical for inner-city teachers, for without it, they are little more than babysitters. If this is the case, educational critics such as Jencks, Kozol, Holt, and others are indeed correct in their basic assumptions that the school can be a destructive force in the lives of students. It would even seem to be true that the longer a child remains in school, the farther behind he or she falls. Certainly, the reading scores of minority youngsters in inner-city schools bear this out; their scores are lower than the national average. Minority students showed an average percentile of 30 in the sixth grade; when they were tested in the twelfth grade, the percentile average had sunk to 9—a glaring and startling deterioration in six years, particularly when one considers that the impact of the teacher is the single most important factor in learning or lack of learning among youngsters, regardless of their background.

Today's teacher training institutions are largely outdated and unrealistic, immersed in a middle-class philosophy of education, and populated by professors of education who are far removed from the actual battlefield by virtue of their ivory tower existence in academia. There are three areas of concern that should be recognized in the training of inner-city teachers.[14] First, a new teacher must be competent in the subject matter. Since the inner-city teacher has so many responsibilities in a given day, it can be assumed that the job is easier if the teacher does not have to spend too much valuable time learning one's subject. In addition, familiarity with one's subject matter allows the teacher more room to create new, innovative methods and ways of motivating youngsters and

---

14. See Miriam Goldberg, "Adapting Teacher Style to Pupil Differences: Teachers for Disadvantaged Children," in *The Culturally Disadvantaged: Perspectives in Urban Education,* Alfred Lightfoot, ed. (New York: Simon & Schuster, SAR, 1970).

presenting material. Schools of education must insist upon competency in one's subject matter as a minimum requirement.

Second, the new teacher must acquire an understanding of the major concepts, and theories, of the social and behavioral sciences that have special relevance to the culturally different child. With this understanding should come a repertoire of teaching strategies that are especially geared to students from backgrounds different from those of the teacher. A grounding in the language and culture of the child you will be teaching is essential. It is not enough to know the languages, but one must also have an appreciation of the culture. The two are coterminous if success with the child is to be achieved.

In addition to learning a language other than English, the language of the peer group should be penetrated, understood, and used. Black English is certainly relevant as is standard English or Spanish.

It is essential that new teachers be exposed to courses in sociology, psychology, history, black studies, Chicano studies, and languages. These courses will, in the long run, prove far more useful than the general, theory-based courses such as foundations of education or school and society. Teacher training is a cooperative enterprise that ideally must be shared with all the departments of colleges and universities. Its current exclusive control by schools of education, which are out of touch with other academic disciplines, must be changed.

Third, the new teacher must have maximum exposure to the realities of the classroom, to children, and to the actual community that the teacher will be teaching in. It is not enough to require only one student teaching assignment which may or may not occur in a cross-cultural setting. It is essential that systematic exposure be given to potential candidates for inner-city teaching assignments. From these exposures comes an openness to and acceptance of differentness, a warmth and respect for cultural differentness, a keener awareness of one's own ethnocentricity, and above all, a flexibility and the willingness to adapt and to become an agent of change. In a recent study done at Indiana University by Mahan and Chickedantz (1975), 54 student teachers went into an observation-participation preservice experience in inner-city schools. The students were tested before and after their experiences to determine the validity and relevancy of some of the stereotypes that they held regarding minority youngsters. The findings, which follow, are just one of numerous replicating studies done on the exposure factor.[15]

1. Teachers increased their positive response-attitude towards inner-city youngsters from 54 percent to 61 percent and reduced their negative response attitude from 27 percent to 7 percent.

2. Positive descriptive adjectives describing inner-city youngsters were changed from a low of 12 percent to 65 percent; negative adjectives were reduced from a high of 64 percent to a low of 12 percent.

3. When asked to indicate their interest in teaching inner-city youngsters, the responses changed from 39 percent in the pre-experience phase to 53 percent in the post-experience phase.

Mahan and Chickedantz drew several conclusions:

The most notable overall change was in the feelings of the pre-service teachers toward the students in the inner-city schools. The percentage of positive descriptors of students increased over 300 percent from July to December.

The social and educational interchange promoted by the field experience sensitized 54 pre-service teachers to inner-city teaching and may be the impetus for getting eager, enthusiastic first-year teachers into the inner city —where they are sorely needed.

This author's study[16] at Loyola Marymount University in Los Angeles with 50 graduates exposed to inner-city teaching brought forth several conclusions:

1. Student awareness of the necessity for different approaches and methods for inner-city youngsters, especially in the area of discipline, increased by 90 percent.

---

15. James Mahan and Penny Chickedantz, "The Impact of Inner-City Field Experiences on Preservice Teachers," *Phi Delta Kappan* (October 1975): p. 127.

16. Alfred Lightfoot, "An Area Report: The Impact and Potency of the First Year's Operation of the Master of Education Degree in Inner City Education" (Los Angeles: Loyola Marymount University, 1975).

2. Student sensitivities to the experiences and needs of the community surrounding the school increased by 85 percent.

3. Student commitment to quality education in the inner-city and the on-site learning approach to teacher training was increased by 90 percent.

4. Student acknowledgment of the necessity to attain more knowledge and expertise in language, culture, and historical background of minorities increased by 95 percent.

5. Student approaches to teaching inner-city youngsters showed greater flexibility, creativity, and innovation with a greater emphasis on individualized instruction.

Success in the inner-city school is basically dependent upon the recognition (1) that inner-city youngsters need specially prepared teachers, (2) that systematic study must be done regarding the personal qualities, the competency knowledge and skills, and the cultural experiences of minority students, (3) that the development of reconstructed, innovative teacher preparation programs both on campus and in inner-city schools are necessary functions of teacher training, (4) that the careful screening and eliminating of candidates not suited for the inner city must begin early as a means of preventing the large teacher dropout rates in inner-city schools, and (5) that colleges and universities must engage in inservice, extension programs to raise the morale and effectiveness of those teachers already in the field.

Point five is particularly important, because there are thousands of teachers in the inner city right now. What is being done for them? Sewell (1972) did a study using 748 certified and tenured teachers in three southern California districts. He asked what incentives would attract a balance of experienced teachers to inner-city schools and keep them there.[17] He concluded that the following incentives would induce teachers to remain in inner-city schools:

1. have a lower class size than that of suburban schools

2. have specialists available in such areas as reading, health, educationally handicapped, etc.

---

17. Orville Sewell, "Incentives for Inner City Teachers," *Phi Delta Kappan* (October 1972): p. 129.

3. be staffed with paraprofessional aides

4. be staffed with teachers who have selected the grade level and the subject they will teach, and,

5. allow teachers to depart, as necessary, from prescribed courses of study to meet the needs of poverty area youngsters, utilizing new programs, materials, or approaches such as greater use of community resources.

The Screening Process

Obviously, the most difficult task of education schools is the screening of potential teachers for inner-city schools. The screening process, of necessity, must take into account that the market has gone from one of need to one of surplus and from one of quantity to one of quality. There are now appropriate numbers to teach, but many educators are not certain that the quality exists, a problem that is increasingly acute for administrators in inner-city schools. Administrators should take the following criteria into account when hiring inner-city teachers, and would-be teachers would do well to ask themselves how well they meet these criteria.

1. What is their academic background and training?

2. Do they meet your staff needs academically?

3. Have they had experiences with culturally different youngsters or have they had specific training in this area? If not, what promise do they show for future training and progress?

4. What is your assessment of personality, values, beliefs, and sense of reality regarding inner-city youngsters?

5. Are there personality factors that would inhibit good teaching?

6. Are there any beliefs or prejudices that would contribute toward a negative self-fulfilling prophecy or inhibiting learning?

7. What are assets of your school that can be used in order to attract and retain those that you want to teach at your school? Specifically, what facilities and materials are available? What degree of flexibility does the teacher have? What accessibility does the teacher have to help and inservice?

Remember that, even with the teacher surplus, it is difficult to recruit and keep teachers in inner-city schools, and care must be taken in their selection.

Attitudes of Teachers

Recent studies have shown that one of the most potent factors in the education of minority youngsters is instructor behavior or teacher attitude. A few years ago, people believed that if a child did not learn, it was his fault. The child was disadvantaged, lacked motivation, or came from a limited background. Many educators are coming to see that perhaps a child's failure is due largely to the disadvantaged teacher.

Studies from the Hispanic Urban Center in Los Angeles have shown that it is the teacher's behavior that acts as the barrier to a child's development.[18] Such studies show that the teacher prevents the minority youngster from succeeding in school because of his or her attitudes toward minority children, a failure to understand their cultural background, the favoring of children that reflect his or her own image and social class—all of which lead to a negative, self-fulfilling prophecy with regard to expectations for minority youngsters. This is especially true if a teacher is from an ethnic group other than the one he or she is teaching, but it is also common when the teacher and child are from the same ethnic group and different social classes. The Laosa study even went further and stated: "Recent empirical evidence suggests that mere membership in a particular cultural-linguistic group does not insure superior teaching ability and success with pupils from the same cultural linguistic group."[19]

Laosa (1974) stated that, although the 1973 U.S. Commission on Civil Rights revealed that teachers in southwestern schools were failing to interact effectively verbally with Chicano pupils to the same extent as with Anglo pupils, "a closer scrutiny of the findings further revealed that Mexican-American teachers praised and encouraged Anglo pupils to a strikingly greater degree than their Anglo colleagues did, and conversely,

---

18. *Los Angeles Times,* October 25, 1971.

19. Luis Laosa, "Toward a Research Model of Multicultural Competency Based Teacher Education," in *Multi-Cultural Education Through Competency-Based Teacher Education,* William Hunter, ed. (Washington, D.C.: American Association of Colleges for Teacher Education, 1974), pp. 138–139.

these same Mexican-American teachers praised and encouraged Mexican-American pupils less than the Anglo teachers did. . . . It seems clear that similar teacher-pupil ethnic group membership is no assurance of multicultural teaching competency."

Indeed, if teacher attitude is a prime factor in assessing pupil growth, then we must use teacher's attitudes as a prime factor in assessing teacher competency. The questionnaire that follows is one of the instruments used in assessing teacher attitudes before going into an inner-city program. Take fifteen minutes and write your responses to the questionnaire. Do not go back and reanalyze your responses and do not change any of your original responses.[20]

Inner-City Questionnaire

Following are several statements about inner-city education, inner-city schools, inner-city youngsters, and inner-city teachers. In light of your own viewpoint and perspective, how do you feel about them? Answer each in response by using *one* of five possible responses:

1=Strong agreement
2=Mild agreement
3=Not certain; don't know
4=Mild disagreement
5=Strong disagreement

_____ 1. No matter how you teach inner-city youngsters, they will be slow learners.

_____ 2. It is better to work in the inner-city school because a teacher can be more creative and innovative.

_____ 3. Inner-city parents are not really interested in how or what their children do in school.

---

20. This questionnaire is taken from Murray Levine and M. George Feeney, "The Effect of Practice Teaching in Inner City Schools on Attitudes Toward Teaching in Inner City Schools," *Notre Dame Journal of Education* (Fall 1971): pp. 244–255. The modifications, changes, and analysis are those of this author.

_____ 4. Peer group pressures are far more intense than in middle-class schools.

_____ 5. A teacher must make children in inner-city schools work or obey.

_____ 6. By and large, more creative teachers can be found in inner-city schools.

_____ 7. The effort it takes to reach an inner-city child is too great for the return.

_____ 8. Children in inner-city schools are not interested in learning.

_____ 9. The home environment of inner-city youngsters has to be changed before any learning can take place in the school.

_____ 10. The difference in achievement between inner-city kids and others can be attributed to genetics and heredity.

_____ 11. Most teachers in the inner city today are mere babysitters.

_____ 12. Teachers should not expect great strides of achievement from inner-city youngsters because they are not capable of the same standards as others.

_____ 13. Children are exposed to more violence and immorality in the environment than are middle-class youngsters.

_____ 14. Kids in inner-city schools do not respect adult authority and constantly seek to erode it in school.

_____ 15. Gang violence is more a reality than in middle-class schools.

_____ 16. The financial rewards for teaching in the inner city should be much higher than in other schools.

_____ 17. A teacher must be on top of an inner-city class every minute or else the children will get out of control.

_____ 18. Less academic work should be required of inner-city kids because they are poorly endowed intellectually.

_____ 19. Most teachers in inner-city schools today have been well trained for their assignments.

_____ 20. Environmental factors are primarily responsible for the difficulties inner-city kids experience in going to school.

_____ 21. Children in the inner city are more open, spontaneous, and are instantly gratified.

_____ 22. Inner-city schools will only improve when we have local community control.

_____ 23. Inner-city kids are usually dirty, use filthy language, and operate with a value pattern that condones dishonesty and non-competition.

_____ 24. Knowing my capabilities and values, I could not teach in the inner city.

_____ 25. Most inner-city youth are affectionate and prefer more personal contact.

_____ 26. Administrative turnover in the inner city is an asset rather than a liability, especially if the persons are inexperienced.

_____ 27. Children in the inner city are loud, raucous, and easily excitable.

_____ 28. Teachers should be more concerned with teaching values than academic subjects to youngsters.

_____ 29. It is important for survival that inner-city youngsters be taught middle-class values.

_____ 30. Different standards of discipline have to be utilized with inner-city kids than are used with middle-class kids.

_____ 31. Inner-city youngsters have as many stereotypes about teachers as teachers have about them. Both are self-fulfilling.

_____ 32. If I had my choice, I would prefer working with inner-city kids rather than with kids in a suburban system.

_____ 33. More tracking should be utilized in inner-city schools, and slow learners should be quickly identified.

_____ 34. Children in inner-city schools must be taught respect for property.

_____ 35. Black teachers are better teachers for black students just as Chicano teachers are better for Chicano students.

_____ 36. Black students are as bilingual as Chicano students are.

_____ 37. Most of the problems in inner-city schools could be reduced through having smaller classes.

_____ 38. Inner-city youngsters smell differently.

_____ 39. Inner-city youngsters are less creative than other youngsters.

_____ 40. Women should not be assigned to inner-city schools.

_____ 41. The first priority for inner-city schools is greater security through the use of security dogs, electronic devices, and more police attention.

_____ 42. For security purposes, it is wise to use parents or former students in the school for various responsibilities regarding discipline.

_____ 43. Inner-city schools are usually in bad physical condition because the students deliberately make the building that way.

_____ 44. More attention should be given to increased health and social services for inner-city schools.

_____ 45. Bilingualism is a problem for students and should not be a problem for teachers. Students should learn correct, usable English.

_____ 46. Because the vast number of youngsters coming to inner-city schools are poor, it is sound educational policy to provide free lunch and breakfast programs. Empty stomaches foster empty minds.

_____ 47. Inner-city youngsters have greater problems regarding school attendance, truancy, and tardy bells than do other youngsters.

_____ 48. Most inner-city schools are segregated and should remain so to avoid the downgrading of other schools.

_____ 49. Since inner-city youngsters use unacceptable language patterns, it is imperative that the school program stress correct speech, proper writing, and elementary reading skills above all other content.

_____ 50. When inner-city youngsters graduate from secondary school, they should be given Certificates of Attendance rather than a Graduation Diploma since it is obvious that their educational background is inferior to that of the middle-class youngster.

_____ 51. Black youngsters can only effectively learn in classrooms if they are sitting next to white youngsters.

In analyzing your answers to this questionnaire, especially watch for the degree of polarization that exists, indicated by large numbers of 1 and

5 responses; the degree of consistency in answers to different questions, such as items 1, 8, 18; the level of prejudice manifested in value judgments, shown in items 11, 13, 23, 38; or the level of reality regarding the inner-city experience, shown in items 15, 19, 21, 47.

Further analysis reveals that a teacher would be highly prejudiced if he or she scored a 1 for items 1, 13, 23, 38, 48.

A teacher in the inner city would be most resistent to change if he or she scored 1 or 2 on items 5, 11, 34, 35, 39.

A teacher's grasp of reality might be somewhat unrealistic if he or she scored a 3 on items 15, 19, 21, 26, 30, 47.

Anyone who scored 1 for item 23 would, in this writer's judgment, be automatically disqualified. Anyone answering 1 to item 24 would be self-explanatory.

Romaine Mackie, William Kvaraceus, and Jack Williams (1957) have provided us with a set of teacher behaviors that suggest sound teaching, especially for those teaching in difficult settings.[21] Such a teacher has the following characteristics:

> 1. A strong liking for children, including the disturbed and disturbing; attracts children and is attracted by them.
>
> 2. Does not feel a compelling urge to be loved by every child.
>
> 3. Can distinguish between the child and his behavior; rejects misbehavior without rejecting the child as a person.
>
> 4. Realizes there are at least three phases to an action: what one does, how one does it, and why.
>
> 5. Has some knowledge of the variations in child-rearing practices among different cultural groups and has some understanding of the relation between child rearing and per-sonality formation.

---

21. Romaine Mackie et al., *Teachers of Children Who Are Socially and Emotionally Maladjusted* (Washington, D.C.: Office of Education, 1957): pp. 52–62. Also see William Kvaraceus et al., *Delinquent Behavior: Culture and the Individual* (Washington: NEA, 1959), pp. 110–111.

6. Has some overall knowledge of modes of living of the local community and their implications for child and school program.

7. Can define and maintain his role as teacher.

8. Has adequate awareness of his own problems and takes care not to work these out through the child.

9. Is able to distinguish between delinquent behavior that reflects cultural influence and that which reflects emotional disturbance.

10. Accepts the child as he is and encourages his healthy aspirations.

11. Recognizes that all behavior is functional for the child.

12. Has sufficient strength to absorb some direct hostility and defiance, recognizing that hostility and defiance can be an essential part of growth.

13. Has some perception of his own academic, cultural, and personal limitations.

14. Can establish limits that are neither overrestrictive nor overprotective.

Why Teachers Fail in the Inner City

Urban schools in general are in bad shape when it comes to teaching the fundamental skills of reading, writing, speaking, and listening. But why is the problem so much more severe in the inner city? Why are teachers unsuccessful with slum children? Why is the greatest teacher turnover in the inner city? Why is it difficult to keep teachers in inner-city schools?

Over the past several years, many educators have studied those questions, advancing many reasons for teachers failures in the inner city. Howard Becker (1952) maintained that there were distinct social-class variations in the teacher-pupil relationship and that these social-class variations accounted for success or failure patterns in the teacher-learner environment. He maintained that three problems loomed large in the variation between a teacher's social class position and that of the lower social class of students in terms of mutual adjustment: (1) the problems of teaching the students at this level, (2) the problems of disciplining students at this level, and (3) the problems of the moral acceptability of the students by the teacher. Since most teachers consider themselves middle class and are certainly products of a middle-class educational upbringing after 16 years or more of exposure to education, the significant conclusion Becker reached was: "Professionals depend on their environing society to provide them with clients who meet the standards of their image of the ideal client. Social class cultures, among other factors, may operate to produce clients who, in one way or another, fail to meet these specifications and therefore aggravate one or another of the basic problems of the worker-client relation."[22] The social class self-perception of the teacher is perhaps the single most potent force operating in determining the success or failure of the teacher-pupil relationship.

Other reasons for teachers' failure or lack of success in the inner city can be attributed to large classes, lack of communication with parents and community, failure to understand the culture and language barriers, false standards, or simply the self-fulfilling phophecy. Corwin and Schmidt (1970) did a study on teachers in the inner city and advanced four hypotheses for the high rate of failure in the inner city.[23] They are as follows:

The Culture Gap Hypothesis calls for the advancement of the argument that teachers are middle-class products who exhibit a tremendous social distance between themselves and their students. They exhibit a life-style and psychology that clouds their perception of youngsters and allows negative stereotypes of an academic, cultural, racial, and structural nature to predetermine educational outcomes. To a certain extent, the solid WASP teacher experiences culture shock when he or she steps into an inner-city classroom.

---

22. Howard Becker, "Social Class Variations in the Teacher-Pupil Relationship," *Journal of Educational Sociology*, Vol. 35, 1952, pp. 451–65. See also Alfred Lightfoot, "The Potency of Social Class in Determining Educational Inequities," in *Inquiries Into the Social Foundations of Education*, Alfred Lightfoot, ed. (Chicago: Rand McNally, 1972), pp. 157–162.

23. Ronald Corwin and Marilyn Schmidt, "Teachers in Inner-City Schools," *Education and Urban Society*, February, 1970, pp. 131–155. See also B.E. Patrick, "Ghetto Schools Are Different," pp. 211–218, and Bernice Waddles and Dale Robinson, "Teaching in Inner City Schools," pp. 206–210, in *Inquiries Into the Social Foundations of Education*, Alfred Lightfoot, ed. (Chicago: Rand McNally, 1972).

The Horizontal Mobility Hypothesis maintains that most teachers seek a higher and better status in the school system hierarchy and look unfavorably upon positions in the inner city. Then, too, the system tends to reward these people for their loyalty by promoting them to middle-class schools. It is certainly no secret to any personnel department in any urban school system that the majority of requests for transfers come from inner-city schools.

The Inequality Hypothesis maintains that school systems do not distribute their resources equitably and that the inner-city schools are always left wanting. Generally, this is the Conant thesis revived from his book, *Slums and Suburbs*. How accurate this is today might be questionable in the light of overly generous treatment of inner-city schools in the disbursement of federal funds under Compensatory Education. Indeed, researchers such as Coleman and Jencks even raise doubts that these so-called inequities have any significant influence.

The Self-Fulfilling Prophecy Hypothesis is a reaffirmation of the Rosenthal Pygmalion Effect. Children tend to achieve at the level expected of them by their teachers. If their teachers' perceptions of them are negative, then the teachers will teach in a perfunctory way and convey their attitudes in a variety of ways. Children will sense this and adjust their own expectations and performance accordingly. The results will affect learning, discipline, attitudes, and personal self-image.

The author feels that a major reason for teacher failure is that teachers are ill-prepared for meeting the needs of inner-city youngsters. They are ill-prepared to work with racially and culturally different youngsters, ill-prepared to handle and cope with discipline problems, and certainly ill-prepared to communicate with youngsters who think, value, and speak differently than they, whether that be Ghettoish or Spanish. What is particularly devastating to any educator is explaining why experienced, credentialled professionals can so inadequately influence the personal lives of students, so poorly judge the needs and relevancies of youth, so incompetently judge the abilities of students, and so prejudicially discriminate against students because of race, color, language, culture, or social class.

In fairness, it should be stated that the public expects too much from its inner-city teachers and schools. The schools are expected to alleviate all our social problems from crime to segregation; in addition, the realities of urban living are so great that they tend to overwhelm the educational system. They serve to doom many educators to failure before they even begin to tackle the problems of living in the inner city. Because society has come to view the schools as the chief vehicle for social mobility, it also feels that the schools are the chief agents for social change. Far too many expectations are put on the shoulders of urban teachers, and this acts as a self-fulfilling prophecy for failure. The urban teacher has enough to contend with in terms of survival and managing the day-to-day problems of his or her particular teaching situation.

Why do some stay in the inner-city schools, combatting these challenges? Why do some feel compelled to seek an inner-city assignment in the first place? Answers are as variable as are the reasons for leaving. Some stay because of an accommodating principal or for altruistic reasons; others stay because they like to dominate others and can do this through the level of discipline required in these classrooms. Still others stay because of inertia. Others stay because such an assignment brings deep personal satisfaction, or in the belief that they can be creative, innovative, and exercise a certain degree of professional autonomy. There are many who stay because they like it; they like the kids, the challenges, the freedoms and the lack of hypocrisy—and they are usually the good teachers. There are good teachers as well as bad teachers in any school. Unfortunately, the bad teachers do a considerable amount of damage.

Exercises

I. Questionnaires such as the one on teacher's attitudes about the inner city are only one means of making some judgments regarding teacher attitudes. Following is the Los Angeles City School System's Human Relations Quiz (Office of Urban Affairs, Los Angeles City Schools, 1973). Compare the two questionnaires in terms of how well they assess teacher attitudes. Can such assessments be made with questionnaires?

In the space provided, please check that answer that, in your opinion, is the correct one. If none of the choices, in your opinion, is the proper answer, mark an N in the margin. On the true-false questions, place a check between the parentheses.

1. The races of mankind are:
( )   Black, white, red, and yellow.
( )   Oriental, African, European.
( )   Caucasoid, Mongoloid, Negroid.

2. Variations in cultural patterns, such as food, clothing, customs, and social organizations, are the result of:
( )   Natural inclinations and abilities inherent in different racial and ethnic groups.
( )   Environment and tradition.
( )   There is no variation in the cultural pattern of the different racial and ethnic groups.

3. Intercultural contacts are valuable because they:
( )   Demonstrate the inherent superiority of some cultures.
( )   Provide us with examples of customs and habits that are socially undesirable.
( )   Enrich our own culture by widening experience.

4. The G.I. Forum is:
( )   A group interested in the benefits of American Veterans.
( )   An organization founded to better conditions of Mexican-Americans.
( )   A memorial to the war heroes of World War II.

5. The Urban League is:
( )   A group interested in city planning.
( )   An organization founded for the betterment of blacks.
( )   A Jewish welfare group.

6. The word *Aryan* correctly applies to:
( )   A group of languages.
( )   A racially pure ethnic group.
( )   A heretic schism in the Christian Church.

7. Gordon Allport, the noted sociologist, has estimated that the following percentage of the American public holds some appreciable degree of racial prejudice:
( )   45 percent
( )   10 percent
( )   80 percent

8. A child of normal intelligence in the ninth grade who is achieving at the fifth-grade level:

( ) Will probably never catch up with his grade level before he completes high school.

( ) Could, with intensive work, close the gap by one or two grade levels at most.

( ) Reflects an inherited incapacity to learn in an average public school.

9. In his dealings with black students, the average white teacher:

( ) Is somewhat uncomfortable because of a lack of understanding of them.

( ) Is uncomfortable at first, but overcomes this feeling and treats them just as other children are treated.

( ) Rarely has a sense of inadequacy in dealing with them.

10. The low economic status of some minority groups is the result of:

( ) Their inability to adjust to American society.

( ) Social discrimination in education and employment.

( ) Their refusal to compete in terms of education and efficiency.

11. Integration in our schools is good as a matter of:

( ) Educational necessity.

( ) Political expediency.

( ) Integration has no particular educational or political value that could not be obtained in other ways.

12. If minority group children feel that there is prejudice directed at them by teachers and other students, this feeling is probably due to the fact that:

( ) Prejudice actually exists to some degree against them.

( ) They simply imagine this to be true.

( ) There is a combination of some actual prejudice and their own feelings of inadequacy.

13. Children with behavior problems growing out of cultural deprivation will probably tend to change their behavior if:

( ) Teachers insist that they conform to middle-class standards of behavior.

( ) They feel that they are an integral part of the mainstream of community life.

( ) They are permitted to act out their hostility.

14. More Mexican-American than Caucasian youth become high school dropouts because:

( )   Of the lack of proper motivation.

( )   Their inability to adjust to the Anglo schools.

( )   A multiplicity of these and other factors.

15. Intelligence tests given to black and white Army recruits during World War I showed that:

( )   Northern blacks scored higher than southern whites.

( )   There was no substantial difference between the scores of blacks and whites from the various regions.

( )   Southern whites scored higher than northern whites.

16. Negroes at one time in our history have served as:

( )   Senators and lieutenant governors of Alabama, Mississippi, and other southern states.

( )   As representatives of southern states in our federal government.

( )   Neither of the above.

Identify five of the following by placing the appropriate number in the bracket describing them.

1. Benjamin Banneker

2. Phillis Wheatley

3. Simon Bolivar

4. Frederick Douglass

5. Crispus Attucks

6. Carter G. Woodson

7. Ralph Bunche

8. James A. Bland

9. Alexandre Dumas

10. Booker T. Washington

11. Stephen Foster

12. James Baldwin

( )   A contemporary black essayist and fiction writer on social topics

( )   The composer of "Carry Me Back to Old Virginny" and "In the Evening by the Moonlight"

( )   One of the commission appointed by George Washington to survey and lay out the city of Washington, D.C.

( )   A noted black woman poet

( )   Author of "The Negro in Our History"

13. Sally Smith   ( ) A black writer of French
14. Francois Dupre   nationality
15. Mary McLeod Bethune ( ) A black educator who
                            established a college in
                            Florida for the training of
                            blacks in humanities

                       ( ) The most noted black aboli-
                            tionist of the pre-Civil War
                            period

                       ( ) The first person to be killed
                            by British bullets in the Amer-
                            ican Revolution

T F 1. U.S. black citizens' annual consumption is greater
         than the Canadian national budget.

T F 2. There are no Orientals in the United States Senate.

T F 3. There are more blacks attending college in the United
         States than there are people attending college in
         Canada.

T F 4. The Mexican-American population of Los Angeles
         County exceeds that of any other minority group.

T F 5. Anthropologically, blacks differ from white persons
         primarily in skin color.

II. Obviously, inner-city schools are different from other schools and
must be so treated in philosophy, orientation, structure, curriculum,
teacher training, and expected educational objectives. Following is a
list of inner-city priorities. Take a few moments to reflect upon what we
have said about inner-city education and then take this priority exercise.
It will help you clarify the issues in your mind.

Inner City Priorities
Following is a list of 25 priority items for improving inner-city schools
and education. List them in *your* order of priority from the first (number
it 1 on the line) to the least (number it 25 on the line) by placing the
priority number on the space provided. All 25 should be listed according

to *your* thinking regarding these priorities. Upon completion, relist the top *five* on the provided lines below. Also list the item of *least* concern in your thinking.

____ 1. One less class to teach to provide more guidance and more supervision.

____ 2. Bonus salary for teaching in the inner city.

____ 3. Reduced class sizes; the class size that I prefer is _____.

____ 4. Have more specialists in needed areas, academic and social.

____ 5. Have use of more paraprofessional aides.

____ 6. Use of more security agents and security devices for protection.

____ 7. Greater involvement of students and community in decision making.

____ 8. Larger raises and "battle pay" for inner-city teachers.

____ 9. Use of a teacher rotation system allowing for easier transfer.

____ 10. Greater flexibility for teachers in selecting subjects and areas that they wish to teach.

____ 11. Assignment of more social and psychological services for schools.

____ 12. Assignment of more competent and experienced administrators.

____ 13. Reduced counselor/pupil ratio.

____ 14. Teacher-selected administrators.

____ 15. Total local community control from central office in decisions.

____ 16. More educational supplies and materials in compensatory funds.

____ 17. Upgraded physical plants and greater maintenance attention.

____ 18. Greater priority for inner-city teachers for transfers and sabbaticals.

____ 19. Greater teacher independence in classroom instruction and innovation.

_____ 20. Deemphasizing academic programs and emphasizing career education.

_____ 21. Greater attention to better teacher training and inservice training of inner-city teachers.

_____ 22. Require all future teachers to have some inner-city teaching experience.

_____ 23. Maintain and enforce balanced, integrated teaching staffs.

_____ 24. Maintain and enforce balanced, integrated schools via the students.

_____ 25. Place a greater emphasis on bilingual-bicultural educational programs.

My top five priorities are:

1._____
2._____
3._____
4._____
5._____

The item I believe to be of least importance in priority is:

_____

Cultural Disadvantagement and the Culturally Different

Chapter 8

When you have finished this chapter, you should be able to perform the following tasks.

1. Define the concept *equal educational opportunity.*

2. List the basic educational premises that are consistent with the belief that the school is an instrument of the dominant society.

3. Characterize and differentiate between the values of the lower class and the middle class.

4. Identify the themes or labels that have hampered progress in educating lower-class youngsters.

5. List the various types of deprivation found in society, as well as the various forms of disadvantagement.

6. Define *cultural disadvantagement.*

7. List a composite portrait of the disadvantaged that has emerged from numerous studies and describe any inconsistencies in these studies.

8. Describe and identify the four models or schools of thought that deal with the concept of *disadvantagement.*

9. Cite characteristics of the poor as indicated by several studies.

10. Describe several positive advantages of disadvantaged youth.

To talk about urban education is to talk about the many problems facing society and the unprecedented threat that these problems pose to the continuance of public education. These problems can no longer be constrained by the forces of conservatism nor laughed off as figments of the imagination by liberal educators. City systems are currently faced with a major cleavage similar to those faced by social systems in this industrial and technological age, namely, the great social, economic, and educational distance between the haves and the have-nots in our society.

Urban schools have not given adequate service and attention to the have-nots in our society. The equality lag within city systems becomes more glaringly apparent each year as evidence of educational inequities becomes more ominous—and more controversial.[1] City planners seem all too preoccupied with urban renewal and not enough concerned with educational renewal. Citizens, as well as educators, although interested and indignant over the lack of success in our schools, are less imaginative and energetic than before and tend to perpetuate institutional drabness and the status quo.

Some educators, on the other hand, have found a new avenue of research in the problems of the disadvantaged, and a new wave of interest and scholarship among educators, writers, and social workers has swept the term *cultural disadvantagement* into the educator's vocabulary. The problem is not new, but it has become more visible as city slums grow and fester, as the issues of desegregation divide school systems and communities, and as dropout statistics increase and those who remain in our schools to be educated fall further and further behind

1. See Christopher Jencks, *Inequality: A Reassessment of the Effect of Family and Schooling in America* (New York: Basic Books, 1972); Alfred Lightfoot, *The Culturally Disadvantaged: Perspectives in Urban Education* (New York: Simon and Schuster, SAR, 1970); Alfred Lightfoot, *Urban Education: Inquiries Into Changing Patterns* (New York: MSS Publishing Co., 1971); Michael Harrington, *The Other American: Poverty in the United States* (New York: MacMillan, 1962); Benjamin Bloom, Allison Davis, and Robert Hess, *Compensatory Education for Cultural Deprivation* (New York: Holt, Rinehart, and Winston, 1965); Francesco Cordasco and Maurie Hillson, "The School and the Children of the Poor: A Bibliography of Selected References," pp. 389–410, in William Brickman and Stanley Lehrer, *Education and the Many Faces of the Disadvantaged* (New York: Wiley and Sons, 1972).

in academic and minimum reading skills required for survival in today's world.

Identifying or designating certain pupils or schools as culturally disadvantaged and acting positively upon that identity is a problem and a controversy for most educators. The basic and primary problem of what to do after identification constitutes a greater challenge for educators and society. This chapter will attempt to tackle the problems of identification, and in so doing, will try to put into perspective the various schools of thought on the subject. Not everyone will agree on these classifications, but they will at least have begun some creative thought regarding some of the problems in the instructional domain. It is hoped that the reader will be able to advance certain suggestions for feasible teaching strategies.

Perspectives for the Problem

The public schools have historically and traditionally had the responsibility of taking all youngsters, regardless of their backgrounds, educating them, socializing them, and making them functional members of society. This has frequently meant changing them, and the schools have been the principle agents of change in our society. As agents of change, the schools have been the primary instruments of cultural assimilation.

The school also became the chief transmitter of culture. Several researchers have developed a model that supports the contention that public schools are instruments of the dominant society and that certain basic educational premises are consistent with that model.[2] Among them are the following:

1. Native intelligence in children is measurable and therefore predictable.

2. Devices of standardization are sufficiently accurate and can

2. See the following: Nathaniel Hickerson, *Education for Alienation* (Englewood Cliffs, N.J.: Prentice-Hall, 1966), p. 23; William Ragan and George Henderson, *Foundations of American Education* (New York: Harper and Row, 1970), p. 222; David Gottlieb and Charles Ramsey, *Understanding Children of Poverty* (Chicago: Science Research Associates, 1967), pp. 30–35.

be relied upon for labeling and establishing systems of instruction.

3. Not all youngsters are of the same backgrounds and intelligence, and thus, not all youngsters are capable of completing an academic program.

4. Programs other than the academic, such as vocational, should be provided for children incapable of completing the academic.

5. The school must help each student to adjust realistically to his own abilities and to be a good citizen by making a meaningful contribution to society when he takes his place in that society.

6. Students must conform to a class behavior pattern that assimilates and inculcates such mores and folkways as the use of decent, formal language as opposed to vulgar, informal language; the use of grammatically correct language; the development of proper attitudes toward sex, drinking, adults, drugs, and patriotism; the need for hard work, productivity, efficiency, and competition; and the denial of physical aggression in the solving of problems.

Consequently, the public school system characterized middle-class values as the appropriate value system and ignored other value systems as it attempted to fit all youngsters into the melting pot. The poor or working class were alien to the school system and were relegated to an inferior position in society as a whole and in the schools in particular. Sociologist Joseph Kahl (1961) defined a five-class structure in America using a single characterizing word or phrase for each class. This categorization has typified the thinking of society and schools ever since.[3]

Upper class: graceful living
Upper-middle class: career
Lower-middle class: respectability
Upper-lower class: getting by
Lower-lower class: apathy

---

3. Joseph Kahl, *The American Class Structure* (New York: Holt, Rinehart, and Winston, 1961), Chapter 7.

In an article summarizing the literature dealing with patterns of child rearing and academic performance, sociologist Catherine Chilman (1965) concluded that lower-lower class families develop few attitudes toward one another that are conducive to good academic performance. Such a home tends to be unintellectual, nonexploratory, and uncommunicative, all attitudes that do not fit into the role model that the public school expects. She offers a comparison of the patterns found in the middle-class home with those of the lower-class home.[4] It follows:

Middle Class	Lower Class
1. Child given freedom to explore and experiment	1. Limited freedom due to crowded environment
2. Much verbal communication	2. Little verbal communication
3. Discipline chiefly verbal, mild, reasonable	3. Discipline harsh, inconsistent, physical
4. Sensitivity to feelings and attitudes of others	4. Slight awareness of subtleties of interpersonal relations
5. Good impulse control	5. Poor impulse control
6. Cheerful, happy, self-assured attitude	6. Low self-esteem, distrust, tendency to hostile aggression and withdrawal
7. Social skills in dress, manners, speech, etc., according to middle-class norms	7. Little skill in prevalent middle-class behavior
8. Goal commitment and belief in long-range success potential	8. Fatalistic, apathetic attitude
9. Educational and occupational success of parents; a parental model	9. Tendency to educational and occupational failure; reliance on personal attributes vs. skills in vocational success
10. Stability in family	10. Instability in family, high separation rate

---

4. Catherine S. Chilman, "Child Rearing and Family Relationship Patterns of the Very Poor," *Welfare in Review* (January, 1965), pp. 9–19.

Educational studies such as these have had their effect upon the school system. Unfortunately, what has emerged in education today is a mind-set regarding the lower-class, one that has labeled all lower-class children as culturally disadvantaged. In this mass labeling, certain beliefs have emerged to hamper the progress of educating lower-class youngsters:

1. Cultural differentness from that which is accepted as the dominant culture is viewed as cultural inferiority.

2. Schools can do little for the youngster who comes from the lower class because of the accumulated deficiencies of his environment.

3. The terms *culturally disadvantaged, culturally deprived, socially handicapped, slow learner,* and *culturally different* are interchangeable and really mean the same thing, namely, that youngsters in this category have an inferior culture (or no culture), are intellectually and socially retarded, and have negative self-images.

4. The culturally disadvantaged are uncreative, unintellectual, and uncommunicative.

5. The culturally disadvantaged should be segregated from the other students and be given a different kind of education, emphasizing occupational training.

The Nature of Deprivation and Cultural Disadvantagement

Educators have long recognized several forms of deprivation and disadvantagement. Researchers have felt that account should be taken of the various categories of the disadvantagement and deprivation in matters of culture and education.

Deprivation has many sources and takes many forms.[5]

5. See the following: Sidney Lens, *Poverty—America's Enduring Paradox* (New York: Crowell, 1969); Frank Riessman, *Social Class and Social Policy* (New York: Basic Books, 1968); Robert Havighurst, *Education in Metropolitan Areas* (Boston: Allyn and Bacon, 1966); C.W. Hunnicutt, *Urban Education and Cultural Deprivation* (Syracuse: Syracuse University Press, 1964).

Affectional deprivation occurs when a person is deprived of affection, attention, or emotional support; the result of such deprivation is temporary or permanent damage to one's self-identity and ego.

Model-person deprivation relates to the absence of persons in the child's life who are good examples for the child to imitate while growing up. The deprived child fails to find such models from adults, other children, peers, or from fantasy heroes.

Intellectual deprivation relates to the lack of challenging intellectual stimulation that can be derived from books, newspapers, discussions, and media instruments. These are absent from the environment, or they are there, but the person lacks the skills in using them.

Nutritional deprivation occurs when a child is not eating adequate food or receiving a balanced diet; disease and illness occurs frequently, immobilizing the child and keeping him or her out of school.

Socioeconomic deprivation refers to the acts of discrimination within society that prevent a person from achieving social mobility.

Educational deprivation refers to the failure of a school system to offer equal educational opportunity, thereby stifling achievement and attainment of goals and levels of aspiration, objective placement in an educational system (tracking), and future opportunities for education.

Deprivation is a condition of being dispossessed, divested, or denied some valued condition. Failure to attain the goals generally prescribed by the culture represents the essence of cultural deprivation. A person is deprived when he or she is hindered in competing for the required ends of society and when a competitor is given an unfair advantage. We are competitors in society—and in a democratic society, all should be given equal opportunities for competition. Obviously, all persons are not equal in capabilities or backgrounds, but equal opportunity refers to the circumstances and conditions surrounding the competition and not the competitors.

Disadvantagement takes many forms, as does deprivation. The two terms are often interchangeable and have come to be almost coterminous. The use of one term over the other has become a matter of preference, which has, unfortunately, only added to the confusion.

Brickman (1968) has broken disadvantagement into several categories.[6] He describes the disadvantage of geography as referring to the advantages or disadvantages that one experiences as a result of living in a city or a rural area, the South vs. the North, an island vs. a continent, a liberal area or a conservative area. One is restricted according to the geographic boundaries of one's region.

The disadvantage of sex refers to the advantages or disadvantages that being male or female bring to a person in a given society. The women's liberation movement is seeking to mitigate some of the disadvantages traditionally assigned to women.

The disadvantagement of political participation refers to the denial of political rights to citizens or the weakness of some groups against other, more organized power blocks. Watergate shows the disparities between political groups.

The disadvantagement of race refers to the victimization of persons because of their race and the denial of access to the same opportunities granted to those of other races.

The disadvantagement of physical differentness refers to discrimination exacted against the physically handicapped within our society and could also apply to those who are mentally or emotionally handicapped.

The disadvantagement of social class refers to the caste-like social structure that many societies have and enforce in order to reduce social mobility. Such stratification, by its very meaning, connotes separateness and inequality.

The lists describing disadvantagement and deprivation are hardly complete. They are complete enough for one to see that, no matter how you want to categorize them, they all have substantial influence upon education, and all take their toll upon school children. The educationally disadvantaged are those who are unwilling participants in the aforementioned injustices.

---

6. William W. Brickman, "Editorial: The Educationally Disadvantaged," *School and Society* (March 30, 1968), p. 196.

How then do we come to a definition of the culturally disadvantaged, a definition that is linked to the aforementioned areas of concern and yet does not inherently become self-fulfilling? This writer suggests a composite definition that consists of three parts. Culturally disadvantaged refers to: (1) the conditions under which a person is forced to socially interact in the total culture, but denied complete access or acceptability in that culture by virtue of the person's differentness; (2) a differentness that is based upon characteristics that put the person at a social, political, and economic disadvantage in the total culture; (3) a set of variables used to determine the differentness, which are broadly construed to be race, social class, religion, geography, heredity, sex, health and nutrition, culture and environment, and education.

The term *culturally disadvantaged* has come to mean many things to many people and has caused a great deal of controversy and name calling. Any discussion of the culturally disadvantaged is meaningless unless the future teacher can seriously answer three questions to his or her satisfaction:

What does the term mean to you?
What do you feel it should mean?
What do you feel it should not mean?

If we were more precise in our search for answers to these questions, educators might not be as confused as they are today over the issues confronting this group of youngsters.[7]

Characteristics of the Educationally and Culturally Disadvantaged

Educational literature since the 1970s has been fairly consistent in its definition of the culturally disadvantaged child. But while uniformity and consensus pervade the literature, disharmony and denial abounds on the lecture circuit. Nonetheless, a composite portrait of the culturally and educationally disadvantaged person emerges, fair or not. It is

7. Master of Education in Inner City Education, Graduate Degree Program, 1976. Loyola Marymount University, Los Angeles, California.

based on several studies.[8] Such people display many of the following characteristics:

1. Language inadequacies, including limited vocabulary and syntactical structure; inability to handle complex symbols and formal communication; heavy reliance upon a restricted sub-cultural language form that substitutes as a second language (e.g., Ghettoish).

2. Visual and perceptual deficiencies, including problems of spatial organization and lateral orientation.

3. A mode of expression and thinking that tends to more concrete, sense-related, and motor-oriented than abstract, conceptual, and symbolic.

4. A preoccupation with immediate gratification and the present rather than the more acceptable deferred gratification.

5. A low self-image, denigrating one's potential as a person and as a contributing member of society; a feeling of alienation and uselessness.

6. Low motivation, limited levels of aspiration, and unrealistic goals in terms of present and future orientations.

7. Restricted attention span, inability to cope with the demands of school, and erratic attendance at school; potential dropout.

---

8. Richard De Blassie, "The Counselor and Cultural Pluralism," *Educational Leadership* (December, 1974), p. 188; E. Casavantes, "Pride and Prejudice: A Mexican-American Dilemma," *Civil Rights Digest* (Winter, 1970), pp. 22–27; Kenneth Johnson, *Leading the Culturally Disadvantaged* (Palo Alto, Calif.: Science Research Associates, 1970), pp. 20–25, 34–35, 103–04; Edmund Gordon, "Characteristics of Socially Disadvantaged Youngsters," *Review of Educational Research* (May, 1965), pp. 377–388; Basil Bernstein, "Language and Social Class," *British Journal of Sociology* (September, 1960), pp. 271–76; Martin Deutsch, "The Disadvantaged Child and the Learning Process," in *Education in Depressed Areas,* by Harry Passow (New York: Teacher's College, 1963), pp. 163–79; Frank Riessman, *The Culturally Deprived Child* (New York: Harper and Row, 1962); Patricia Sexton, *Education and Income* (New York: Viking, 1964); Stanley Charnofsky, *Educating the Powerless* (Belmont, California: Wadsworth Publishing Co., 1971); Robert Havighurst, "Who Are the Socially Disadvantaged?" *Journal of Negro Education,* 1964, pp. 210–17; John Langer, "The Disadvantaged, the Three R's, and Individual Differences," in Brickman's *Education and the Many Faces of the Disadvantaged* (New York: Wiley and Sons, 1972), pp. 47–51.

8. Limited I.Q. range, somewhere between 75 and 90.

9. Limited imagination, with unsystematic thought processes and very little creativity.

10. Limited powers of independence, initiative, and resourcefulness.

11. Living in extended families with a poor home life and environment and few adult models at home.

12. A nonjoiner of organizations and activities.

13. Marked antiintellectualism, attitudes that are antischool, antiauthority, antipolice, antiinstitutions.

14. Use of physical force to settle arguments or control children; a general display of machismo and a need for peer-group identity (primary peer group).

15. Feeling of little control over events, institutions, and their own lives.

16. An experiental background that does not fill the expectations of curriculum oriented to the middle-class.

17. An economically impoverished background; caught up in self-perpetuating spiritual, moral, aspirational, educational, and poverty cycles.

18. A negative environment that is ugly, crowded, filthy, noisy, and disorderly.

19. A home environment that lacks the necessary cultural artifacts associated with school readiness.

20. Parents that fail to support their children's academic pursuits and are not vitally interested in the school.

21. Basic skills such as reading, writing, and arithmetic that are depressed below national norms.

Teachers tended to perceive parents of disadvantaged pupils as generally not encouraging high academic achievement and sometimes even working against it. They scorn teachers and do not attend school organization meetings such as the PTA. They cannot provide school community leadership when given tasks to perform. They are cruel to their children and ignorant of many aspects of child development. They are difficult to deal with, unreasonable, and sometimes drunk and violent.[9]

From the studies on the culturally disadvantaged, one would believe that such students are hopeless morons, come from homes that do not care about them, and are brought up in a subculture that is alien, foreign, and against the finest of American ideals. Some educators would have us believe that this group of youngsters represents 30 percent or more of the children in our urban schools.[10] If this is the case, how do we account for such recent findings that point out that the decline in educational achievement nationwide is substantial, that only 49 percent of the 18–29 age group in our society have the skills and knowledge needed to function effectively in the day-to-day struggle to make a living and maintain a home in contrast to 60 percent in the 30–39 age group? Another study points out that 20 percent of Americans cannot really cope in our society because they cannot read or understand what they have read. Reading skills and writing skills were way down for students aged 13–17. In addition, other startling statistics indicate that:

- 39 million people were functional but not proficient in such tests as reading a newspaper grocery ad.
- 13 percent of the persons in the study could not address an envelope properly for mailing.
- 30 percent could not pick the proper airplane flight to make a meeting in another city.
- 49 percent did not know that each state has two senators.
- 28 percent could not figure out the amount of change due them by subtracting the cost of a purchase from a $20 bill.[11]

---

9. Research Committee of the Coordinating Council on Human Relations, Detroit, "The Challenge to Education in the Multi-Problem Neighborhoods" (Detroit, April 20, 1961).

10. Robert Havighurst, "Who Are the Socially Disadvantaged," in *Inquiries Into the Social Foundations of Education,* Alfred Lightfoot, ed. (Chicago: Rand McNally, 1972), p. 201–02.

11. "Washington Report," *Phi Delta Kappan,* January, 1976, p. 355; *Los Angeles Times,* October 30, 1975; Department of Health, Education, and Welfare, Education Division, University of Texas Report and National Assessment of Educational Progress, 1975.

Such findings lead one to question if there is really such a group in our schools as the culturally disadvantaged.

The Models for Disadvantagement

Educators view the culturally disadvantaged from varying perspectives and have managed to establish well-defined paradigms. Although these theoretic models are numerous, four seem to stand out. These four can be identified as the culturally disadvantaged paradigm, the genetic pathology paradigm, the social linguistic pathology paradigm, and the culturally different paradigm. The four are bound together by a concern about the child that seemingly has some or all of the characteristics previously mentioned. Let us briefly explore their differences as well as their similarities.[12]

The Culturally Disadvantaged Paradigm

This model is the most traditional model and the most widespread in its usage and acceptance. Its title suggests that there is a mainstream culure and that those outside of that mainstream are at a disadvantage. Those who adhere to this model are careful to identify the character of the mainstream or dominant culture, its values, norms, folkways, institutions, and patterns of role playing. Those that are unable to function in that culture are unable to function because they are not representative of the dominant culture and represent a subculture. When they attempt to interact in the dominant culture, they are unsuccessful because they do not have the requisites for successful interaction. This model posits the theoretical premise that persons of low socioeconomic status, irrespective of racial or ethnic origin, are characterized by noted deficits when evaluated according to the culturally determined norms of the dominant culture. Obviously, the dominant culture is that of the middle class. Some supporters of this model are cumulative deficit theorists, who believe that children in subcultures accumulate marked deficiencies from their environment before they enter school and continue to accumulate these deficiencies as they move through school because the system is basically dominant-culture oriented. Such deficiencies have an accumulative effect and may eventually reach a point where they are irreversible. Standardized tests are often used

---

12. These models are an outgrowth of a study done by Dick Puglisi, in which he described two of these models. I prefer to extend these theoretical divisions into four distinct models. See Dick Puglisi, "Two Approaches to Minority Education," *Educational Leadership,* December, 1974, pp. 173–175.

to identify those who are disadvantaged. This model of identification would be the quickest to list children as disadvantaged by simply looking for the overall characteristics of the culturally disadvantaged child. A social scientist and urbanologist such as Robert Havighurst is a good example of a representative of this model.

The Genetic Pathology Model

This model is the most controversial paradigm and is least accepted by social scientists and educators. It states that the single greatest influence upon intellectual differences is heredity. The genetic pathology model seriously questions the value of environment and rejects its influence upon the variances of learning. Research into possible genetic influence upon intelligence had been academically and socially taboo until Arthur Jensen revived it. Jensen postulated that an inherited G-factor helps to explain the variance of 15 points in the intelligence testing of whites and blacks. He said that the G-factor helps persons perform tasks and problems that require mental manipulation and transformation of ideas, and that whites inherit more of this factor than blacks.

The G-factor is not a new concept, having been hypothesized in psychology at least 25 years ago to explain intelligence tests measure. Jensen resurrected this concept to explain racial differences in I.Q. test achievement and popularized it. Jensen maintained that the G-factor is found in all standard I.Q. tests, regardless of the diversity and content of tests; he further maintained that the less the test problem is based upon habit and the more complex it is, the more important the role of the G-factor.[13] Needless to say, the Jensen thesis erupted like a volcano upon the educational arena and Jensen was called everything from unscientific to a racist.

The entire question of genetics relationship to intelligence raised the spector of eugenics once again and brought into the educational arena such diverse people as William Shockley of Stanford and John Higham

---

13. One of the most readable articles Jensen has ever written can be found in *Psychology Today*. See Arthur Jensen, "The Differences Are Real," *Psychology Today*, December, 1973, pp. 80–86. In the same issue, Berkeley Rice examines the storm of controversy Jensen caused in his article, "The High Cost of Thinking The Unthinkable," pp. 89–93, while Theodosius Dobzhansky, in "Differences Are Not Deficits," pp. 97–101, takes exception to the Jensen thesis.

of Harvard. While Higham advanced the Jensen thesis and tried to apply it to the American Indian, Shockley advanced his own thesis regarding dysgenics.[14] Overlooked in the entire controversy was the Jensenism that traditional modes of instruction for the black youngster were not workable and that a new emphasis should be placed upon concrete learning for disadvantaged youngsters. This argument gave greater credibility to the forces for compensatory education and the organization of educators who believed in the doctrine of separate but equal education.

The Social Linguistic Pathology Paradigm
This model, due largely to the research conducted by Martin Deutsch, has generated considerable support and acceptance.[15] According to this model, the disadvantaged are those low in socioeconomic status, mainly minority group members, and are in need of compensatory assistance. It emphasizes the point that deficits characterize the physical and social environment of the lower socioeconomic strata and have the effect of retarding the child's intellectual development. This retardation is most noticeable in cognitive and linguistic difficulties experienced by lower-socioeconomic-class children. One of the principle areas of concern of this model is the linguistic area, where it is believed that ethnic environments produce severe linguistic deficiencies for minority youngsters that are especially apparent when they are expected to experience, appreciate, and understand formal English.[16] Other language styles such as black English are viewed as deficient versions of standard English, even though they are valid language forms that communicate. When the monolingual child (Chicano or black) is forced to become bilingual by learning his subcultural language *plus* the formal English, in order for him to reverse his monolinguality from the subcultural to the dominant culture for acceptability, the child runs the risk of becoming alingual. The same is true in the cultural sense: monoculturality forced into biculturality leads to monoculturality and possible aculturality. What should be happening, in essence, and what would be

---

14. John Higham, *Strangers in the Land: Patterns of American Nativism* (New York: Atheneum, 1967).

15. See Martin Deutsch, "Perspectives on the Education of the Urban Child," in *Urban Education in the 1970s,* A. Harry Passow, ed. (New York: Teacher's College, 1971), pp. 103–19.

16. Puglisi, p. 173.

educationally desirable, would be monoculturality that led to biculturality and to a multicultural syndrome. Unfortunately, this is rarely the case.

The social linguistic pathology model advocates early intervention programs such as Head Start and is a champion of compensatory education and early childhood education. Educators such as William Labov and Dorothy Seymour emphasize the linguistic model;[17] Martin Deutsch emphasizes both the linguistic and the social model.

The Culturally Different Paradigm

This model is the most current model and reflects the most recent trends in education.[18] Its most current advocates are academicians such as Horace Kallen and contemporary education critics such as Herbert Kohl, Jonathon Kozel, and Charles Silberman. It is largely based upon Kallen's cultural pluralism concept, which states that the differences between minority groups and the dominant group are largely cultural.[19] The purpose of the school is not to eliminate the deficiencies discussed earlier, which in reality do not exist, nor is it to impress upon the child the incorrectness or inappropriateness of his culture. The purpose of the school is to emphasize every group's cultural heritage and the necessity for bicultural existence. All cultures have legitimacy and importance; no culture is dominant or subdominant; all are equal in richness, tradition, and educational purpose. Each group has as its responsibility the integration of its culture with the fabric of the society. In the truest sense of the word, the school, the curriculum, the home,

---

17. See Dorothy Seymour, "Black Children, Black Speech," *Commonweal,* November, 1971, pp. 175–178; William Labov, "Academic Ignorance and Black Intelligence," *Atlantic Monthly,* June, 1972, pp. 59–67; William Labov, *Language in the Inner City* (Philadelphia: University of Pennsylvania Press, 1972); Helaine Dawson, *On The Outskirts of Hope* (New York: McGraw-Hill, 1968).

18. In 1969, California enacted a revolutionary statute. The law stated that every school district in the state that has one or more schools with 25 percent or more minority enrollment must provide its staff with 60–90 hours of inservice preparation in the history, culture, and current problems of diverse ethnic groups. See *Education Code,* State of California, Article 3.3, Section 13344.4. See also Enid Blaylock, "Article 3.3: California's Answer to Cultural Diversity in the Classroom," *Phi Delta Kappan,* November, 1975, p. 203.

19. See Horace Kallen, *Culture, and Democracy in the United States* (New York: Boni and Liveright, 1924); Seymour Itzkoff, *Cultural Pluralism and American Education* (Scranton, Pa.: International Textbook Co., 1969).

and the community are multicultural in thrust, purpose, and achievement. A school attending to this model would have several characteristics.[20]

They are:

1. To reflect the pluralistic nature of our society, both past and present.

2. To present diversity of culture, ethnicity, and custom as strong positive facets of our society.

3. To present the cultural, sexual, and racial groups in our society in a manner that will build mutual respect and understanding.

4. To portray people, whatever their culture, as displaying various human emotions, both negative and positive. Individuals of different cultural groups should be described working and playing together.

5. To provide a balanced representation of cultural groups and avoid stereotyping.

6. To present members of various cultural groups in positions of authority.

7. To examine the societal forces that operate to maximize or minimize the opportunities of minority groups.

8. To help students gain knowledge and appreciation of the many contributions to our civilization made by members of various cultural groups.

9. To portray cultures other than from a "special occasion" point-of-view (e.g., Is there usually a pinata when studying Mexico? Are Native Americans presented mostly around Thanksgiving? Is the study of blacks confined to Black History Week? Are Asian-Americans studied around the Chinese New Year?).

10. To present a wide variety of representation in a consistent form of the many cultures of the world in the total curriculum from K–12.

---

20. See Gloria W. Grant, "Criteria for Cultural Pluralism in the Classroom," *Educational Leadership,* December, 1974, pp. 190–192; see also Itzkoff, *Cultural Pluralism and American Education,* and Lightfoot, *The Culturally Disadvantaged.*

11. To include an equal representation of the cultures presented in the U.S. in the total curriculum from K–12.

12. To examine real problems and real people of the various cultures, not just heroes and highlights.

13. To provide experiences that will help build positive attitudes of a student's own cultural group and acceptance of other cultural groups.

14. To use words and phrases that are complimentary and honestly descriptive of the culture.

15. To make certain that cultures are not presented in isolation from each other. A pluralistic curriculum should provide experiences that show how people of one culture have adopted food, clothing, and language from other cultures.

16. To present all sides of an issue using primary resources whenever possible.

17. To provide opportunities for children of one culture to interact in another child's culture through a reality experience.

18. To examine and use the various language forms that children have adopted and integrate them into classroom experiences.

19. To develop a curriculum library of materials and sources regarding different cultures and have it available. The library should contain scientific as well as nonscientific studies, fiction as well as nonfiction.

The Culture of Poverty

It has been estimated by some that anywhere from one-fifth to one-fourth of the U.S. population is poverty stricken. Figures differ according to the tests used and the criteria.[21] In a recent study by the Roman Catholic Church's antipoverty agency, it was pointed out that there are 40 million

---

21. Ragan and Henderson, *Foundations of American Education* (New York: Harper and Row, 1970), p. 173. See also Michael Harrington, *The Other America: Poverty in the U.S.* (New York: Macmillan, 1962); Sidney Lens, *Poverty—America's Enduring Paradox* (New York: Crowell, 1969); Henry Miller, *Poverty American Style* (Belmont, Calif.: Wadsworth, 1966); Daniel P. Moynihan, ed., *On Understanding Poverty* (New York: Basic Books, 1969); James Sundquist, *On Fighting Poverty* (New York: Basic Books, 1969).

	Culturally Disadvantaged	Genetic Pathology	Social-Linguistic Pathology	Multicultural
Heredity vs. Environment Influence	Environment most influential	Heredity most influential	Heredity (physical) and environment (social) influential	Environment most influential
Norm of Society	Middle class sets the norms	Middle class standards for tests, but I.Q. is a matter of genetics	Middle class sets the norms	All classes should set the norms
Assimulation vs. Pluralism	Assimulative society	Pluralism (elitism based upon intelligence)	Assimulative society— integrate the weak and the strong	Pluralism
Culturalism	Monocultural (dominant cultural pattern)	Acultural (dominance based on intelligence not culture)	Bicultural	Multicultural
Remediation Approach	−separate facilities −compensatory education −tracking −limited integration	−elitism and tracking −cognitive education for brighter students; concrete for slower −ability grouping	−intervention programs at early stages −language programs −compensatory aid −integration	−strengthening one's own cultural heritage first −learning about other cultures next
Possible Extremes	overstandard- ization	eugenics— dysgenics	forced integration	separatism in learning one's culture

Figure 8-1. Summary of Four Models

poor persons in the United States, approximately 65 percent more than the government figures show. The government figures listed 24 million poor in the U.S. as of 1974. The Church report, "Poverty Profile, 1975," indicated that the government's yardstick is unrealistic, given any of the variables listed such as real cost of living, provision of adequate diet, and habitable housing. The study noted that in 1959 the poverty level income (poverty index) represented 54 percent of the average median family income, but that in 1974, it represented only 40 percent.

The relative capability of the poor to participate in society, using the government's poverty standard, is far lower than in 1959. If the poverty index were 54 percent of the median income now, the number of poor Americans would be almost 46 million. According to the study, a more equitable poverty index would be half of the average median income for families—$6,420. This standard, according to the study, would con- servatively estimate the number of poor people at about 40 million, or about one in every five Americans.[22]

Poverty permeates every facet of our society and takes its toll upon every institution in American life. Our schools, being the most public of all institutions, take the greatest beating because of poverty. Educa- tors overwhelmingly agree that poverty affects the lives of children and, in turn, creates a culture of poverty in our schools. Whether rural or urban, school systems are affected. Realistically speaking, the culturally disadvantaged, as a category or group of youngsters, is made up of the poor. Children and youth from the culture of poverty are truly the deprived, the disadvantaged. When educators seek to list the character- istics of youngsters who are disadvantaged, they must seek out those characteristics that are coterminous with the culture of poverty.

Several recent studies are noteworthy for doing just that. These studies have concentrated upon children from the culture of poverty and are most revealing in their conclusions about the deprived and disadvantaged youth of poverty. What follows is a summation of these conclusions as they relate to four areas of concern: (1) home and family structure, (2) personality and social characteristics, (3) learning characteristics, and (4) general school relationships. In essence, they attempt to describe the children of poverty and offer some important implications for education in our schools.[23]

---

22. "Poverty Profile, 1975" Campaign for Human Development, Roman Catholic Church, Washington, D.C., 80 pp. See also *Los Angeles Times,* December 22, 1975; "U.S. Census, 1970," Bureau of the Census, Department of Health, Education and Welfare, Washington, D.C.

23. The most significant conclusions are drawn from the exhaustive research studies of Newton Metfessel and his "Project Potential." See Newton Metfessel, "Project Potential," University of Southern California, 1965. See also "Conclusions on Research on the Culture of Poverty," Student Achievement and Student Opportunity Centers, Charles Drew Junior High School, Los Angeles, October 19, 1965 (mimeographed paper); Alfred Lightfoot, "Identifying Youth, Disadvantagement, and Poverty," Loloya Marymount University, Los Angeles, 1970 (mimeographed paper).

Home and Family Structure

Such children typically have parents who do not have the language skills to enable them to foster their children's language and cognitive development. These children do not hear long sentences, sentences with complex grammatical structure, or patterns of sequential sentences. This affects the development of these children in both receptive and expressive language abilities.

The child's conceptual formation development may be adversely affected by lack of objects. For the purpose of the Project Potential research, concepts were defined as abstractions from things (concrete objects). This demands that a subject have concrete objects on which to build abstractions (identify similarities and differences) in order to generalize to new situations.

Their level of curiosity is also affected. One develops curiosity, generally, by having things to be curious about. The lack of curiosity affects both motivational patterns and the development of creative behavior.

Language development is crippled because they do not perceive of the concept that objects have names, and, indeed, that the same object may have different names. This may be one of the major reasons why poor children have later difficulty in coping with instruction in reading.

Questions are not asked or answered in the family. Consequently, these children do not perceive of adults, in general, as people from whom you ask questions and receive answers, a fundamental postulate on which the school culture is organized.

They come from homes where there is a sparsity of objects, such as toys and play materials of different colors, sizes, and shapes. Consequently, the children receive little or no training in the concepts of color ("bring me the blue one"), directionality ("bring me the one on the left"), position ("bring me the middle one"), or relative size ("bring me the small one").

They are disciplined by physical force. In the school culture, discipline is invariably issued through reason (insight building) or by deprivation of privileges. Since reason is generally not used in the poverty home, the child has had little opportunity to build insights into the causes and consequences of his own behavior. In school settings, he reacts to reason in a discomfited way.

Such children have little encouragement of their fantasy lives. Middle-class parents generally accept a child's imaginary playmate and may even enter into imaginary play. The parent from the culture of poverty tends to remain neutral and, occasionally, in the instance of imaginary playmates, may discipline their child for lying.

The parents work at jobs that require little education; this frequently gives the child the impression that school is not particularly important in terms of preparation for life.

The children have little or no out-of-school experiences that are translatable to the school culture. Out-of-school resources such as zoos, museums, libraries, and exhibition halls were found to be unfamiliar to the majority of the children. Over half the children in this study had never been to the Pacific Ocean, although it was less than twenty-five miles away.

Frequently parents are concerned that too much formal education may spoil their child. Anxiety over losing status in the eyes of their growing offspring as educational differences increase is a particular manifestation of this concern.

The parents often feel that the family is preeminent over school attendance laws. Consequently, what is defined as truancy by the school, may be viewed as a sign of family loyalty by the parents. Also, the observed truancy of older brothers and sisters in situations unrelated to family welfare or family well-being contributes to patterns of poor attendance.

The parents frequently communicate negative appraisals of the school establishment because of their own difficulties in coping with the school culture. By a process of horizontal acculturation demanded by the school establishment is facilitated.

Frequently the parents lack a basic understanding of the educative process to such an extent that the school is perceived as a place where magic occurs, e.g., the child learns to read, write, and spell. One of the major benefits of having parental participation in school programs, particularly preschool, is the eradication of this belief which occurs·in inverse relationship to their understanding of the educative process.

These children frequently come from homes in which the physical environment mitigates against the development of listening skills. The home is so noisy that the child learns to tune out. This not only occurs in situations of yelling and screaming, but also in the general noise level that is increased by cramped living quarters and radio and television. The kind of television watched in the homes of the poor has little in it that is translatable to the school culture.

Personality and Social Characteristics

Such children typically are characterized by weak ego-development, a lack of self-confidence, and a negative self-concept. Conflicting feelings about themselves frequently result in exaggerated positive and negative attitudes toward others.

They have great difficulty in handling feelings of hostility through the use of words rather than through force.

Typically they have poor judgment because of their meager experiences. They have had little experience in making small decisions, so they are unequipped to make larger ones.

These children frequently fail because they expect to fail, which only tends to reinforce their feelings of inadequacy.

Learning Characteristics

Such children have a cognitive style that responds more to visual and kinesthetic signals than to oral or written stimuli.

They need to see concrete applications of what is learned related to immediate sensory and topical satisfactions. The use of a nutrition period as a formal learning experience is of special importance here.

They learn more readily by inductive rather than by deductive approaches. Learning experiences that move from the part to the whole, rather than from the whole to the part, are invariably the most successful.

They persevere in a task only when they are engrossed in a single activity. They have poor attention span. A teacher should not give instructions in sequence, such as, "First do this, and then this, and then this." Such children will typically respond to the last thing that they have heard.

They have significant gaps in knowledge and uneven areas of learning. Teachers generally believe that, if a middle-class child knows Fact A, it is highly probable that he or she will know closely related Fact B. But a child from the culture of poverty who knows Fact A may not necessarily know Fact B.

The cycle of skill mastery, which demands that successful experiences generate more motivation to perform and, in turn, guarantees levels of skills sufficient to prevent discouragement, may be easily reversed so that the achievement habit ends prior to its ever beginning. One of the major objectives of the preschool for these children, consequently, is the sequential attainment of success experiences.

They frequently have had little experience in receiving approval for success in a learning task, an assumption on which the school culture is based. Teachers should be sensitive to the fact that these children frequently perceive praise in context of evaluation rather than reward.

They frequently learn less from what they hear than their middle-class counterparts.

General School Relationships and Characteristics

Such children are at a marked disadvantage in timed test situations. Clocks and watches have been characterized as "middle-class gods."

They use a great many words with fair precision, but not those words representative of the school culture. The child who says, "I'm going to carry him home," is using a term alien to the school establishment but well-founded in such familiar songs as "Carry Me Back to Old Virginny," and the song line, "I looked over Jordan and what did I see, Comin' for to carry me home." The role of the teacher is to explain alternative ways of saying things rather than to reject the alien terminology.

Strengths of Disadvantaged Youngsters

Unquestionably, our white, middle-class oriented educational milieu is going to have to reevaluate itself if it is going to live up to the most basic of educational tenants: respect the individual differences in values, ability, and environment of the child. Since the school cannot possibly mobilize society's resources for improving the environment of the child, it will have to reorder its priorities and mobilize the resources of the child himself. To overlook the strengths and resources of the child seems a natural thing to do for educators since it then becomes easy to blame someone else for your own shortcomings. Society is more easily blamed, as is the home, or the gang, or violence on television. But until schools look directly and objectively at the children themselves and use their strengths and resources, very little can be accomplished in learning or behavior modification.

Too often the school atmosphere is wrought with negativism, defeatism, or a self-defeating philosophy regarding these children. Educators are prone to oversimplify the situation, too quickly labeling a child and assigning him an inferior status, a second-class citizenship role in our society. We don't seek to build the talents and creativities in these youngsters. Such children do have resources; they have strengths; and they have vast potential for adjustment to almost any situation. Let us examine some of these strengths and resources.[24]

The poverty youngster must be independent, self-reliant, and creative early in life. Because responsibilities fall on him early, he must learn to do things for himself. Survival is the name of the game, and he has a keen sense of adjustment and readjustment to the realities of survival. The relevant is the meaningful, and the meaningful is the day-to-day necessities of survival. In learning to do things for himself, he does not

---

24. See Michael Obsatz, "Can We Break the Class Barrier?" *Changing Education* (May, 1973), p. 14.

remain dependent for long. Those who survive have to be creative; those who are not creative in their adjustments do not survive.

The poverty youngster matures earlier than other youngsters. Family responsibilities (caring for brothers or sisters) and social responsibilities (earning a living) thrust him into earlier adulthood and makes him responsible for tasks in life that are usually reserved in a middle-class culture for older persons.

The poverty youngster must be strong, self-defensive, and aggressive. He must defend himself, his possessions, and his freedom of action. This aggressiveness is the child's attempt to maintain a sense of order, a sense of direction, and a degree of control over his life. Survival in his family, in his neighborhood, at school, or on the streets depends upon his inventiveness and strength.

The poverty youngster is socially oriented and is spontaneous in his verbal interactions. He must learn to interact effectively with others and to contend with a variety of behaviors, personalities, and associations. Crowded conditions at home or at school do not afford him the luxury of leading a sheltered, quiet life; he cannot limit his associations because of intense peer pressures, and because of these pressures, he feels compelled to speak bluntly and frankly when he and the group deem it appropriate. This may mean he is easily distracted, but that is because much seems to be going on around him that he can relate to. He can laugh easily at himself and finds humor everywhere. The tragedy of poverty environments allows him to see the other side—consequently, he doesn't take life too seriously as others do. Sometimes teachers don't understand this when he doesn't take his work seriously, or doesn't seem afraid of a threatened punishment.

The poverty youngster usually is physically strong and basically well-coordinated. Physical ability and stamina are coterminous with survival. Because of this ability, he is more spontaneous, more responsive to physical stimuli, and more sensitive to spontaneous activities such as sports or music.

The poverty youngster has more adaptive mechanisms and is more in touch with reality than his middle-class counterpart. Unemployment, crime, disease, drugs, sex, and starvation are not isolated parts of his community. He is taught that to win out over his environment, he must fight and survive these elements. To do this, he must know himself, his limitations, his strengths, his weaknesses. Life is all around him; it is vital, real, pragmatic, sometimes overwhelming. This inner honesty and awareness, coupled with his ability to view life realistically, help him adapt to changes and to survive under the most trying of circumstances. The poverty youngster is an adult before his time.

Poverty youngsters have the kinds of strength and perserverance to survive the social disorganization of their community and the social disconnectionism and dysfunctionalism of the school. They survive in spite of the forces outside the school and in spite of the forces inside the school. If schools and teachers would capitalize on the strengths of these youngsters rather than on their weaknesses, there would be some startling results and changes in our schools and in society.

Conclusion: Raising Some Questions

Should the school be the instrument of cultural assimilation or the change agent for cultural pluralism? This question his dogged educators for the past twenty years, especially when it comes to educating the minority child, the disadvantaged child, the deprived child, or the poverty child. What should be the role of the school in our society, which has a dominant culture and many subcultures, and which also has a democratic ethic about equality? Are we truly a pluralistic society when we see Anglo-Americans dominating all walks of life, encapsulating ethnocentrism in its most extreme forms, yet professing the democratic ideal? Will we be truly pluralistic when we maximize cultural options; develop ethnic literacy regarding other cultures; revise and implement culture-free proficiency tests; respect cultural and linguistic differences; and provide equal social, educational, and economic options to multiethnic populations? Where do we begin, or perhaps, where do we end what we are doing—in our schools or in society? We return to the basic philosophical question raised before: Should our schools be the agents of social change, or should our schools simply react to social change? Think carefully before you answer for it will determine the course of public education for the next 100 years and will determine the validity of the American ideal of equal opportunity for all.

Exercises

I. Many writers have suggested that, in early childhood, the minority child becomes aware that differentness is a mark of inferior status in our society. It is claimed that this consciousness of inferiority becomes a part of the child's developing personality and affects his academic motivation, as well as his aspirational levels. On the other hand, some critics claim that this is an exaggeration of the facts, that not all minority children have damaged egos, and that schools can no longer point to a poor environment as the cause of inferior achievement.

> 1. To what extent are the critics right? Can the school motivate and instruct the disadvantaged child despite environmental handicaps and deficits?
>
> 2. What type of programs can a school promote in an effort to promote a more positive self-image?
>
> 3. A teacher must always start where a child is in terms of language, knowledge, understanding, and interest. How can this basic educational principle be applied in the teaching of the disadvantaged child?
>
> 4. Reissman has suggested that teachers of culturally disadvantaged children build upon the common strengths of children rather than expend energies in helping them overcome handicaps or defects in their backgrounds. Do you agree? Enumerate some of those common strengths that minority youngsters have and discuss school and classroom techniques for utilizing these strengths in the school.

II. Assume that you are part of a Board of Education that has complete control over a community school system. The Board is made up entirely of blacks, and blacks are 43 percent of the school population. Other groups break down as follows (in percentages): Chicanos, 26; Puerto Ricans, 15; American Indians, 1.5; Oriental Americans, .5; middle-class whites, 12; mentally and physically handicapped, 2.

> 1. Describe in detail the possible changes that you would make in your system in staffing, supervision, accountability, organi-

zation, expenditures, curriculum, and materials. Be specific. Be innovative.

2. Can you develop an adequate educational and school program without resolving problems of minority segregation (de jure and/or de facto)? What are the advantages and disadvantages of such segregation?

3. In terms of teacher and school accountability, what objectives would you insist upon from each teacher by the end of the year? What measurements would you use to test whether the school is doing a good job?

4. Would you use ability grouping and tracking in your system?

III. Our schools have literally become self-fulfilling prophecy mills for the culturally disadvantaged. In effect, many of the teachers in these schools have become the agents of that prophecy. Following is a questionnaire about attitudes regarding culturally different children. Take the questionnaire and analyze your responses. To what extent are you an agent of social change or a victim of the self-fulfilling prophecy syndrome? There are no exact, absolute answers; the importance of your answer is not in your agreement or disagreement, but in the changes you would make based on your reactions to the statements.

Directions: In the blank at the left of each statement, write A if you agree with the statement and D if you disagree. If you agree with one portion of a statement but disagree with another portion, rewrite the statement in a manner that suits you better.

_____ 1. The classroom should serve as a forum where all types of religious, ethnic, and social-class problems can be discussed freely. Restrictions should not be imposed on the kinds of topics brought up, even if the topics are controversial.

_____ 2. To ensure that children have equal opportunities for education, it is often necessary for a teacher to furnish special activities and extra aid for pupils from disadvantaged minority groups. In short, equality of opportunity is not provided simply by treating all pupils in precisely the same way.

_____ 3. In physical education activities like folk dancing or ballroom dancing, it is best to pair students of the same racial stock to dance with each other rather than mixing students of different racial backgrounds.

_____ 4. Children whose spoken or written English is poor because their parents use a foreign language at home should be given extra individualized help in English by the classroom teacher, either before or after school.

_____ 5. Since the real purpose of language is simply to communicate ideas rather than to meet the requirements of grammatical rules, children from families that use substandard English should not be pressed to change their normal household approach just so long as they get their ideas across.

_____ 6. To avoid embarrassing students of a minority group who may be in the class, the teacher should avoid discussing in class the problems in the community that involve that minority group.

_____ 7. Because children from a low socioeconomic class usually do not have the academic advantages at home (such as books and parental supervision of homework) enjoyed by upper-middle-class children, teachers should use more lenient standards in marking lower-class pupils.

_____ 8. To ensure that students become better acquainted with classmates from varied social class and ethnic backgrounds, the teacher should assign students to desks in a pattern that mixes social class and ethnic groups.

_____ 9. The school's proper role in the field of intergroup education is to provide an arena in which pupils of varied intergroup backgrounds can come to know each other. It is not the school's proper role to create action projects for altering the existing intergroup relations within the community.

_____ 10. The teacher—in attempting to adjust his methods to the subcultural habits of the various socioeconomic levels of his students—should adapt his classroom discipline to the kinds of discipline the particular pupil is accustomed to facing in his own social class level. Thus, the teacher warns upper-middle-class students verbally, because they are used to this form of discipline at home, but the teacher should more often use corporal punishment with lower-class pupils because they are more accustomed to responding only to rough treatment at home.

_____ 11. High school teachers of regular subjects, like mathematics or social studies, should not be expected to alter their teaching methods and materials to accommodate the English-language deficiencies of students from bilingual or foreign-language homes.

_____ 12. Equal opportunities for education means treating all pupils in an identical fashion, regardless of the variations among them in social class, ethnic, or religious background.

_____ 13. In districts where blacks have had equal educational opportunities, their tested intelligence is the same as that of other racial groups. Hence, teachers should expect black students in such districts to meet the same standards of academic performance as are applied to students from any other ethnic group.

_____ 14. Improving intergroup relations is the task of the social-studies teachers, not of teachers in such areas as English, mathematics, science, or foreign languages.

_____ 15. In order to realize the ideal of establishing a single, basic American culture shared by all citizens, the school should teach the same manners, morals, and language usage to children of all social strata. If necessary, teachers should strongly emphasize the need for children to adopt this common culture.

_____ 16. Because certain ethnic minorities had such meager opportunities for a good education in the past, it is desirable for teachers to give pupils from these minorities somewhat higher marks than usual in order to provide the extra encouragement they need to seek advanced schooling. These minorities need a helping hand in the form of a more-than-equal chance, which can help make up for the educational poverty they have suffered in the past.

_____ 17. If a student, either in the corridor or on the playground, calls a classmate a derogatory name that labels a group of which the classmate is a member (wop, nigger, spik, polack, greaser, hebe), the teacher who overheard this should not interfere, for it is none of his business.

_____ 18. Children from lower socioeconomic-level homes should be expected to attain the same standard of English-language usage as is required of children from middle- and upper-class homes.

_____ 19. The school's prime function is to further students' academic progress. This means that classroom activities should focus on subject-matter goals. The task of improving relationships among social classes and ethnic groups should be left to the home or to outside groups such as clubs and churches.

_____ 20. Students from Spanish-speaking homes should be given aid with English language in a special class that is substituted for one of the student's elective courses. The school should not expect the regular classroom teacher to devote extra time to aiding such students.

_____ 21. Because blacks on the average have lower intelligence than white children, it is appropriate for the teacher to design less difficult assignments for them than for the rest of the class.

_____ 22. In a classroom of mixed ethnic groups, a student who does not wish to accept membership on a committee with classmates of different ethnic stock should nevertheless be required to be on the committee.

IV. The following is a test given to graduate interns in a master's program for the training of inner-city teachers. Take the test on the basis of what you presently know about culturally disadvantaged youngsters.

True or false:

_____ 1. The phenomenon of the self-fulfilling prophecy tends to make children live up to what is expected of them.

_____ 2. Each subculture has unique characteristics that influence its style of learning, behavior, and language.

_____ 3. Cultural background becomes a handicap whenever an individual leaves his primary group.

_____ 4. A middle-class white is as disadvantaged in the black ghetto as a black is in the dominant white middle-class culture.

_____ 5. One's chances of being disadvantaged are greatly increased if one is born into a minority group.

_____ 6. The culturally disadvantaged child is handicapped in the typical school setting and usually achieves less.

_____ 7. The belief that culturally disadvantaged children cannot learn is probably attributable to the I.Q. test given.

_____ 8. When specifying culturally disadvantaged, the most potent force in determining that label is social class affiliation.

_____ 9. There is no significant or scientifically reliable data to support the thesis that minority children, especially blacks, are innately inferior in intelligence.

_____ 10. When attaching poverty as a characteristic of disadvantagement, it essentially refers to economic, moral, aspirational, educational, and social poverty.

_____ 11. Negative physical environment plays a strong role in the development of a negative self concept.

_____ 12. Aggressive behavior is learned.

_____ 13. Teachers have the tendency to teach disadvantaged youngsters that they are inferior.

_____ 14. Culturally disadvantaged youth tend to favor instant over deferred gratification and value physical rather than intellectual prowess.

_____ 15. It is conservatively estimated that the disadvantaged constitute anywhere from 40 percent to 60 percent of our urban school population today.

_____ 16. Of all the disadvantaged school groups, the most segregated, and thus the most deprived, are the American Indians.

_____ 17. Of all of the minority groups in our public schools, the Chicanos rank highest in school dropouts, with tenth grade being the level most commonly attained.

_____ 18. The poor white is as impoverished economically and educationally as the poor black or poor Chicano.

_____ 19. Academically speaking, educational retardation of the disadvantaged is normally characterized by a minimum of three years reading retardation at a given age-grade level.

_____ 20. Bilingualism and biculturalism are not solely the handicaps of the Chicano student but are also those of the black in our inner-city schools.

Schools and Community:
The Future of Urban Education

Chapter 9

When you have finished this chapter, you should be able to perform the following tasks.

1. Suggest how the school systems of the 1970s are better than the systems of generations ago.

2. Identify several critics of public education.

3. Define and describe who the members of the underclass are in urban society and how they became so.

4. Describe how the finances of an urban center determine its very existence and that of its schools.

5. Compare the general problems of the cities with those of the schools and tell how they are interrelated.

6. Suggest how higher service costs in the city often result in higher educational service costs as well.

7. Name several characteristics or symptoms of youth today that have implications for our schools.

8. List several of Heather's suggestions for educating youth in the future.

9. Define several suggestions for reform offered by the author and comment on their logic.

American cities were once represented as the most attractive, sophisticated, cultural, and technologically advanced center in which one could live, work, and play. Immigrants streamed into these melting pots looking for a better life; farmers and laborers moved to the cities in hopes of getting their share of the good life; minorities left their small-town existences and prejudice for what they hoped would be a new life with greater possibilities of the American dream of equal opportunity. People came from all parts of the country and all parts of the world to our cities in hopes of attaining a better life, a better job, and a better education. The American metropolis once represented the dream of a lifetime: to reach the city was to reach for the pot of gold at the end of the rainbow.

It is neither insignificant nor inconsequential that these dreams and expectations were seldom realized. Urban communities grew rapidly until the beginning of the twentieth century when we were indeed an urban nation. Startling, by contrast, were the realities of urban life—decaying, ramshackled, and overcrowded living conditions; declining social and welfare services; environmental stagnation; overcrowded and overburdened public transportation facilities; a sweeping increase in crime; a hardening of class lines reflected in segregated housing patterns; and a public school system that was unable to adjust to the realities of swift social change.

The urban crisis has now been with us for at least a century or more. The cities of the 1850s and 1870s suffered from the conditions of poverty, slums, pollution, noise, deteriorating buildings, and declining social services. By the late 1860s the United States had economically advanced to the point where urban agglomerations could and did support the majority of people in America. American industrialization fueled further economic development, which fueled further urbanization. Society, as is often the case, was overwhelmed by the changes; cities became overwhelmed by the rapid industrialization and the tremendous immigration of human bodies into its boundaries. Schools, often the last to react to social change, fell further behind.[1]

As more generations grew up in the cities, escape to the suburbs became the answer for many who believed that the cities would inevitably get worse. The late 1950s and early 1960s saw an explosion in the suburban

---

1. For an excellent treatment of the historical origins of the urban crisis, see James F. Richardson, "The Historical Roots of Our Urban Crisis," *Current History* (November, 1970).

population. Escape became the natural predilection for a large body of middle-class citizens who could no longer contend with the urban problems.

But escape to the suburb was as artificial as the original migration to the city. By 1980, 90 percent of all Americans will be urban dwellers. Cities will still grow, although certainly not at the rate they once did during the 1940s and 1950s; suburbs will continue to grow as well, probably faster than ever before, although we are beginning to see a return of the middle class to the cities. Inescapably, however, will be the reality of the trend toward increasing urbanization of the suburbs, bringing with it the problems of the cities. And their noise, air pollution, crime, transportation, taxes, and high population density will also extend their claims upon the suburbs as well.

So far, city governments have been incapable of meeting these ever increasing demands put upon them by the advancing twenty-first century and its baggage—a more complicated kind of inflation, the energy crisis, and environmental and consumer problems. The urban schools have also failed to meet these demands, and the public school system is presently going through the ultimate test of its survival: Will it have two systems, one for the haves, who will mostly live in the suburbs, and another for the have-nots, most of whom will live in the cities? As suggested previously, the urban problems will ultimately become the suburban problems as well, and until urban school systems recognize this, little hope exists for a renaissance in public education. The problems of the schools of the have-nots are as much the problems of the schools of the haves. They are all interwoven, and no one can escape reality by simply moving from one neighborhood to another. The challenge of urban education systems is to provide appropriate learning experiences for the various life-styles of their vast number of students. It is within this context that urban education within the cities and suburbs must be reconceived, integrated, revitalized—and adequately financed.

Education is the largest single industry in the U.S. in terms of people involved and monies spent. Since 1971, education spending has surpassed defense spending. In 1975, 120 billion was spent for education, and 87 billion was spent on defense. Millions of Americans are employed in one way or another in the field of education. Education accounts for approximately 8 percent of the gross national product. There are 17,500 public school systems and 15,000 private school systems throughout the U.S.[2] Charts 9–1 and 9–2 respectively show the population changes for the years 1790–1975 and the participation of persons in public schools for the years 1870–1972.

Chart 9–1. Estimated Population of the United States: 1790 to 1975 (In thousands)

Year[1]	Total popu- lation[2]	Year	Total popu- lation	Year	Total popu- lation	Year	Total popu- lation
1790	3,929	1840	17,120	1890	63,056	1940	132,054
1795	4,607	1845	20,182	1895	69,580	1945	139,767
1800	5,297	1850	23,261	1900	76,094	1950	151,135
1805	6,258	1855	27,386	1905	83,820	1955	164,588
1810	7,224	1860	31,513	1910	92,407	1960	179,386
1815	8,419	1865	35,701	1915	100,549	1965	193,223
1820	9,618	1870	39,905	1920	106,466	1970	203,849
1825	11,252	1875	45,073	1925	115,832	1975	213,641
1830	12,901	1880	50,262	1930	123,188		
1835	15,003	1885	56,658	1935	127,362		

1. Estimates as of July 1.
2. Includes Armed Forces overseas.
Sources: U.S. Department of Commerce, Bureau of the Census, *Historical Statistics of the United States: Colonial Times to 1957; Projections of the Population of the United States: 1975 to 2050,* Series P-25, No. 601.

The school systems of the 1970s are better than the systems of the 1930s or 1940s: The illiteracy rate has been cut in half; students are spending more time in school than ever before; large numbers are going on to higher education and graduate work; teachers are more adequately and professionally trained; accrediting agencies, as well as state agencies, are demanding more accountability; desegregation has become a reality that systems can no longer turn their backs on; and schools are offering more vocational and adult education. Nearly one out of every three Americans is engaged in some form of schooling and education.

Our schools have moved from the more traditional modes of expectation to more relevant, current concerns. Not only are our schools expected to

---

2. Allan Ornstein, *Teaching in a New Era* (Champaign, Illinois: Stripes Publishing Co., 1976), pp. 1–5; *The Condition of Education,* National Center for Education Statistics (Washington, D.C., 1976), pp. 2–3.

Chart 9-2. Participation in Public Elementary and Secondary Schools: Selected Years, 1870 to 1972

	School year ending											
	1870	1880	1890	1900	1910	1920	1930	1940	1950	1960	1970	1972
Average length of school term (days)	132.2	130.3	134.7	144.3	157.5	161.9	172.7	175.0	177.9	178.0	178.9	179.3
Percent of population 5–17 years enrolled	57.0	65.5	68.6	71.9	74.2	78.3	81.7	84.4	83.2	82.2	86.9	88.1
Percent of enrolled pupils attending daily	59.3	62.3	64.1	68.6	72.1	74.8	82.8	86.7	88.7	90.0	90.4	90.2
Average attendance as percent of enrollment	33.8	40.8	44.0	49.3	53.5	58.6	67.7	73.2	73.8	74.0	78.6	79.5

Source: U.S. Department of Health, Education, and Welfare, National Center for Education Statistics, *Statistics of State School Systems, 1971–72.*

perform all the traditional tasks of education, but they are asked now to prepare the young to solve the problems of local, national, and international affairs and to live in an uncertain, rapidly changing society. To a large extent, schools today reflect the demands and expectations of the communities they serve. We live in a pluralistic and diverse society, and the clash between provincial expectations of some communities with that of the broader pluralistic communities of others has often brought contradictory expectations and demands. Public education has increasingly accepted responsibility to soothe those problems and has sometimes made promises greater than it could fulfill. This responsibility also belongs to society itself, which has required schools to do far more than they can realistically, given the limited resources allocated to them. Society has come to expect from schools solutions to social problems that society itself has been unable to comprehend, let alone solve. The result has been chaos in the schools, as well as in society, and a nagging sense that the schools have failed us.

From this gloomy picture have come the critics of our public schools with their messages of doom. The critics have charged the schools with every conceivable crime. Alvin Toffler, Marshall McLuhan, and Everett Reimer have warned that schools are irrelevant and are not keeping pace with cultural, social, and media changes. Reimer contends, "The contradictions of such a world are becoming apparent. They are best illustrated in the school and best corrected by freeing education from the school so that people may learn the truth about the society in which they live."[3]

James Herndon, Jonathan Kozol, Herbert Kohl, Kenneth Clark, and Patricia Sexton have cautioned us that public schools are institutions fostering an inequality and a racism that are destructive to minority youngsters and that, regardless of the tremendous strides made by the courts over the last several years, minority youngsters are falling further and further behind. Whether the issue be sexism, black vs. white, desegregation, or bilingual education, minorities continue to be minorities, and they become increasingly more visible.

Charles Silberman, Paul Goodman, Edgar Friedenberg, Jules Henry, and Stanley Charnovsky have told us that our schools are repressive

---

3. Everett Reimer, *School Is Dead* (New York: Doubleday and Co., 1972), Foreword, p. 11.

institutions, noncreative and alienating, that they continue to create impotent members for the powerless groups of society. These critics tell us that the worst part of schooling is the need and desire for mass conformity, and that this need and desire fosters hate, alienation, rivalry, competition, and bigotry within our system.

Neil Postman, Elizabeth Eddy, John Holt, and William Glasser tell us that schools are dull, boring, meaningless, routine-oriented, nongoal directed, and deliberately crush students' creativity and aspirations. Schools facilitate students' learning not to learn. Christopher Jencks even questions the value of schooling in terms of getting and keeping a job and has raised serious questions about what it is that schools are actually doing. Ivan Illich, like Everett Reimer, calls for the total dismantling of the schools. Robert Coles, Nat Hentoff, James Koerner, and Peter Schrag are other educational critics with gospels that are antiteacher, antischool, antiestablishment, and anticompulsory education.[4] Yet the school remains the singularly most pervasive element in a child's life. If the urban school is, as Ray Rist calls it, "a factory for failure," then there is a policy implication of some magnitude that future educators had better analyze and change.[5]

To what extent are the critics in tune with the public and the mood of the public? Are the critics writing only for the benefit of their educational peers, or do they truly sense the concerns and moods of the public at large? From the aforementioned list of critics, note the following chart on what the public perceives to be the main problems [see Chart 9–3]. Perhaps this is why urban schools have not basically changed over the years: the perceived problems of the educational critics and that of the public are good examples of what sociologists label "social distance" in communication.

---

4. See the following: Paul Goodman, *Growing Up Absurd* (New York: Random House, 1960) and *Compulsory Miseducation* (New York: Horizon Press, 1964); John Holt, *How Children Fail* (New York: Pitman, 1964), *The Underachieving School* (New York: Pitman, 1969), *Escape From Childhood* (New York: Dutton, 1974), *What Do I Do on Monday?* (New York: Dutton, 1974); Jonathan Kozol, *Death at An Early Age* (Boston: Houghton Mifflin, 1967); James Herndon, *The Way It Spozed to Be* (New York: Simon and Schuster, 1968); Ivan Illich, *DeSchooling Society* (New York: Harper and Row, 1971), *After DeSchooling, What?* (New York: Harper and Row, 1974). Charles Silberman, *Crisis in the Classroom* (New York: Random House, 1971).

5. See Ray C. Rist, *The Urban School: A Factory for Failure* (Cambridge: MIT Press, 1973).

Chart 9–3. The Major Problems of Public Schools

From national samples asked,
"What do you think are the biggest problems with which
the public schools in this community must deal?"

The percentages of respondents citing problems were:

1970	1972	1974	1975
Discipline 18%	Discipline 23%	Discipline 23%	Discipline 23%
Integration/ segregation 17%	Integration/ segregation 18%	Integration/ segregation 16%	Integration/ segregation 15%
Finances 17%	Finances 19%	Financial support 13%	Financial support 14%
Teachers 12%	Teachers 14%	Use of drugs 13%	Teachers 11%
Facilities 11%	Large school/ large classes 10%	Difficulty of getting "good" teachers 11%	Size of school/ classes 10%
Dope/drugs 11%	Parents' lack of interest 6%	Size of school/ classes 6%	Use of drugs 9%

Source: National Center for Education Statistics, The Conditions of Education (Washington, D.C.: U.S. Government Printing Office, 1976), p. 52.

The Present and Future Condition of Urban America

American cities are changing from centers of educational and creative life to catch-areas for the urban poor, the elderly, the unemployed, and the minority group member. This has become a radical departure in the function of central cities. In addition, race and class have become institutionalized attitudes that have shaped our present cities. They have determined housing patterns and social mobility, schooling and school districts, leisure and recreational activities, and financial income for most large urban communities.

As a larger disadvantaged population emerges in our central cities, revenue capacity diminishes and service costs increase. The white middle-class has left while the black middle-class has moved into select housing areas. The emerging occupants of the central cities seem to be the undereducated, the unemployed, the unemployable, the poor, the elderly, the handicapped, the alienated and frustrated, the lower-class, and the minority group member. Our present society has created this class, taken advantage of it, and is now trying to deny it equal opportunities and is running away from it to the outer confines of the central city. Society has created what Mel Ravitz has called "the underclass."[6]

The underclass is a resident of the central city, lured there by promises of gain and advantage that were once part of the American dream. If society does nothing to resocialize this emerging population, this population will spread, creating problems throughout the community. The underclass threatens the established classes unless the big cities are able to tackle their internal problems and resocialize the residents of the central city. These problems persist regardless of minority leadership that we see in cities such as Detroit, Gary, Newark, and Los Angeles that have black mayors. Cities and suburbs will have to become more nearly like each other in socioeconomic composition, opportunities, and educational programs if urban community life is to survive.

There is no doubt that urban big cities lack the resources to restore themselves. A report prepared by David T. Stanley of the Brookings Institute and issued by the National League of Cities noted that eight American cities were financially troubled because of poor municipal leadership, short-term debts, and inadequate tax support. The troubled cities are New York, Buffalo, Detroit, Newark, St. Louis, Boston, Cleveland, and Philadelphia. Stanley said, "Their economies are going nowhere and their people are going elsewhere."

The Stanley report said that money problems could impair the cities' "borrowing ability, require reduction of municipal services, pose a threat to public health and safety and thus diminish the quality and satisfaction of urban life. . . . City trouble has a widespread impact. The city government tries to solve its budget-balancing problems by raising taxes, imposing fees, reducing its work force, and cutting down on purchases and construction. This is bad for the local economy."

Possible solutions, Stanley said, include emergency cash grants to cities by legislatures, state authorization of new taxes or special bond issues, and stiffening of state control over city financial decisions. He said the federal government could be asked for operating cash, guaranteed loans,

---

6. Principal ideas taken from the keynote address of Dr. Mel Ravitz, "The Cities, A National Perspective: Past, Present, and Future," November 22, 1976, The Second Annual Conference on Urban Education, Milwaukee, Wisconsin.

or a one-time cash grant, although he considered the cash grant "a bail-out idea" that would be "hard to justify and hard to enact."

The report said New York City was unable to borrow needed cash and might be unable to balance its budget. It noted that Buffalo had a high short-term debt and Newark was troubled by residents angered at the level of city services. St. Louis' economic base was considered shaky, and there were signs that its municipal payroll would be increased. He said Boston faced high payrolls, pension liabilities, and poor morale of residents. He said Detroit needed more state aid; Cleveland suffered from inept fiscal management; and Philadelphia faced money troubles due to past mistakes within its administration.[7]

When one thinks of finances, one often forgets about the size of some urban public school systems. In actuality, public school enrollments in the largest U.S. cities exceed enrollments in many states. For example, only 14 states have a larger enrollment than New York City schools, and Los Angeles city schools have a larger enrollment than that of 23 states.

It is estimated that, by the year 1980, an additional 24 billion dollars will be required annually to sustain the 1964–74 rate of improvement in urban public schools. According to some experts, sustaining this rate would require the addition of at least another 1 percent added to the approximately 8 percent of GNP already earmarked for education. Robert McBride has given us some useful and valuable figures to look at regarding this dilemma (see Chart 9–4).

Toledo, as another troubled urban center, closed its schools in early December, 1976, sending 56,000 pupils home on an early vacation because of the lack of money. Voters had refused for the third time to increase taxes to pay for the school system's bills, and this refusal added 13 school days to the regular winter holiday. Dr. Robert Jackson, School Board President, noted that this was "just a harbinger of things to come." School administrators in Toledo, not unlike other districts in Ohio and Oregon, said that closing the schools in 1976 would mean more problems in 1977 if additional money is not found. Toledo schools estimated a deficit of $10 million for 1978.[8]

---

7. *Los Angeles Times,* December 3, 1976; see "Report of the National League of Cities" (Washington, D.C.: HEW, 1976).

8. *Los Angeles Times,* December 4, 1976.

Chart 9–4. Enrollment and Cost Forecast—Minimal Expenditures Model

	1976–77	1977–78	1978–79	1979–80	1980–81
K–12 enrollment in millions	44.1	43.4	42.4	41.5	41.0
Expenditures per student ADA*	1,700	1,790	1,900	2,030	2,140
Total expenditures in billions*	72	75	78	81	85
Increase vs. 1974–75 in billions	8	11.5	14.5	17.5	21.5

* Current dollars

Cost Forecast—Continuing 1964–74 Trends

	1976–77	1977–78	1978–79	1979–80	1980–81
Expenditures per student ADA	1,970	2,160	2,380	2,660	2,860
Total expenditures in billions	80.5	87	94	103.5	109.5
Increase vs. 1974–75 in billions	16.5	23.5	30	39.5	46

Source: Robert McBride, "Where Will the Money Come From? Financing Education Through 1980–81," *Phi Delta Kappan* (November, 1976), pp. 248–53.

Higher education, as well as other levels of schooling, has been affected by financial problems. New York City is a classic example. If New York had declared bankruptcy, it was estimated that nearly 15,000 public school teachers would have lost their jobs. New York did not declare bankruptcy, but it was forced to tighten its belt regarding city services. City University of New York was one of the hardest hit institutions. A university system with a long-standing open-door policy and a free tuition policy had to impose tuition and other economic moves. Since the budget crisis began in late 1975, CUNY lost 13,000 employees. Amid the latest financial pinch and the loss of free tuition, 9,000 full- and part-time faculty, administrators, and other staff members have been fired—many with only a 30-day notice of termination. This is the largest faculty dismissal in U.S. academic history.[9] As is so often the case in this age of teacher surplus, the schools have become the safeguard for the older, tenured teachers at the expense of the younger, nontenured ones. Its future effect on education could be devastating.

9. *Los Angeles Times,* December 20, 1976.

Obviously, schools and their budgets are affected by a myriad of problems peculiar to the cities, as well as by problems inherent in the educational establishment. The general problems of the cities affect the general problems of the schools. Briefly, they are:

1. Cities face financial deterioration as migrations take place. These patterns include the exiting of business and professional populations.

2. Filling this gap are economically disadvantaged populations that pay less taxes and require costlier services than do suburban persons. Among the services requiring more funding is public education.

3. The loss of business, high unemployment, lower land values, and tax revenues are factors that make the cities' budgets too small to deal with the needs of their new inhabitants.

4. Cities simply cannot afford as much money per pupil for education as can suburban communities. Because problems that accompany cities' density and deterioration demand expensive solutions in other areas than education alone, schools automatically receive a smaller share in proportion to the total city budget than do suburban schools.

Few would dispute that education in the cities costs more than education in the suburbs. The poor, the minority, the handicapped, the "underclass" need greater priorities for special educational attention. Higher service costs in the city often result in higher costs of educational personnel, maintenance, construction, and services. Several areas alone illustrate this inequity.[10]

Maintenance costs more. Violence, disruption, and vandalism in urban city schools was more than $600 million in 1975 alone. The 1974 figures were as follows: $102 million to repair vandalism, $243 million to recover burglary losses, $109 million in arson costs, and $140 million for such things as locker thefts and student extortion. Cities such as Los Angeles

---

10. See the following: "Washington Report," *Phi Delta Kappan,* June, 1976, pp. 707–708; *Los Angeles Times,* July 14, 1976; National Education Association, *Education Neglect* (Washington, D.C., 1975); Birch Bayh, "An Overview of Violence and Vandalism in Our Schools," in Leonard Golubchick and Berry Persky, *Urban, Social, and Educational Issues* (Dubuque, Iowa: Kendall Hunt, 1976), pp. 17–22.

and Chicago are forced yearly to spend some $7–10 million apiece as a result of vandalism.

Personnel needs are greater. Despite declining enrollments for the past four years, the number of teachers employed by urban school districts continues to rise. The NEA tells us that in the 1975–76 school year, the number of teachers totaled 2.46 million, .5 percent more than the year before. The average salary for classroom teachers was $12,624, which was 7.4 percent more than the preceding year. Alaska had the highest average salary at $19,880, and New York was second at $15,950. Mississippi and South Dakota bottomed out the list with average incomes of $9,314. As the teacher surplus grows, urban school faculties will become increasingly more tenured, and fewer and fewer places for new, nontenured teachers will be available. Salary commitments for tenured personnel will become large, placing still another burden on city budgets.

The need for services will grow. Increasing demands for health and social services are placed on urban school systems. With violence and drug problems rampant in some urban districts, social services are vitally needed. Financial difficulties experienced by private and parochial schools have created additional problems for large public urban schools. As private schools raise tuition or run into financial difficulties, students from these schools enroll in public schools. Yet public school budgets and facilities do not increase proportionately. Add to the service list the ever increasing demands upon urban centers for better reading remedial programs and the whole new broader range of mandated programs in multicultural and bilingual programs for urban youngsters, and you have increased services and declining revenues at an alarming pace.

Desegregation is a cost problem. Since most large urban central cities have large minority populations, the question of desegregation becomes a fundamental concern, especially since its cost is astronomical. Busing alone can increase the costs by millions of dollars for just one school system. Add to that the costs of inservice training, multicultural materials, and the added security precautions facing systems going through the desegregation cycle, and you have costs that any large urban system is simply unable to handle.

State-aid formulas do not offset the disparities between central city and suburban city educational costs. Unfair burdens and restrictions are often placed on the cities since states still operate on the assumption that cities are rich and rural areas are poor. Property tax as a basis for support, the organization of school districts, tax and debt limits, responsibility for retirement funds, and statutory limits on bond issues often favor suburban and rural areas. In addition, federal aid has not really assisted urban schools to any large degree. Aid levels are low in proportion to the total cost of education and the amount of per pupil expenditures. The uncertainty of the availability of funds has minimized future planning, and the administrative procedures attached to such funds have diluted the effects of any such aid. Wealthy districts receive aid as do poor districts, and the funds for many federal programs are not distributed to urban areas in shares proportionate to the school population. Most important, the federal government, as well as many state governments, has no systematic way of measuring its own overall resource allocation priorities and their effects in education. Denver School Superintendent Louis Kishkunas has called this "a national disgrace." According to one educational association, urban school financing is characterized by "high educational overburden, high municipal overburden, high concentration of disadvantaged, limited local resources, aging physical plants, rapid population shifts, and a diminishing tax base."[11]

Frankly, big cities lack the resources to restore themselves; a city administration can do only minor things to restore itself. Cities require major changes initiated by the federal government, and this is unlikely. Cities are symbols of national problems, a reflection of major social problems, and a unity between the city and the federal government is vitally needed. We have long known about race and class problems in our society and have done nothing about them; now we find that something is wrong with our economic system as well. Inflation, an energy crisis, high unemployment, and starvation thrives in a country that is one of the richest and more proficient in the world. Outdated remedies such as tax rebates, tax reform, price controls, and work programs do not seem to work any more. Americans are unable to make their economy run well during peacetime, and they cannot have a revitalized urban school system until they get a revitalized national economy. Society must deal with the underclasses of its central cities; they must be integrated and resocialized into the total society. Decaying inner cities will not go

---

11. *Education U.S.A.* (Washington, D.C., National School Public Relations Association), November 29, 1976, pp. 97–104.

away, but will fester like a cancer, growing and eventually engulfing the suburbs. Americans must be made to realize that there is no escape from the central city—the central city is everywhere, and the problems must be dealt with on a massive scale or the blight will touch us all. John Adams said, "The whole people must take upon themselves the education of the whole people, and must be willing to bear the expense of it."

Provisions for Educating Changing Youth

Education is still seen as an instrumental activity and valued accordingly by society. This does not mean that education is viewed the same way as it was 30 years ago. Today, society is more expressive, more alert to the relevancies of modern life. These changes have come about as a result of the social, economic, political, and intellectual changes of the last ten years. Vietnam, Watergate, inflation, the energy crisis, the environment—all have taken their toll upon American youth. Robert Havighurst has drawn a sharp contrast between what he calls emerging values and receding values. Among receding values are the values of individual saving and thrift, work as a major source of self-respect, nationalistic attitudes and policies of military power, and religious separation and sectarian loyalty. In contrast, emerging values are experience for the sake of experience, "doing your thing," esthetic activity, tolerance of complexity and ambiguity, domestic justice and opportunity for the disadvantaged, and service to society.[12]

Fred Wilhelms finds other significant symptoms among the youth of today.[13] Among them are:

1. Revulsion against the subhuman repetitiousness of factory labor.

2. Determination to stay out of the rat race of single-minded careerism.

3. Widespread anomie; feelings of being lost in a vast, impersonal machine hostile to personal identity.

---

12. Robert Havighurst, "The Future of Education: Image and Reality," in *The Future of Education, 1975–2000,* Theodore Hipple, ed. (Pacific Palisades, Calif.: Goodyear Publishing Co., 1974), p. 90. Reprinted by permission.
13. Fred Wilhelms, "Tomorrow's Assignment," p. 211, *The Future of Education, 1975–2000.*

4. Revulsion against materialism; austerity with regard to material possessions, especially status-related ones.

5. Criticism of virtually all institutions, even of institutionalism itself.

6. Rejection of future orientation in favor of living for the present.

7. Rage against all forms of injustice and oppression, including racism and also against class discrimination and the cruelties of war.

8. Emphasis on personal authenticity, coupled with a struggle to break through to a new openness of communication.

9. Enormous dedication to preserving and restoring the environment.

10. Search for a new politics, a determination to take charge and build a new society in which persons will be of equal importance.

11. New emphasis on the affective side of life, with tendencies to reject the more coolly cognitive.

12. Hunger for love, with visions of an all-loving world.

13. Search among religions and philosophies for a dimly envisioned better way of life, exemplified by a life of desperate groping for answers, accompanied by much faddistic scurrying from one solution to another.

As we look at these emerging values, the fact that American society has moved from an economy of scarcity to one of abundance and back again to one of scarcity is of particular interest. Although the productivity of the American economy is high and is even held down by government in some quarters to avoid overproduction, we have one of the higher rates of unemployment and inflation since the Great Depression. We have created through our schools an educated work force for nonexisting jobs. We continue to train thousands of teachers, for example, for nonexistent jobs.

Traditional education, on the other hand, is being questioned by the very youth we are educating. They are asking such valid questions as, Why should I go to school? Why should I train to be someone I can't become because of the needs of the market? Can you guarantee me a job? Schools are unable to provide viable and relevant alternatives to traditional schooling.

The schools of the future are going to have to take into account the realities of the 1970s. Schools are going to have to become learning laboratories no longer confined to the classroom. The community will be the source of immediate reward for educational activity. Schools will have to provide services such as community planning, information, and action programs; programs for public health and social service needs; a range of cultural, communication, and recreational services; a range of athletic services; a range of services related to city agencies of government, welfare, police, fire, sanitation, and urban planning; and services for career planning and vocational guidance and retraining programs. The school must, of necessity, become closely integrated with the total community and not, as it has been traditionally, be isolated from the relevancies of life in the community. A school system of this nature has the potential for becoming one of the most potent socioeconomic-political instruments for dealing with urban problems and day-to-day living.

This will not happen overnight, but a start must be made to change our schools because our students have changed, our cities have changed, and the American dream, as we once knew and understood it, has changed. Glen Heathers in his *Research for Better Schools* suggested certain provisions needed in education for the future.[14]

Following are ten of Heathers' provisions:

> 1. Teach all students competencies in problem solving in the various curriculum areas. Skills should be taught in identifying and analyzing problems, then in devising and testing solutions, using both academic and real-life situations.
>
> 2. Offer all students career education involving study of various occupations that includes work sampling in real or simulated situations. Regular individual career counseling should be offered as a basis for planning the student's program of studies.

---

14. Glen Heathers, "Education to Meet the Psychological Requirements for Living in the Future," in Christopher Lucas, *Challenge and Choice in Contemporary Education* (New York: MacMillan, 1976), pp. 368–370.

3. Offer all students systematic citizenship education, including the analysis of issues and societal problems in terms of values involved and consequences of alternative decisions. Students should participate in political processes through student government and through taking part in real or simulated elections and government activities.

4. Teach students competencies in interpersonal relations, group participation, and intergroup relations. This instruction should give particular attention to studying and interacting with individuals and multicultural groups differing in race, national origin, sex, age, and other characteristics.

5. Involve all students in community study and participation in community activities. This school-in-community approach should provide for a regular interaction of the school with both formal and informal community agencies and organizations.

6. Teach all students to understand and appreciate people and cultures elsewhere in the world, with emphasis on industrially less-developed countries in Africa, the Middle East, the Orient, and South America. Stress should be placed on teaching how individuals grow from infancy to adulthood in the different societies, using data obtained by cultural anthropologists.

7. Offer all students education directed toward self-knowledge, a positive self-concept, an integrated set of values, and qualities of initiative and independence enabling them to accept challenges and take needed risks.

8. Teach all students to develop leisure-time interests and skills including physical, intellectual, and esthetic expression and [give] attention to both social activities and private experiences.

9. Individualize or personalize each student's educational program in terms of courses of study, learning goals, learning methods, and rate of advancement. Instruction should stress in full development of the student as a unique individual.

10. The schools should treat each student as a person of worth and dignity, recognizing that, at any age, the student is the client whose interests the school's staff serves. Students should participate in decision making about the school program as fully as their maturity allows.

The author has tried to show that the only true reality of effective urban education is an effective urban teacher. Even after considering Fred Wilhelm's youth characteristics and Glen Heathers' provisions for schools of the future, one is still left with the key essential for the success or failure of urban education. That essential is the effective teaching style of the urban teaching specialist. It is the author's firm belief that there are certain skills that *all* urban teachers must develop for success in teaching urban youngsters.[15] Among these are the following groups of teaching coping skills:

A. Pre-Instructional Skills

The ability to understand and use developmental and remedial reading procedures.

The ability to reconstruct syllabi, textbooks, and reading materials in terms of the backgrounds of students.

The ability to construct and use concrete materials for classroom work.

B. Managerial Skills

The ability to organize and make routine, if necessary, classroom procedures.

The ability to work effectively with small groups within the classroom and to know when to use such procedures.

The ability to handle aggression and violence.

The ability to use individual and group procedures in gaining classroom discipline.

C. Cultural and Psychological Skills

The ability to adjust new entrants to the classroom situation quickly.

The ability to know when a child should be referred and to whom.

A knowledge of the language patterns in an area and the ability to work with them.

A knowledge of the neighborhood and families to see the effect this has upon classroom work and procedures.

---

15. Partly taken from Vernon Haubrich, "The Culturally Disadvantaged and Teacher Education," *Reading Teacher* (March, 1965), pp. 499-505. Groupings and modifications are those of the author.

The ability to translate the academic knowledge of children from different cultural backgrounds into specific procedures for classroom use.

D. Instructional Skills

The ability to organize self-contained classrooms and to shift to individualized study centers and the open classroom.

The use of varied and multicultural materials at all levels of ability.

The ability to individualize one's instruction and to engage in day-to-day pupil-teacher planning.

The ability to use and disregard, if necessary, standardized evaluation instruments.

The ability to use and prepare urban-oriented materials so as to clearly picture, through vocabulary and stories, experiences to which all types of urban youngsters can relate.

E. Professional Skills

To engage in preservice and inservice professional training when dealing with new materials and innovations.

The ability to use special personnel such as paraprofessionals, student teachers, parent aides, and community volunteers.

To continue one's training and learning about the urban child and the urban milieu.

The urban teacher must cope with a battery of related problems. Coping with such varied problems as negative attitudes, discipline problems, motivation, parental pressure, aggressiveness, inattentiveness and boredom, emotionality, instability, hyperactivity, attendance and truancy problems, lack of support at home or school, individualized instruction, building self-concept, understanding culturally and lingually different youngsters, and intergroup relations in a desegregated setting are concerns that will determine the success or failure of urban teachers. This success or failure will ultimately determine the success or failure of urban education for the next generation.

Urban schools have been the victims of certain educational myths explored in this book. These myths have helped to perpetuate the school's legitimacy as an educational agency. In review, they are

(1) that public schools exist basically to give all citizens an equal educational opportunity to get ahead in the world and a chance to be socially mobile, (2) that education is a process and a system that seeks to reach each child and to help each child identify his or her own inner potential and to realize it, (3) that education prepares all its citizens for a future and significant role in society and that those with initiative, independence, and the ability to solve problems will be successful in later life, and (4) that the function of the public schools in respect to the poor and the minorities is to bring them into the mainstream of American economic and social life.

If these ideals were true, then the grim, joyless, irrelevant, and often antagonistic atmosphere of the classrooms would instead be one of happiness and reward such as Robert Owen fostered in New Lanark and New Harmony[16] during the 19th century.

Some Suggestions for Basic Reform
One of the worst problems facing urban education today is the training of urban teachers. Teacher training institutions are doing a miserable job; their main goal seems to be to preserve the status quo. Much has been written of the weaknesses of schools of education. Here are some specific proposals for reform that educators should carefully consider:

1. Teacher training institutions should require all candidates for a teaching credential to have inner-city teaching experience.

2. All teacher training institutions should have carefully prepared competency-based training programs.

3. All college-level educators should be required to return every four or five years to the battlefield (the urban classroom) for at least a year to update their knowledge of the teaching world. This is especially important for tenured professors of education who have not been in the classroom in years.

4. All candidates for a teaching credential, upon completion of student teaching, should be required to engage in a full year of substitute teaching before entering the classroom as a full-time teacher.

---

16. For a treatment of Owenism and his system of successful education, see Alfred Lightfoot, *Robert Owen: Schools and Society for a New Age* (Washington, D.C.: University Press of America, 1976).

5. Teacher training institutions should prepare teachers for particular and specialized areas, such as junior high school or the lower elementary grades, remedial teaching, bilingual teaching, substitute teaching, private school teaching, or career education.

6. Schools of education should make their programs as realistic as they possibly can. Grade-point averages for acceptance to schools of education should be tightened; with the current surplus, educators have an obligation to accept only the best candidates.

The above list is, of course, controversial, and many persons will choose to disagree with it.

On a state and national level, several proposals can be made to improve the school systems. They are as follows:

1. Eliminate standardized testing and the abuse of the intelligence quotient as a standardizer. Or failing this, admit the cultural bias of such tests and construct other appropriate culturally biased tests for subgroups of youngsters. Schools have sanctified the I.Q. test, and this, in turn, has propagated controversy over whether or not minority groups are innately inferior to their white counterparts in intelligence. Such debate detracts from the real business of the schools: learning.

2. Eliminate the property tax as a basis for support and apportionment of monies for public education. The sweeping inequities between rich and poor neighborhoods, based on the tax base, are tragic and unconscionable.

3. Eliminate tenure for teachers and eliminate the life credential. No teacher should be automatically guaranteed a job or credentials for life, especially those who have done little to update and maintain their skills. Instead, substitute a system of merit evaluations, whereby teachers evaluate teachers, administrators evaluate teachers, and teachers evaluate administrators. An era of teacher surplus is an ideal time to rid ourselves of dead weight.

4. Integrate the schools and do so on the premise that desegregation is a cross-district proposition and not solely confined to the inner city.

5. Use teacher surplus to reduce class sizes and offer more elective offerings, guidance services, and remedial facilities. Enough of this nonsense that there is not enough money. Education is too important to our future life-styles to skimp on it.

6. Establish evening programs of continuing education at schools for dropouts, parents, remedial cases, or just for recreational pursuits. It is a travesty to permit school buildings to sit idle half a year while society has such demanding educational needs.

7. Make significant curriculum changes within schools to incorporate such diverse proposals as individualized instruction, year-round schools, accelerated graduation, modular scheduling, smaller classes and professional aids, use of media centers and open campuses, more early childhood education programs, greater emphasis on bilingual and bicultural programs, more electives and a breakdown of traditional course groupings, and a reevaluation of graduation requirements to establish minimum criteria for each grade division (primary, elementary, middle, and secondary) and a requirement to stick to them as necessary prerequisites for attainment of graduation.

8. Place less emphasis upon the distinctions between grade levels. Allow students to move across levels when they have achieved the competencies and skills necessary for each level. If a grading system is to be used, devise one that tells something about the student. Cahn and Kitcher have suggested a system based upon three components: (1) the grade received, (2) the number of students enrolled in the class, and (3) the percentage of students who received an equal or higher grade.[17] A student's transcript might look like this:

	1	2	3
English:	C	(#35	57%)
Math:	B	(#85	94%)
History:	A	(#35	85%)
French:	B	(#25	10%)

9. Greater funding of specialized and compensatory programs

---

17. Steven Cahn and Patricia Kitcher, "There's No Percentage in College Grades," *Chronicle of Higher Education,* September 27, 1976.

in such areas as reading, bilingual education, special education, early childhood education, and exceptional education.

10. Develop some sort of national standard regarding teacher training and the accreditation of schools. Regional and state differences are currently so varied that persons in one state can get a teaching credential with minimal training while persons in other states have to go through a five-year program. Also, some states do not recognize credentials from other states and impose restrictions on candidates who move into their states.

Obviously these suggestions are neither exhaustive nor complete. Not everyone will agree with them, especially professors of education. Many will say, "But we're already doing this." But are they?

A final thought: the U.S. is one of the few nations in the world that does not have a national system of education. Perhaps it is time to look into the merits and demerits of a national system. Appendix 1 lists some reform suggestions for California proposed by the RISE Commission (Reform of Intermediate and Secondary Education). These, too, have merit and should be looked at in terms of the problems presented to you in the context of this book.

In conclusion, urban schools have not functioned as agents of social mobility; they have not provided equal educational opportunity for all; they have basically failed to contribute significantly to solving the many social problems facing schools and society.

Make no mistake about it, the schools of today will be radically different from the schools of tomorrow. We may not even recognize them as the same institutions that we have come to know as schools. Change will come, and today's youth will be part of that change. The reader may not fully agree with many of the positions taken in this book, but if they have encouraged the reader to think and to criticize, then they have accomplished the author's purpose.

Hugh Prather put it best when he wrote: "Negative feedback is better than none. I would rather have a man hate me than overlook me. As long as he hates me, I make a difference."[18]

---

18. Hugh Prather, *Notes to Myself* (Moab, Utah: Real People Press, 1970).

Exercises

I. Read the proposals in Appendix 1. What are your reactions to these suggested reforms? What implications do you foresee if these suggestions are carried out?

II. Following are several questions and problem areas for reading, research, and discussion:

> 1. Consider the proposition that academic freedom should be extended to the teacher who, while thoroughly competent in his or her field, is:
> a. strongly anti-Semitic.
> b. an extreme religious fanatic.
> c. a communist.
> d. a homosexual.
> e. an avowed social and moral nonconformist.
>
> 2. What has caused such widespread unrest and alienation among youth? How are the youth of today different from those of a generation ago? How can we make education more relevant to today's youth? To what extent should youth be involved in educational decision making (curriculum planning, hiring or firing of teachers, making rules)?
>
> 3. Some critics argue that special education for the segregated is inherently undemocratic and educationally unsound. Would you agree regarding: (a) segregation by sex as opposed to by coeducation, (b) segregation by social class and income, (c) segregation by race, (d) segregation by age level (junior high), (e) segregation by ability level.
>
> 4. Should there be local (decentralized) state, federal, or professional control over our schools? What are the merits and the weaknesses of each kind of control? Should there be a national system of education? If so, what should be its features?
>
> 5. How do we improve teacher training? What should be the requirements to be a teacher? How should we handle the problems of teacher surplus?

III. Following is a comprehensive list of research topics and projects in urban education. You might wish to explore any one of them further through reading or writing on the topic.

Urban Demographic Problems and Patterns

1. Role of housing relevant to the energy crisis

2. Role of the neighborhood school system in fostering de facto segregation and residential housing patterns

3. Relationship between environmental protection and the nation's housing needs

4. The impact of socioeconomic factors on the behavior of mortgage lenders (the red lining issue)

5. Increasing equal opportunity in housing

6. Innovative site planning concepts for urban schools

7. Neighborhood preservation of cultural and ethnic traditions

8. Impact of suburban growth on central cities

9. Impact of crime on central city growth

10. Racial and socioeconomic separation in urban centers

11. Impact of population decline on central cities

12. Causes and consequences of rural to urban and intermetropolitan migration

13. Impact of revenue sharing on local government programs

14. Local government taxation problems

15. Public services: allocation of priorities and effectiveness (welfare, rapid transit, police, fire)

16. Specialized public service needs of citizens

17. Evaluation of the impact of specific HUD programs

18. Default and bankruptcy of major urban centers

19. Legal constraints on community growth (zoning, land use, population shifts)

20. Human responses to natural and man-made physical environments

21. Equalization of metropolitan school financing

22. School boards as policy makers: reflective of the community and school needs

23. Zero-based school (or city) budgeting

24. The property tax as a base for support for public education (*Serrano* decision)

25. Current demographic population patterns in major urban centers

Multicultural/Cross-cultural Education

1. Subcultural influences upon a minority group

2. Middle-class stereotypes of minority and/or lower-class children

3. Potency and import of busing to achieve equal educational opportunity

4. Bilingual-bicultural programs mandated by law

5. Treatment of minority cultures in classroom content and textbooks

6. Influence of the media on multicultural learning

7. The debate over academic or vocational education for minorities

8. Contract performance and culturally different schools

9. The free school/alternative school movement and multicultural education

10. Local community control over schools and multicultural education

11. Reasons for Chicano/black gang rivalries and unrest

12. Education and the American Indian: assimilation or pluralism

13. Use of the community in planning cultural curricula

14. The public schools as monocultural and assimilative elements

15. The education of Japanese, Chinese, Korean, and Vietnamese children

16. Inservice training for teachers and administrators for multicultural programs

17. Status of state education laws at the present time, e.g., California and its 3.3 requirement

18. Sociolinguistic patterns of a select minority group

19. The cultural deprivation controversy

20. Component parts of an effective bilingual/bicultural school program

Inner-City and Minority Schooling

1. The social pathology of the ghetto

2. Educational techniques used to improve slum children's education

3. Reasons that inner-city teachers fail

4. Validity of I.Q. and standardized tests for minority youngsters

5. Drug usage in the central city schools

6. Ability grouping in inner-city schools

7. Language deficiencies of the pre-school and middle-school inner-city child

8. Peer group pressures upon behavior, values, and achievement

9. Gang warfare and leadership tendencies

10. Influence of the home on achievement

11. Parochial schools and their treatment of minorities

12. Compensatory programs: impact and effectiveness

13. Teacher training for inner-city schools

14. The social structure of the ghetto

15. Ghetto children's reading and language problems

16. Discipline problems (violence, vandalism, etc.) in inner-city schools

17. The impact of teacher surplus upon staffing needs for central-city schools

18. Innovations in inner-city schools

19. The I.Q. controversy and Jensen

20. Identifying the gifted and creative in central-city schools

21. The poor white in Appalachian schools

22. Psychological health of inner-city teachers: research studies

23. Poverty and minority status: interrelationships

24. Coping as a substitute teacher in the inner city

25. Teacher aides; school dropouts as assistant teachers

26. Strategies for teaching inner-city youngsters

27. Sensitivity and inservice training for teachers transferred to inner-city schools

28. The Black Dialect and Language as an alternative language

29. Segregated faculties and administrations in central-city schools: appraisal and reassignment

30. Facilities, materials, curriculum, health services in the inner-city school; are all schools in an urban community the same?

Sociopsychological and Interdisciplinary Research

1. Effect of segregation upon self-image and ego development

2. Effect of segregation upon achievement and level of aspiration

3. Effect of desegregation on self-image

4. Effect of desegregation on achievement and level of aspiration

5. Successes or failures of integrated schools

6. Race as a factor in intellectual differences

7. Socioeconomic status as a determiner of opportunity and achievement

8. Sociological analysis of the school dropout

9. Social distance as a factor in teacher-parent relations in the culturally different school

10. Means of protest of the urban and rural poor

11. Racial superiority and social scientific evidence

12. Influence of the family (size of and/or lack of a parent figure) upon success of children

13. Poverty, mental health, and school performance: inter-relationships

14. Early childhood education and school performance

15. Teacher expectations/perceptions: self-fulfilling prophecy

16. The Coleman Reports: then and now

17. How to combat racism in our schools

18. The middle-class black or Chicano teacher in the lower-class, urban minority school

19. Prejudice and self-concept: racial awareness

20. Paraprofessionals in the classroom: utility and effectiveness

21. Role of teacher unions in bettering urban schools

22. Legal and judicial decisions affecting urban school systems

23. Present status of desegregation

24. Empirical evidence on the effects of desegregation and policy implications

25. Urban school decentralization: selected attempts

26. Are culture-fair or culture-free standardized tests possible?

27. Bloom's Cumulative Deficit Theory

28. Schools and declining achievement/performance levels: extent/causes/reasons/implications

29. Violence in society: its impact upon schools and pupils

30. Class size and its import on learning and achievement

Appendix One

RISE Commission Report

I. Following are highlights from the report of the RISE Commission in California.

The student should be involved in formulating school rules, which should be minimal in number and precise.

School systems should develop competency-based curricula requiring students to achieve specified learning outcomes.

When a student has met the objectives of a subject, he or she should receive credit and the course should be considered completed.

Each student should be required to demonstrate competency at or above the minimal level established by the school district in each basic skill area.

A wide variety of educational alternatives should be made available to students, including optional learning formats.

First-hand learning experiences on the job or at places where students can witness actual functions being performed should be increased as part of educational programs.

Hours, days, and months of school operations should be flexible and diverse. School sites should be open on a year-round basis and be open beyond the traditional school hours.

Grade and age groupings should include people of all ages and encourage a mixture of adults and children in learning situations.

Instruction in the basic skill areas ("communication and computation") should be the highest priority for all students.

Each student should demonstrate competency in these basic skills.

School systems should offer opportunities for students to be in contact with people of different racial, ethnic, socioeconomic or cultural backgrounds.

School systems should emphasize the relationship between subject matter and career opportunities and should help students formulate "appropriate attitudes about the personal and social significance of one's own work and the world of work."

School systems should equip all students with the knowledge, experience and skills necessary to begin implementing their career objectives.

Students, teachers and citizens should participate in the selection of new teachers hired by schools.

Students and parents should participate in establishing procedures for the evaluation of all educators in schools.

Local school boards should adopt well-publicized means for considering the views of interested persons at all stages of the decision-making process. Advisory councils are "obvious vehicles" for public involvement.

School systems should adopt plans that assure teachers, parents, citizens and students in each school community "an active and effective role in establishing policies for their local school's program."

Appendix Two

Educational Journals

Adult Education

Arithmetic Teacher

American Biology Teacher

American Education

American Psychologist

American School Board Journal

American Sociological Review

Audio Visual Instructor

Bulletin of the National Association of Secondary School Principals

Business Education World

California Education

Catholic Educational Review

Catholic School Journal

Changing Education (A.F. of T.)

Child Development

Childhood Education

Clearing House

Commentary

Comparative Educational Review

Education

Education and Urban Society

Educational Horizons

Educational Leadership

Educational & Psychological Measurement

Educational Theory

Elementary English

Elementary School Journal

English Journal

English Language Teacher

Exceptional Education

Harvard Educational Review

High Points

High School Journal

Hispania

History of Education

Instructor

Integrated Education

Journal of Abnormal Psychology

Journal of Counseling Psychology

Journal of Educational Psychology

Journal of Educational Research

Journal of Experimental Education

Journal of Higher Education

Journal of Marriage & the Family

Journal of Negro Education

Journal of Personality

Journal of Political Economy

Journal of Reading

Journal of School Psychology

Journal of Secondary Education

Journal of Social Issues

Journal of Social Psychology

Journal of Teacher Education

Junior College Journal

La Raza

Liberal Education

NEA Journal

NEA Research Bulletin

National Schools

National Elementary Principal

Notre Dame Journal of Education

Peabody Journal of Education

Personnel & Guidance Journal

Personnel Psychology

Phi Delta Kappan

Phylon

Psychological Abstracts

Psychology Today

PTA Journal Magazine

Reading Teacher

Research Quarterly

Review of Educational Research

Saturday Review (Education section)

Scholastic Teacher

School and Community

School and Society

School Review

Science Education

Social Education

Social Problems

Social Studies

Sociology of Education

Speech Teacher

State Journals

Studies in Philosophy and Education

Teachers College Record (Columbia U)

Urban Education

Urban Review

Author Index

Subject Index